FISH & SHIPS

My life in the Royal Navy

ALF PICKUP

Published by:
RealTime Publishing
Limerick, Ireland
ISBN: 978-1-84961-094-0

Dedicated to my wife Hermione who passed away in February 2011, daughters Helen and Theresa, and grandchildren, Emily, Anna, Megan and Joel, without whom this book would not have been written.

All proceeds of the book to go to my wife's favorite charity: "THE GIFT OF SIGHT"

Chapter One

The twelfth of July, 1961 – twelve days before my 16th birthday – I find myself in Newcastle doing a second interview to join the Royal Navy. My first interview a year earlier had gone well, but at that time I was Austrian by birth, and so I was deemed to be an enemy of the state, and was refused entry. My schoolmaster, Captain Tribe, and the Lord Mayor of Scarborough, pulled a few strings and I was granted a second go. Obviously, by this time Austria and Britain had become friends, so I was in the clear.

I was given a full medical and pronounced a perfect specimen. I was then ushered into a room and given a pencil and an exam paper; I was told I had an hour to complete the paper. Now, I'm not saying the questions were easy, but...! What is the odd one out, a knife, a fork, a door? Christ, there had to be a catch; I thought I was joining the Royal Navy, not a bloody lunatic asylum. I had just spent four years at the Graham Sea Training School in Scarborough learning navigation, Morse code, ship construction, and seamanship, and they hit me with this rubbish. Anyway, ten minutes later I handed in the paper; the dumb buggers took half an hour longer than me to mark it. I can't say I was too surprised when they told me I had passed. I now had to sign a load of forms which, in turn, made me a Junior Electrical Mechanic 2nd class. After this, you have two weeks to change your mind; the only thing is they don't tell you this till you've done three weeks. By this time it's too late; you're in for twelve years with no remission. I was issued a railway warrant to Portsmouth Harbour railway station; I was also given ten shillings for food and drink. I caught the train at Newcastle and headed south. The journey was a bit daunting, as I had only been out of Scarborough three or four times since I was three years old, once to a book company in Hull, and once on a day trip to Blackpool, and twice to Newcastle trying to join the RN.

The next few hours were spent on a British Rail steam train, steaming to Kings Cross. I finally arrived, and was totally gobsmacked at the amount of people rushing around, seemingly going nowhere. I found a porter and asked him, "Where is my train for Portsmouth?" He kindly explained that I needed to catch an underground train to Waterloo. I found the escalator to the underground; I didn't realise they had mines in London; it seemed there was a people factory down there churning out people by the thousand, all different nationalities and colours. This was something new to a backwoods boy from the Saxon settlement of Scarborough.

I somehow managed the maze of the underground and found Waterloo station; from there I caught the Pompey train. I bought a stale cheese sandwich and a cup of stewed tea for the price of a bottle of champagne, robbing bastards, at least it would take the hunger pangs away for a little while, till I could get to my next meal, I thought, hopefully! An hour and a half later, the train arrived at Portsmouth Harbour. I woke to the train hitting the buffers, a novel way of making sure that passengers wake up on arrival. Once off the train, I made my way to the exit and handed in my one way ticket to the collector. Outside the station a group of lads about my age were milling about looking as lost as I was. A few minutes later, a smart looking petty officer came up and addressed us, "Right you lot, get fell in," and no please or thank you. I ask you, how rude.

By now, I was looking around and finding it hard to believe there were no cliffs; the whole place seemed to be at sea level, all very strange to a Saxon cliff dweller. The petty officer had rounded up about forty lads; he led us down the ramp to the Gosport ferry. He obviously had some arrangement to get forty passengers onto the ferry for nothing, because the ticket collector let us on for free. The ferry set off and headed towards the harbour entrance; we were all thinking, 'where the hell are we going?' This guy driving had obviously done this before because the incoming tide turned the ferry to where we originally thought we were going: Gosport.

At this point, all we new lads were hanging over the ferry's side in awe of the Navy ships berthed alongside and at anchor in the harbour. Some were in commission, some were reserve fleet, and others were waiting for the scrap yard. There were battleships, cruisers, aircraft carriers, destroyers, and frigates – you name it and we had it. Not having done much homework on the Royal Navy, I was in awe at the size of the ships. The biggest ship I had seen previous to that day was the pleasure ship Coronia running from Scarborough to Whitby, which was about the size of a minesweeper. It was a bit like graduating from pedal cars to a Rolls Royce in one go. I've got to say, I was pissing myself with excitement at the thought of being part of all this.

Alf Pickup

The ferry finally arrived at the pontoon at Gosport. A big blue lorry with Royal Navy stamped on the side was waiting for us, and we were herded into some semblance of a squad and marched up the gangway to the lorry. Civilians looked on in amusement, all a big bloody joke to them; they probably knew what we were in for. Anyway, the tailgate on the lorry was dropped and we all climbed in. The drive to HMS Vincent took about ten minutes, probably due to the fact nobody had cars in 1961. We arrived at the main gate; the establishment was surrounded by a huge wall topped with barbed wire that should keep the burglars out, eh, what? Once through the gate, we disembarked the lorry and were lined up again. In front of us was a figure head of some famous Admiral; behind him was the parade ground where we would spend many a happy hour in the months to come (not). At the end of the parade ground in the middle, was the mast; behind the mast to the left and right were the accommodation blocks named Hawk, Anson, Blake, and Duncan, all named after famous Admirals of yesteryear.

Well, there I was, in the clothes I left home in with eight shillings in my pocket, left over from my travelling expenses. It seemed like I had come to a different planet. The nice people at the recruiting office had turned into nasty bastards here at Vincent. A Petty Officer started shouting at us, letting us know in no uncertain terms that he regarded himself as ever so slightly superior to us. You could tell he considered us to be a very low form of pond life, and by the time he was finished with us, we would all be proper little sailors, all thanks to him and his sadistic mates.

We were now in three lines and marching to the slop room, the place where they kit us out with our new uniform. The guestimators behind the counter were piling up kits on the side, and asking our sizes. Of course, every 16-year-old knows their inside leg, their neck size, and hat size, don't they? Anyway, the kit that was issued as follows: 2 milk churn lids (caps), one for work and one for best, 2 silk HMS Vincent cap ribbons, 2 Navy style collars, 2 silks, 2 white lanyards, 4 white fronts, 1 rough serge number 2 suit, 1 smooth serge number 1 suit, 4 sets of woolen vests and underpants, a Burberry raincoat, 2 sets of overalls, 3 sets of number eight working shirts and trousers, 1 canvas money belt, 4 pairs of socks, 2 sets of blue knee length stockings...don't go away, there's more...2 sets of sports gear shirt and shorts, 1 oilskin, razor, toothbrush, shoe brushes, polish, duster, and 2 blocks of pussers hard soap (not exactly dove cream bars), a housewife (sewing kit) and name types for marking the aforesaid mentioned.

For our evening attire, we slipped into something more comfortable: 2 pairs of pooftas overalls (pajamas). Footwear consisted of 1 pair of shoes (for best), 1 pair of 17th century deck slippers, complete with buckle; presumably someone in Nelson's day over ordered and there was a surplus to be used up; a pair of studded marching boots made from rough crocodile skin finished off the clothing side. A Royal Navy seamanship manual (used to measure the exact width of your kit at musters) and a pussers dirk, (like a heavy duty Swiss army knife) were the last things to be issued.

The next few days were spent marking our kit – this included everything – clothing was marked with black paint using our wooden types. Tape was cut and stitched onto our socks and stockings, then marked with our tiny metal types. Shoes and boots were taken down to the cobbler, and our names stamped into the leather. Once the marking was done, we had to embroider the letters with red silk, a thing that comes naturally to 16-year-old boys. It was important to mark things in the correct place, as all the names had to be in line when laying out your kit for muster. We were shown how a kit was supposed to look when your locker was open for daily inspection and kit musters. All kit had to be the width of the seamanship manual when laid out. Shoes and boots had to be brought up to a mirror finish; this took weeks of constant spit and polish. Lessons were given on how to iron clothes, and get seven creases in your bell bottom trousers. Personal hygiene was taught; some of the smelly buggers needed lessons on how to wash, and there was no such thing as deodorants in those days.

Our entry was number 42; we were split into the four divisions mentioned earlier; I became part of Duncan division, and from then on there was always a healthy rivalry between divisions. All our civvies and anything personal were packed up and sent home; everything we had now was pussers' issue.

The trip to the barber was an interesting experience. Two ex-Belson guards armed with sheep shears took great delight in relieving us of our golden locks, or in my case, dark brown locks. They were remarkably quick; I bet they sold the hair to some top Mayfair salon to be used as hair extensions; this was our first and only free haircut. Getting up at 5 o'clock every morning to the sound of a bugler playing reveille took some getting used to, especially when we had to go down to the unheated pool twice a week to have swimming lessons. All this was because the Navy required you to pass a swimming test. This consisted of jumping in the pool in a pair of overalls, then swimming two lengths of the pool, climbing out, jumping in again, then floating for five minutes before climbing out again. I spent the whole year at Vincent trying to pass this test; I failed because I could not float, and I guess I must have had too much shark DNA in me. You know, keep moving or sink. Anyway the training instructors, not liking failures on their watch, eventually gave me a pass certificate. I think they felt sorry for me, I know I did. I often wonder how my old next door neighbour got on, having been torpedoed three times in the Second World War and not able to swim a stroke. I recall him saying, "Where are you going to swim to?" I rest my case.

On the second week, everyone was required to climb the mast, up one side of the rigging to the button on the top, then down the other side. No problem, except I had to do it twice; some twat had got himself to the top and decided he didn't want to come down. I was volunteered with another lad to persuade him that it would be nice if he could maybe loosen his grip and follow us down, and stop crying all over us. After 20 minutes, we managed to get him down, which wasn't easy with a 12 stone lump hanging round your neck. I must admit I did feel sorry for him; I think they called it vertigo.

By that time I had been given an ID card with my photo on it; lose this piece of easily forgeable card and you were dead; punishment knew no bounds, and a heavy fine was also given. I was also given an official number and a station card making me the second of port. This meant some trivial duty every four days, as if we didn't have enough to do already, what with all that washing, ironing, and polishing.

Getting up on a morning was usually helped by the duty Petty Officer giving us words of encouragement, like, "come along, you chaps, rise and shine, time for your swimming lessons…" You're right, I'm joking.

It was more like the ranting of the local lunatic, shouting and screaming as if the end of the world was at hand; to us it certainly felt that way. One Petty Officer in particular will stand out in the memory of all who came across him. His name: Stallard. The name might suggest he was a Nazi; he certainly acted like one. Now, I'm not saying this guy was mental, BUT, he was an absolute bastard. Evidently he had spent time in a Japanese prisoner of war camp, some of it in a tin box in the tropical sun, which obviously turned him slightly. After the war the Navy decided to put him ashore, rather than risk him on a ship, or a lunatic asylum. When he was on duty, this man would come into our dormitory on the first note of reveille with a broom handle, which he used to crack us sleeping beauties across our legs, with the dire warning that if we were not up in the next two minutes, death awaited us. If, per chance, someone did not quite make the two minute deadline, his bed with him in it was tipped over, and his locker complete with all contents scattered over the floor. This was usually followed with a kit muster within the hour, not easy when some sick sod has trampled over it.

His other favourite trick was to open all the dormitory windows, nice in the summer, not so clever in the winter with a force 8 gale blowing through. This guy seemed determined to get back at the Japs by taking his anger out on us. I expect by now the Devil is having a hard time keeping him in check.

The first few weeks were spent on the parade ground learning our left from our right, how to march in step, turn left, right, and about. Breaking in the new boots was probably the hardest bit, doing all this crap with feet full of blisters was no joke. Once the marching bit was sorted out, we were given Royal Enfield 303 rifles; these were single shot, bolt action jobs, left over from the second world war and probably earlier. To a 16-year-old it was like giving candy to a baby; after all, we were only just out of the cops and robbers stage of our short lives, and giving us a gun made us feel like real warriors.

All this training made us proficient in the art of looking good as a group. Divisions were a daily occurrence, always accompanied by the Royal Marine and Vincent's bugle band; the Marine band was totally professional, while the bugle band was volunteers; it was all very impressive. Once everyone was fell in on the parade ground, the band would march on to a rip roaring military tune and stop in the centre. Us Catholics would then fall out for prayers in the drill shed, while the Church of England service continued without us. I expect these days of political correctness they have to have prayer mats and all that sort of crap available. After Divisions the band would flash up and we all marched off to instruction; the idea of this was to get everyone up to the standard to pass the educational test for leading rate. My rank at this time was junior electrical mechanic 2nd class, not bad for someone who didn't know the difference between an electric plug and a bath plug. One or two of the instructors were a little insane, not quite on par with Stallard; a certain Lt Commander who shall remain nameless had a habit of telling us that the text books were wrong if someone pointed out an error in his teaching. He also had a habit of returning a salute with a Nazi salute, shouting hail Hitler. Even scarier was when he ordered some young lads to his cabin to play with his dinky cars.

War time rationing was still in force in Vincent; either that or the catering officer was making a fortune at our expense. Meal times were cordon bleu, not in quality but in size; one thing you would always remember at Vincent was permanent hunger. They made you burn 4,000 calories a day while giving you 2,000; this is the nearest you can get to a perpetual motion machine, e.g. getting more out than you put in. The dining hall was a draughty drill shed, 95 degrees in the summer, and minus 10 degrees in the winter, not exactly the Ritz. Meal times consisted of 600 starving teenagers queuing up with metal trays; hats were taken off and placed on racks and the duty PO would go round and spike any hat that did not conform to the Navy regulation milk churn lid, e.g. no fancy bow waves. Once the queue got moving, the chefs, all old sea dogs complete with tattoos and attitude, would slap some overcooked crap on your tray; a bin of sliced, two-day-old bread was always at the end of the line, presumably to bulk you up for the missing rations. This, of course, was limited to two slices, and next to the bread was the margarine, which consisted of 3 pounds of marge whipped up with milk to give the appearance of a tray full. Once this marge hit the bread, it tended to vanish.

Any form of indiscipline or lateness was rewarded with 14's or 9's; 14's consisted of an hour's doubling round the parade ground with a 303 rifle, usually in the afternoon; two hours' extra work was also done, one hour in the morning, and one hour in the evening – normally this was done in the galley to help those lazy bastard chefs. All this was fairly easy for a fit young teenager; that is, unless you got that psycho Stallard, who used to have his own little variations on the rifle drill, like making you hold it over your head, or out in front of you while doubling on the spot in front of a wall; his stick would come into play when you got dizzy. Years later, I heard a rumour that he had managed to kill a young lad, evidently through a ruptured stomach; bet that didn't reach the papers. The only good thing was that they did away with the rifle bit after that. The worst punishment apart from 14's and 9's was a dishonourable discharge, or the cuts. This was metered, in a walled courtyard; the guilty individual would be leaned over a chair with his trousers down and given six lashes with a leather cat. The story went, if you survived without crying you were given 10 shillings, but I don't recall seeing anyone smiling with ten bob in his hand after that.

During the first few months I joined the bugle band, and under the marine band officer's guidance, learnt to play the bass drum. We would practice every morning, then lead the marine band out on divisions; I looked the dog's bollocks in my tiger skin, especially when it was ceremonial and everyone had their best uniforms on. It was quite something knowing you were responsible for dictating the marching pace with the base drum.

Crime in Vincent during 1961-1962 consisted of someone breaking and emptying the one and only fag machine, so it was promptly removed. Thanks a bunch. The other incident was when a young, ex-cat burglar from the next dormitory climbed through our dorm's window onto the heating pipe, and made his way over to the NAAFI shop across the road; he consequently came back with enough goodies to keep us in snacks for days. Fortunately, the police were unable to find the culprit – a bit like today's

13

police, really. The powers that be decided to keep the NAAFI open for legitimate transactions. Basic training in seamanship was the main aim of teaching at Vincent; we were taught Morse code, and semaphore. This was a bit of a waste on me, as my four years at the Graham Sea Training School consisted of practicing this twice a week and I was quite proficient at it, as I was to show the instructor when he hauled me in front of the class for not paying attention. It seemed I could read his Morse code, but I was a bit too quick for him, which was most embarrassing (for him).

We spent many a happy hour learning to sail in Portsmouth Harbour. I recall one particular day when the wind was a bit fresh and variable, I just happened to be the coxswain of a whaler happily sailing along, when my crew and I decided to go and have a look at the Royal Yacht Britannia. Well, everything was going well as we sailed by, that is till the wind dropped and the current took us alongside. Try as we might, there was no way we could stop the top of our mast putting a huge scrape down the beautiful royal blue paintwork of the yacht's side. By now, we had the oars out and were rowing like hell before anyone could spot us. I heard from a dockyard worker some years later that the special paint used on the yachts could not be touched up, and a total paint job had to be done on any hull damage, oops!

You would have thought things could not have gotten worse, wrong! Having scarred the yacht we decided to go to the opposite side of the harbour out of harm's way. We ended up by the Flandroyant, a training ship anchored midstream. We somehow managed to get our mast caught up in her forward anchor chain and the boat was heeling over at a dangerous angle. That damn current had the better of us yet again, and suddenly there was an almighty crack as the mast splintered. The boat was now full of sail, wooden shrapnel, and sprawling sailors, but at least we had broken free (literally). By the time we had untangled ourselves we found ourselves now drifting towards the Gosport ferry; Jesus, when would this nightmare end? We eventually managed to recover the oars and headed back to shore.

The instructors were not pleased with us; I could tell this by the fact I was put on Commanders' report for damaging government property. The Navy didn't do accidents in those days; there was always someone to blame, and in this case, as captain of my ship, it was me. I ended up with seven days of number 14's; this went well for five days, no problem, same routine every day; that is, till day six. I arrived to do my rifle drill only to find Saturday's routine started an hour early and I was adrift. I ended up on defaulters again in front of the Commander, so I explained my dilemma and he let me off. The regulating Petty Officer was given a bollocking for not giving me a card with punishment times on it. He was not best pleased with me I can tell you, I know this because he told me I was a little bastard. He had obviously been reading my personal notes, as I was born one, but I don't know what his excuse was. Anyway, I kept well clear of him for the rest of my stay.

One evening after lights out we organized a raid on the next dormitory. Pillows in hand, we hit them; the ensuing pillow fight resulted in feathers everywhere, and obviously the noise that was generated attracted attention and the duty Officer and Petty Officer duly arrived. We were all fell in on the parade ground, which was followed by two laps of the parade ground; now we had a nice sweat on in our jimjams, and we were told to change into our number one uniform. This was followed by another two laps, then a change into overalls, two laps later into another outfit; this carried on till we had been through our whole kit, and after two hours, the nice Officer said we could now fall out and go to bed. He then added, "By the way, you will all have a kit muster at 8 o'clock sharp." Strange sense of humour, I must say. The rest of the night was chaos, with everyone trying to wash, dry, and iron their sweaty kit to be ready for the morning inspection, oh, joy.

Sport in Vincent was varied; it covered most things, football, rugby, hockey, swimming, running, and boxing. I was nominated to play rugby because I had a bit of pace. My first match ended in a 52-nil loss, but I was hooked and played for most of the ships I was on during my naval career. We had an annual sports day against HMS Ganges, our sister establishment, and they usually won, due to the fact they had five times the ratings we did; the recruits there were training to be seamen as opposed to us technical types in Vincent. Mornings were spent under instruction, and afternoons doing either drill or sport; the sport time was the only time we left the establishment apart from four hours on Sunday. One of the toughening up processes was pairing lads up and making them knock ten bells of shit out of each other in the boxing ring. I, personally, did not get involved as our class had an odd number in it, and that was me. I did however do well at our interdivisional sports day. I won the hundred yards (no meters in those days), the two twenty yards, and the long jump. I was a bit of a ringer, really, as I had previously run for Yorkshire as a schoolboy. Prizes consisted of medals and chocolate, and being a cocky, hungry little toe rag, I decided to go in for the mile race as well. Unfortunately, distance running was not my forte, and I ended up in sick bay with exhaustion, serve me right, eh what. Still I had enough chocolate to keep going for a week or two, so I couldn't grumble.

Sundays from 1400-1800, we were allowed out of Vincent for leave. What we were supposed to do with ten shillings a week pocket money, I don't know. Let's face it, by the time you had bought your toiletries, cleaning gear, fags, and sweeties, you did not have much left for a mind bending run ashore. Now and again the local cinema was visited for the afternoon matinee, but mostly Sundays were spent washing, polishing boots, and on the ironing board. I recall one particular Sunday I was pressing my seven cresses in my bell bottoms, when another lad assured me the best way to get really sharp creases was to use brown paper and soap. The idea was to rub soap on the back of the creases, then press over the crease using the brown paper; I stuck to the tried and tested method of a damp cloth. After we had finished, the lad picked up his bells to show me how good his creases were, and the result was fourteen rings of serge on the floor; the creases were so sharp he had gone right through the cloth. He was left with a nice pair of shorts and a bill for another pair of trousers. We all pissed ourselves. No doubt he got a new set off Bernard's Navel tailors who ran a lucrative business exploiting gullible young lads by getting them to open an account with a monthly allotment.

Leave was given at Easter, summer, and of course, Christmas. As we didn't have any civvies, we had to go on leave in uniform, not that anyone minded; we felt top dogs, but only had one little gold star on our arm. Most lads took it on themselves to add a few more badges, little realising anyone who knew anything about the navy would spot us as frauds. Once on the train, it was usual to look for an empty carriage so you and your mates could crash out, having first tipped a can of Campbell's vegetable soup on the floor to deter anyone from sharing your carriage. Once or twice on the way home to Scarborough, I would miss my stop at York and end up in Darlington. This was due to the fact a new invention was being used, welded rail between Doncaster and York; the normal *clickerty click* turned into a soothing *ssshhh* and a deep sleep ensued.

After my final leave, we were issued with tropical kit: two new number six suits, two white shorts, white stockings, and one pair of white canvas shoes. The usual marking, washing, and ironing followed on our Daz white gear, before being packed ready for tropical climes in the future.

My final days in Vincent involved the Passing out parade. Everyone was dressed up in their number one uniform and on the parade ground, while I was in the band, all dolled up in my white gaiters and belt, complete with my tiger skin. Out of the blue, my name is called out. Jesus, what's going on? Evidently, I had won the Captain's prize, which was awarded to the most promising junior of the entry, and I couldn't believe it. Anyway, I fell out of the band and marched up to the Captain's dais to pick up my award, a leather embossed writing case, which I still proudly have 40 years later. The following days were spent packing my kit along with all my

16

classmates. We are bursting with excitement, and the adrenaline is flowing, as at last we are heading for HMS Collingwood.

Chapter Two

Dawn on the twelfth of July, 1962: the lorries are waiting for us on the parade ground; we climb aboard, complete with our suitcases and kit bags, and off we go onto the next part of the adventure. Five miles down the road we reach Collingwood. Leaving behind an establishment with 600 to join one with 6,000 is quite a culture shock, I can tell you. Now Collingrad, as we come to call it, is surrounded by a high wire fence to keep the burglars out; it seems to work as I don't recall anyone getting caught breaking in. Inside the main gate is the usual figurehead representing the quarterdeck; the main road runs from the gate up to the parade ground, Jesus, what a size, reputedly the biggest in Europe, only the Yanks have one bigger; that's a surprise!(not). On either side of the parade ground are dozens of wooden huts on stilts; these were built after the war, when the land was a bog. It took years to drain the land, and was still liable to flooding but for the permanently running pumps. Our lorry pulled up over to the left hand side of the parade ground; we got out and fell in outside an office. A Petty Officer marched us to one of the huts; this was to be our home for the next few months. Inside the hut were two lines of metal beds with a locker on each side, and a pot belly stove in the center, which was the central heating system for the winter. Once settled in our hut, we were marched round to the bedding store to pick up a pillow, three blankets, and a mattress cover, all probably left over from the Crimean war.

The following day we joined the other five thousand or so for morning divisions and morning prayers, usual routine, fall out Roman Catholics; Christ, I wish I'd told them I was a Jew or something, all this falling out crap every day made you feel like a leper. Then the bloody priest trying to get us to do Hail Mary's and all that bullshit. After divisions, we head off for White city; this is the training complex at the back of Collingwood. We are now being given our first taste of electrical Instruction. We start with maths and formulas relating to electrics and electronics; we do valve theory, motors, generators, telephones, AC, DC, low power, high power – all this basic stuff is rammed into our pea brains in the space of four months. During this period we are reminded that parade drill is still part of our training. We are, of course, given watches; this time my station card reads the second of starboard, which means possible duties every four days, although in reality the duties occurred only every eight days. It meant you had to keep a sharp eye on the day's daily orders in case your name appeared.

I recall one particular event when I was on duty on security patrol with another lad; we had just got back to the main gate and in the guard room, when we overheard the Officer of the day talking to the Chief of the watch. Evidently, when he approached one of the patrols a timid voice called out "who goes there," and the duty Petty Officer replied, "Officer of the day and duty Petty Officer." Unsure of what to do next, the two lads started whispering to each other. After a few minutes, the irate Petty Officer yelled, "Come on, you two; don't keep the Officer of the day standing at attention all night!" To which one of the lads called out, "Officer of the day, stand at ease." You see the power a lad with a wooden stick has over his superiors.

I previously mentioned the size of the parade ground; well, it took a good 15 minutes to double round it. The rule was if you crossed the parade ground you did so with a hat on your head and you ran at the double; anything otherwise was rewarded with a day's number 14's punishment. You can imagine the surprise of the Chief gunnery instructor, standing at the south end of the parade ground, when he sees an individual sauntering across the distant north end with his hat on the back of his head and his hands in his pockets.

Staring in total disbelief, he gathers himself together, and then yells out in his considerably loud voice, "That rating report to me!" The rating stops, takes his hands out of his pockets, adjusts his hat, and then places both hands to his mouth and yells back, "feck off!" With that, he legs it for all he is worth off the parade ground to the safety of the surrounding buildings, never to be seen again. This story was related to us by Webby who worked in the armoury; he was one of the few survivors of HMS Hood when she got sunk, and he was spotting in the crows nest at the time.

Since arriving at Collingwood, we became entitled to blue liners – duty free tobacco and cigarettes, all packed in distinctive packets with RN splattered over them so as not to confuse them with woodbines or park drives. These tubes of death were manufactured from the sweepings of the BAT factory; still, at two and four pence a hundred (that's 12p in today's money), you could not really complain. The allowance for evening leave was 25 a night, with a maximum of 200 for leave. One particular weekend, I was all packed to go on a long weekend with my mate, Kirk, to Coventry;

that's 75 fags. Just then the Chief gunnery instructor decided to give me a little call as I was crossing the parade ground. "That rating report to me!"

It seems after all my training, I was not doubling in the correct Naval manner, and was promptly given a days 14's, to start within the hour. The next morning, I'm heading towards the main gate to start my now short weekend, and I'm obviously looking guilty because the scumbag on duty decides my bag needs searching, and guess what? Having packed for the long weekend and now going on a short weekend, the man finds I have 25 cigarettes too many. Now, smuggling in the Royal Navy runs alongside raping the ship's cat in seriousness. I found myself alone back in my hut, waiting for Monday to see the ship's Commander.

Monday arrives; I put on my number one suit and head for the queue waiting for defaulters. I'm called in and marched in front of the commander. I'm charged with smuggling 25 cigarettes. Have I any mitigating circumstances, he asks, and boy, have I. The weekend's story is told and I am given seven days 14's, unsympathetic bastard. What made me even more pissed off was the fact that some Tiff (artificer) was given the same seven days for having 2,000 fags, not exactly an accidental oversight. I guess I should have demanded a retrial.

Princess Anne is due on a visit; the whole camp is on red alert, and grass is painted green, litter scoured for, leaves removed from ground and trees, the usual palaver for a visiting dignitary; I bet they think we live like this all the time. Anyway, she arrives, has a nice lunch in the wardroom, the usual quail in aspic and hummingbirds' tongues in orange sauce. After lunch she is invited to put a spoonful of earth round a sapling to commemorate her visit; a plaque is placed in the ground; she departs in her Rolls Royce silver cloud and heads for home, having done a hard day's work eating and shoveling. The next day, the sapling is hanging from the top of the mainmast, and the Captain is not amused. You can tell this from the fact he stops all leave till someone owns up. Of course, nobody does; why would anyone want 60 lashes for doing such a dastardly deed? Anyway, the married guys are getting pissed off, and their teas are getting cold at home; wives are phoning newspapers, and newspapers are phoning the Captain thanking him for the story. No doubt some lad already doing fourteen days punishment is pissing himself with all the trouble he has caused. Anyway, after a few hours, the Captain relents and lets leave commence; a full enquiry follows with no results.

Sport in Collingrad was not compulsory; physical training was, and pairing us up for boxing was also a requirement. This time I was not the odd one out and I ended up in the ring with my mate, Kirk. Now bearing in mind I was, at this time, ten and a half stone and Kirk was at least twelve and a half stone, I considered this a bit of a mismatch. However, Kirk wore beer bottomed glasses and without them life was a blur, much to my advantage; in fact, he did not hit me once and I knocked ten bells of shit out of him. I did apologise to him afterwards, and he forgave me. After the fight one of the physical training instructors came over and told me that I had to enter Collingrads boxing championships, due to my talented right hand (I had a good uppercut by all accounts). I had four fights and won them all by knockout in the first round, which meant I was now in the finals for middle weight. I was quite chuffed about all this; my class mates were all behind me. What I didn't know at this time was a certain boxer called Paddy Graham was also in the final. Now, this guy was a Navy legend; he was southern area, ABA, and Northern Ireland amateur champion.

The night of the final arrived, I was in my corner dressed in a white Navy t-shirt, a pair of Navy issue sports shorts down to my knees, and a pair of plimsolls, when in came Paddy, dressed in silk shorts, a t-shirt covered in boxing honors, and proper boxing boots. I'm thinking, why me, o lord. My sphincter muscle is tightening up, my mouth is drier than a camels arse, adrenaline is coursing through my veins, the fight or flee mode is kicking in; my loyal mates are giving me a hundred to one chance. Seconds out, round one, Paddy comes out of his corner, blowing air through his nostrils like some insane bull. I move forward, I see a chance, there's a gap between his gloves, I place a perfect uppercut between them, bingo, smack on the end of his jaw, I damn near took his head off, he hits the deck, out for the count; in thirteen seconds of the first round it's all over, I'm not going to die after all. My classmates can't believe it, and neither can I. I did get a bit worried when Paddy was still out after five minutes; smelling salts failed to rouse him, but he did recover and was not very complimentary about my lucky punch, the Irish twat. I got a nice silver medal and a crate of beer, which I celebrated with my classmates.

After I had finished my electrical training on the second of December 1962, I was put on establishment duties till a draft to a ship came through; I was nominated to help down at the pig farm. My duties consisted of mucking out and collecting swill from the galley and cooking it up in huge, gas-fired cauldrons, or the Maggi soup factory, as we used to call it – the guy who thought up this money spinner was onto a good thing. I remember once when a new consignment of piglets arrived, some clown let the tailgate of the lorry down before we were ready, and all fifty piglets made a dash for freedom. Ironically, quite a few were recaptured after running round the wardroom, which seemed apt, as officers were lovingly known by junior ratings as pigs. Once we got settled into our new jobs, we had to move accommodation from the training side of the parade ground to the ship's company side at the other side of the establishment. This meant packing up and borrowing a hand cart to transfer our belongings to our new homes (huts). In hindsight, I should have gone the long way round to my new condo, but to save time I decided to go across the sacred parade ground.

Now, doubling with one's worldly possessions on a two wheeled cart is not the easiest thing to do, but you try telling that to a moronic gunnery instructor, who by definition is thick enough to carry you and the damn cart at regulation pace across the parade ground. Unfortunately, we mere mortals are incapable of such feats, so consequently, I end up with yet another day's 14's for not being up to their high standard.

Enjoyment in Collingwood consisted of going to the NAAFI club for a few drinks or, on paydays, going into Fareham to the "Bird in the hand" pub to get legless on scrumpy, not a pleasant experience I can tell you.

The physical training Officer sends for me, and I am invited to volunteer for the navy boxing championships in HMS Victory. I accept, and having won all my previous fights in the first round, I am a little cocky and consider training a waste of time. I win the first two fights in the first round, and the second fight in the second round; in the semi-final I fight a 6 foot 3 inch stoker who is built like a bean pole. I beat ten bells out of him for two rounds; unfortunately, I did not score any points, but his forearms were black and blue. I came out for the third round and was so knackered I could hardly lift my arms to defend myself, and he consequently won on points. I was a bit disappointed till I found he had Paddy Graham in the final; boy, was that a bit of luck, as Paddy was looking forward to killing me. I was happy not to give him the chance. I heard later he knocked out the unfortunate stoker in the first round. Paddy was bought out of the Navy soon after, and turned professional; no doubt he will remember me.

Having finished my course with 57% overall, and done my farming bit at the piggery, my draft finally comes through. I am to join HMS Wakeful in Portsmouth dockyard on 24th of January 1963. I am issued with a new set of branch badges, an L with lightning flashes from each corner; I still have no idea what the hell L stands for. But I am no longer a junior; I am electrician second class, dizzy heights or what. I know I'm not exactly in charge of the National grid yet, but hey, these things take time.

I join this dilapidated type 15 Frigate, F159, a converted 1945 Destroyer, even from the jetty she seems to be falling to bits. How she escaped the scrap yard I'll never know, but the Admiralty in their wisdom decided to use her as a training ship for budding navigators.

The superstructure is made of aluminium joined to the steel deck; add a little salt water and you have the makings of a battery, good design, eh what. She is powered by steam driven engines fuelled by Fleet fuel oil, the most disgusting, foul smelling, thick, black shit you could imagine. Electricity is produced by five generators, three steam, two diesels, all kicking out 220 volts DC; other motor generators are fitted to produce various DC and AC voltages that supply radar and navigation equipment. As I recall, she was totally disarmed.

I am now heading up the gang plank; I salute the quarter deck and white ensign. I am greeted by the quartermaster who asks for my identity card and joining papers; he tells the bosun's mate to take me to the regulating office where the regulating petty Officer gives me my joining routine. This is a card which takes me all round the ship gathering rubber stamps from different departments letting people know I'm here, places like the pay office, the ship's office, the catering office, the bedding store, the armoury, and of course the electrical departmental office. I am now given my duties, which include my job in the department, my watch port 2 again, my special sea duty for leaving harbour, my action station, emergency station, my damage control station, my boarding party, and other various little bits to confuse the hell out of me. My accommodation for the next six months was to be a mess deck for the electrical department which was the size of two average living rooms. In it was housed twenty-five ratings; you can imagine what it smelt like, deodorant not being readily available in the early sixties. This, by the way, was only the port side of the ship; the starboard side was the seaman's living area, in which was housed another twenty-five ratings. Fitted on the hull of the ship on both sides were nine bunks in stacks of three, the middle ones became back rest to the bottom bunk seat during the day, these were for the mighty three badge men (twelve years service plus) and killicks (leading hands). The two mess tables became platforms for two camp beds, and underneath was space for another two camp beds; the rest of us twelve unfortunates made do with hammocks.

This probably sounds very cosy till you are told the ship is broadside messing. This means you ate in the same area, and it was not much fun to climb out of your hammock in the morning into someone's bacon and eggs. Once up in the morning, all bedding was stowed, the bunks zipped up, camp beds stowed, and hammocks lashed to become floats if the ship sank, or damage repair bungs if required. The after bathroom had eight sinks and three showers, really good with fifty ratings trying to get ready for breakfast and work; the only thing good about this way of living was the fact we got paid hard layers. It was only a few bob a week but it came in handy. Once the mess was cleared, two ratings were nominated each day to do cooks. This meant scrubbing out and tidying up, then ditching the gash. Once this was done, the two had to go to the galley to collect potatoes and vegetables to peel for the mess lunch. At nine o'clock, the duty officer would do his rounds of heads (toilets), bathrooms, and mess decks, whether you got a rescrub or not depended on how keen they were. At lunch and supper time there was the usual rush to try and get one of the nine seats available. Entertainment was board games, cards, or listening to the SRE (ship's radio equipment). A film was shown maybe once a week. It usually snapped half way through, adding to the excitement.

My first job in the magic world of electrics was on the low power section, 24 volts and below; I guess you had to build up trust before they let you loose on the big stuff. One of the duties was switchboard watch keeping; this consisted of keeping the voltage steady at 220 and adjusting loads; these switchboards were all open, and heavy duty spring loaded knife switches operated the ship's equipment. The voltage was adjusted by a small lever, up to raise it, down to lower it. This particular day, the chief electrician was behind the switchboard working on something or other, when I, being nosy, decided to lean over and have a gander at what he was doing.

Well, you can imagine my surprise when the whole bloody ship goes dark and equipment starts clunking off at a rate of knots; all hell is now let loose, bodies running everywhere in organized panic, finally, the generator is restarted and normality restored. It was then that I realized what had happened, I had inadvertently leaned on the voltage regulator and tripped the generator, oops, time to stay stum. Another time, I was helping down at the switchboard when I was just about to pass a very large spanner to the chief working on an interconnector switch, when the ship lurched violently and the spanner slipped out of my hand and ended up across two knife switches. The resulting firework display was something to behold, as we were left with two bakelite handles and about five pound of molten copper on the deck. Strangely enough, I was not prosecuted for damaging government property on this occasion.

My first trip abroad was to the Channel Islands. All went well till we got an emergency recall so we could transport some MP back to the mainland because of the Profumo affair. Unfortunately, a member of the crew had other ideas; he cut all the compass repeat cables rendering our little ship unseaworthy. Little did he know that the mighty electrical branch had the technical ability and the waterproof tape to fix the problem within hours. I heard some years later that the prat who did it was in the Lenox pub in Portsmouth bragging about it one night, when he was overheard by regulating Petty officer in civvies, who promptly sent for a shore patrol and had him arrested; he got 90 days in detention quarters and a dishonourable discharge.

In the early sixties, no civilian clothes were allowed on board ship, so one went ashore in uniform and changed into your Teddy boy suit or whatever at the Trafalgar club, or Aggie Westerns. These were refuges for drunk and weary sailors; you could play snooker or darts or unwind with a magazine or newspaper and have a few drinks before hitting the NAAFI club, which was full of desperate women keen to find a husband. Popular pubs at that time were the Lenox and the Albany, complete with big Sylvie, a nice girl, twenty stone of Pompy womanhood, who would entice you to buy her a drink by grabbing you by the balls and uttering the famous phrase, "Buy me a drink, Jack." Not many refused, strangely enough.

Our next trip abroad was to Copenhagen; I and twenty-three other lucky buggers got trained up to do a guard for some local celebration there. After weeks of perfecting our routine, we arrived and a coach took us with all our finery to the town centre; the local army and navy all had ceremonial guards there. We fell in, dressed off, shouldered arms, and then stood at ease. Now, the other guards had all fallen in, done their dressing off, shouldered arms, stood at ease, and then stood easy. Stand easy, no, not us, we're British, we come to attention and stay there; after all, it's only 85 degrees plus. Unfortunately, the guy to my right doesn't like the heat and decides to flake out; as he falls he forgets to push his bayoneted rifle away from his body, and the bayonet is just about to go through his skull via his left cheek when I, and the guy on his other side, catch him.

I remove the weapon from his head; all this is being done to the sound of the gunnery Officer screaming, "Leave him, leave him," callous bastard; matey on the other side tells him to fuck off, which doesn't go down well. We carry him to a waiting ambulance; the driver piles him in the front and slings his rifle in the back before roaring off, sirens blaring. By this time everything is over, our transport has gone without us, and we're stuck in the middle of Copenhagen fully booted and spurred with a 303 rifle. We pop into a bar for a beer or two and prop our rifles on the counter. I don't know if they thought we were threatening them or not, but the beers were free; he even got us a lift back to the ship, damn nice chap.

The gunnery Officer was intent on reprimanding us for disobeying his order, but obviously changed his mind when the Captain received a message from the local Mayor, praising me and my mate for our heroic action, up yours Guns!

Chapter Three

It is now the ninth of September, 1963. I've completed six months on Wakeful, during which time I have met my future wife, Hermione, on a blind date. Actually, my mate was going out with her at the time, but I didn't fancy my date so we swapped.

I now have a draft to HMS Maidstone, a submarine depot ship with facilities for nuclear boats, she weighs 5,900 tons and was built in 1935, top speed 17 knots. She is stationed at Faslane near Helensburgh on Gareloch. The big future nuclear shore base has recently started construction. I arrive at the ship and complete my joining routine, same, same. The only difference this time was the accommodation: a huge mess deck, a bunk, a dining hall, Christ, it was like joining the Queen Mary; the flats (passageways) were huge, I was well impressed.

My first job on the Maidstone was communal party. I thought great, cleaning party, and this is what I joined up for. I was given a flat to keep clean, washing paintwork, dusting, polishing brass tallies, and damage control clips; sod this, I thought. I removed everything made of brass and took it down to the engineer's workshop, and got permission to use the buffing wheel. The brass came up like burnished gold; my flat was gleaming. The Captain came and did his rounds, and to say he was gobsmacked is an understatement. After rounds, I was summoned to see the Captain. I thought, Jesus, now what have I done? As it happened, he was so impressed he made me official brass cleaner, starting with the Captain's flat. The job I created was carried on when I finished. After three months, I was given a job change to Ring main and generation; it's now January 1964, and I'm just getting used to this newfangled electricity called AC. After my experience with DC, I am finding this new stuff is more dangerous, and hurts like hell if you happen to brush against it; in fact, it tends to throw you across the compartment. Doing routines on some of the ring main switch gear could take all day; you wouldn't believe how many bolts held a lid on these huge boxes. The daft thing was, once you got the huge lids off with blocks and tackle, the inside switchgear was as new, and after inspecting these pristine boxes we had to reseal the lids to make them watertight, then lift them back into position to bolt them up.

Youv'e heard the expression 'if it isn't broke, don't fix it.' Well, that certainly applied in this case. One job I was sent to do was to go down to a steam driven generator which was leaking steam on the armature; this was causing insulation problems, so rather than stop it and fix the problem, I was to draw a bucket of trichoethylene and throw it on the armature to dry it out. This was successful for a little while, and was repeated every four hours.

What they didn't tell you, was this stuff was lethal. In fact, a few years later, six people died in a factory using this solvent, and the Navy then limited its issue to 1 pint maximum per day, thanks for that. After a month or so on generation, I was transferred to the battery section; this included navigation lights. One day someone reported the masthead steaming light was too dim, in other words some of the twelve lamps had blown. The Chief electrician asked for a volunteer to go up and replace the lamps, for some reason no one came forward, so I thought, what the hell? I drew the fuses, got some lamps, grabbed a safety harness and tool bag, and headed for the 140-foot pole. What someone had failed to tell me was the rope ladder up the mast was 100 years old, at least it seemed that way; it was coming apart in my hand on the way up. I eventually reached the first obstacle, the platform half way up, now bearing in mind I have a tool bag, lamps and a safety harness on my person, I now find I have to negotiate the platform by climbing round rigging to get onto it. Once I'm on the platform I take a well earned breather, the old adrenaline has kicked in and I'm getting a bit of a buzz; I now climb the next set of rotten rope to the top platform of the mast, only the rope ladder has run out and the steaming light is still twelve feet above me.

Christ, there is no way I'm shinning up that. How the hell am I supposed to climb up and repair that? It was then I noticed two pins which held the top pole section in place and kept the twelve foot section separate from the main mast. I removed the pins and lowered the top bit between my legs, and now was able to get to the lamp base. I had to hammer ten bells out of it to get the brass ring undone and remove the glass dome. Eight of the twelve lamps had blown, so I swapped them and replaced the dome and ring. My problem now was trying to lift the top back into position to replace the pins; it proved impossible, so I left the mast 12 feet short. It remained this way till the ship was scrapped. I know this because years later the Maidstone became a temporary prison ship for the IRA, in Belfast harbour, and I spotted her on the news, her mast still 12 feet short.

At this time, the nuclear base at Faslane was in the first stages of being built; lots of earth moving machinery was in the area and the whole area was fenced off. During this period, submariners were normally at sea for six weeks on patrol, all with no alcohol, so you can imagine what they were like with six weeks pay in their pockets and gasping for a drink; that's right, they got ever so slightly pissed. On this particular occasion, one of these drunken submariners decided the area in front of the ship needed redesigning, so he somehow managed to start a bulldozer and set off on his tour. After he demolishes the security fence, he sets about driving over the cars, twelve in all, with devastating results. He then turns his attention to the quartermaster's hut and squashes it and everything in it; fortunately, the guys inside heard what was going on and legged it before he arrived. He eventually passed out and crashed into a bollard, which helped the duty watch chasing him to catch up and arrest him. He got the nominal 90 days in detention quarters.

As sport was a bit limited, I decided to join the ship's boxing team to keep in trim. This time I trained, not so cocky after the last fight. I was capable of doing three rounds without dropping of exhaustion. My first fight was against a submariner; I'm not saying he was game, but I must have knocked him down twenty times in the three rounds; I just could not knock him out, and each time he got up, with of all things, a smile on his face. He might have thought it funny, but I was getting a bit demoralized, and was glad when the final bell went. Come the presentation of awards, I was presented with a lovely shoe cleaning kit; it must have cost at least half a crown, tight bastards. I would not have minded so much but for the fact the guy I knocked ten bells out of got a bloody great silver trophy as the best loser of the evening. I'll give him his due, as he was the sort of guy I'd be happy to have along in any situation.

The next event was against an American submarine depot ship. I was paired up with a six foot six windmill, who came out of his corner both arms flailing round in circles, and he caught me unawares. I just stood there gobsmacked. Fortunately, I managed to get out of the way before being hit on the top of my head with one of his sails. I'm not sure, but I think this was probably his first fight. Anyway, after dodging him for two rounds he became exhausted (been there), the bell went for the third round, and I put him out of his misery with an uppercut to his unprotected jaw, goodnight Vienna.

I was now preparing for the next fight when an incident happened that was to cut short my boxing career. It was about 1130 one night, and I was lying on top of my bunk when the mess drunk came off shore. This guy's wife had left him, and he turned to the dreaded booze; he was consequently disrated from Petty officer down to EM1, and had a chip on his shoulder which involved the whole world and everyone in it. He also got very nasty, and everyone was weary of him when he drank. Now for some reason he stumbled in the mess and found his way to me. He mumbled something, and then did what I thought was a bit unusual: he grabbed me by the balls.

Now this is a painful experience, so I politely asked him to let go. "What are you going to do about it?" he said, so I showed him. I gave him my best right full in his face; he let go and ended up on the deck. I then leapt out of my bunk, only to see him get up growling, "Nice try kid, but you'll have to do better than that," and sure enough, he was right. I spent the next ten minutes just hitting the guy, only to watch him get up again each time; I must admit I was crapping myself at this time. The mess deck was swimming in blood, and so were people's bedding and towels; fortunately, it was all his. He kept following me till we ended up in the sailors' mess; I eventually hit him with my best shot and he collapsed unconscious. I honestly thought I had killed him. Throughout the fight, the whole mess was urging me on; I was covered in blood, and my hands hurt like hell. All I was dressed in was my boxer shorts. I was worried, and not wanting to get done for murder, I legged it up to the sick bay. I reported that a guy had fallen down a hatch and was unconscious; they looked at me covered in blood and must have thought, lying little bugger.

Anyway, a stretcher party was sent down the mess, and he was loaded up and taken to the sick bay. I followed to make sure he was still alive; he regained consciousness, lifted his head to me and said, "I'll have you, you little bastard." With that, I ran down to the electrical workshop, locked myself in, and stayed there for the night. The next morning I'm wandering through the ship in my boxers to get to my mess. I arrive, and see people are busy scrubbing blood off bulkheads and deck. I am expecting to be sent for, to be charged with something, but nothing happens. Although the whole bloody ship knows what's happened. I'm amazed. Lunch time arrives and rum is being issued; being only seventeen I am not allowed in the mess during this ceremony. I hear my name being called, I go into the mess, and there before me is the grotesque figure of the guy I fought the night before.

He was unrecognisable, two slits for eyes, a broken nose, and a swollen face, and everything matched perfectly with my swollen hands. He now holds out his tot of rum to me, I refuse, and he whispers to me, "You might as well have it because I can't drink it." I took it as way of apologising for last night. I drank the tot, half a pint of two parts water and one part rum, my very first tot in the RN. I became quite well known on board after the incident. I must admit I would never go to sleep till the man came off shore and he went to sleep first. A month later he came off shore in a foul mood and picked on the smallest lad in the mess. I leapt out of my bunk and approached him; he obviously recognised me through his drunken haze, and went to bed without any trouble.

During one week of storing ship, flagons of neat pusser's rum went missing; this was a little unusual as every doorway and hatch was guarded on the route to the storeroom by senior ratings. An investigation and a search revealed nothing, however, I do recall being invited to the stokers mess for a tot of rum for some favour I had done, and it did have a hint of oily bilge water, I think the clue as to where the rum went could be there.

One night I had just finished the middle watch doing switchboard watch keeping (midnight to four am); I had a quick shower and headed for my bunk. I climbed in, switched my bunk light off, and was preparing to go to sleep when I observed someone coming down my aisle dressed in overalls. I didn't recognise who it was, so I kept an eye out. This character then proceeded to go in my mate's locker and took cigarettes and money; he was obviously a professional thief as he had his name painted on his back, Mitch, DER. I scrabbled to get out of my bunk and managed to thump him hard in the middle of his back; he went down, and I then got out, by then he was up and running. I was after him, and I chased him to the stokers mess shouting and screaming all the way, by now everyone was awake. By the time I had looked round and found Mitch, he was in his bunk, looking as if nothing had happened. I got hold of the leading hand of his mess and explained what had occurred in my mess. The officer of the day and duty Petty officer were summoned, and I told them what happened; they checked his back, and sure enough there was the bruise I had planted there; they also checked his overalls and found the name as I described.

Next they went to his locker – in it they found hundreds of different cigarettes, and piles of loose change and notes, which seemed a little odd as it was a non pay week and most people were on the bones of their arse. He was taken out of the mess and put in cells for the rest of the night. The leading hand of the mess told me that this Mitch character was always volunteering to do the middle watch, and that money and cigarettes were always going missing.

The next morning, the guy whose cigarettes were stolen and I were summoned to the commander's table for defaulters, as witnesses, you understand. I gave my account of the evening's events; this was followed by my mate being asked if he could identify his packet of a hundred senior service, which was on a big pile of other cigarettes and loot on the side table. Probably exhibit A, unfortunately, all packets of senior service look the same, so he said no. My evidence, the bruise, the chase, the named overalls meant nothing to the incompetent prosecution, and thieving Mitch got his case dismissed. He actually left the Commander's table with all his stolen fags and money and smirked at me. I nearly laid him out there and then, but for my mate holding me back. He returned to his mess thinking he'd got away with it, however his messmates were waiting for him and justice prevailed. They took him down to the engineer's workshop and put both his hands in a vice, breaking eight fingers; he ended up in sickbay, and stayed there till he and his reputation left the ship for a medical discharge. The Navy doesn't have much use for sailors who can't use their hands.

The Maidstone used to sail once a year to qualify for duty free fags; the problem was she had extra superstructure on the front end to facilitate the nuclear subs, which made her front heavy, and in rough weather she tended to lurch up a wave and then dive into it. You would lay in your bunk wondering if, after she nosed in, she would ever come up again, but fortunately she always did. One of the places we used to visit was Belfast. I recall on one particular visit, we had just fallen in on the upper deck to dress ship, when this old Irish guy on the shoreline started hurling abuse at us and taking pot shots at us with a double barrelled shot gun. Well, we crapped ourselves to start with, till we realised his shot was falling short by fifty yards or so, then we started taking the piss out of him till we were told to shut up.

A notice was put up, inviting twenty-five members of the crew to visit the Guinness brewery, and I put my name down. A coach picked us up and off we went. They gave us the usual tour of the brewery; they seemed to make everything but Guinness. Afterwards, we were directed to the board room, where a huge, long, oval table surrounded by leather seats lay before us. We all sat down, in front of us were plates of sandwiches, a glass, and a bottle of beer. We started eating the sandwiches and politely sipped the beer, and then this top guy from the brewery came in. "Come on, lads, drink up," he says, and with that he drew the curtains at the end of the room to reveal crates of beer stacked to the ceiling. It took us a few hours to clear them, but clear them we did. I don't remember much of the trip back to the ship, surprisingly.

Back at Faslane, most of my spare time was spent reading or going for bike trips. The weather in the area always seemed to be either raining, or drizzly, or cold or a combination of the three, but despite this, the scenery was spectacular. Going into Helensburgh for a run ashore was out of the question; for a start, it was six miles away, and the bus only ran twice a week if there was a z in the month. Secondly, I was only on £3.10sh a week, and that was needed for the odd weekend. As we were only given four free railway warrants a year, we had to make them last or pay our own train fare. The submariners obviously had a few bob to spare after six weeks at sea with nothing to spend their money on, so when they came in, they hit the town hard. One of the popular pubs had a landlord with one arm, and what an arm; he could lift a barrel with one hand, and if there was any trouble he would go behind the trouble maker and stick his hand between their legs, grab a handful of wedding tackle, and march them out on tiptoe. I'm not sure if the Maidstone was supposed to be the Navy's open prison or not, but more people seemed to be getting into trouble on her than the rest of my future ships put together.

After seven months on the Maidstone, I was drafted to HMS Corunna D97 on the seventeenth April, 1964; at that time she was refitting in Portsmouth dockyard. A battle class destroyer built in 1945; she was fitted with two 4.5 inch twin turret guns, two bofors, and a Sea Cat anti air missile system, the first to be fitted in the RN. This ship looked like a warship: sleek, fast, 36 knots top speed. Being in refit, she was in a bit of a state. The ship's company was being put together in HMS Victory (now HMS Nelson) which was a shore establishment used to accommodate ships in refit. After the refit, the ship's company began to settle in and get her up to fighting readiness; we completed harbour acceptance trails and headed to Portland for sea acceptance trails, and work up, which consisted of testing every capability of ship and crew. We did damage control exercises for fire, flood, and damage, we did lifeboat drills, emergency stations, action stations, boarding parties, landing parties, replenishment at sea (RAS) for stores and fuel, speed trails, breakdown drills, you name it we were tested on it. After the inspection we headed to Plymouth, and once there the Captain allowed weekend leave to the port watch, which was me; I headed to Portsmouth to be with my girlfriend.

It was Saturday when I received a telegram saying stay in Portsmouth; the ship is being brought back by the starboard watch. The ship duly sailed, and got outside the harbour when she had a total machinery failure; she was dangerously close to running aground when the tugs reached her and brought her into Plymouth again. My second telegram arrived telling me to return to Plymouth ASAP, and we were there for a day or two while repairs were carried out. We then sailed for Portsmouth, and on the way we did a RAS with the royal fleet auxiliary vessel (RFA) Tide Pool; now, keeping a parallel course with the ship you are fuelling with is fairly important. Unfortunately, at this particular moment in time we were drifting off course, and the Captain changed course to move in closer to the RFA. An escorting frigate opened up with her 4.5 inch guns and distracted our skipper; he forgot to straighten up and we collided with the Tide Pool. Our starboard side was caved in damaging plates, and disabling one of our switchboards, our bedstead 965 long range radar got tangled up with the tanker's fuelling gib. 'Hands to emergency stations' was piped and damage control parties got on with keeping the ship afloat. One sight I will always remember was the Chief Stoker hanging on the guard rail with his foot on the Tide Pool trying to push her away. We eventually got untangled and broke free to lick our wounds; we limped back to Pompey and into dry dock, where the plates and switchboard were repaired. The boilers were playing up again, so the dockyard maties were back to try and fix them. They replaced the fuel sprayers and the fuel blower fan; unfortunately, the igniters, rods with spark plugs on the ends which gos into the boiler to light the fuel, were defective and no spares were available, and hadn't been since the refit.

After our little tryst with the RFA, and mini ship rebuilding exercise, we sailed for sea trails. We spent the day on one boiler, and everything went well till we were heading for the Solent and the Captain decided to get the second boiler flashed up. Well, due to the fact we had no working igniters, the emergency routine was to get a steel pole, wrap an oily rag round the end, and light it. Next, the fuel sprayers were turned on, the burning rag was now thrust into the igniter hole, and the fan switched on to draw the flame onto the fuel thus lighting the boiler. Unfortunately, the dockyard had wired the fan up back to front; the flaming rag was blown into the bilges where it quickly set fire to fuel, and all hell now broke loose.

The massive cooling fans in the boiler room soon had the fire raging; the watch on duty were soon legging it at a great rate of knots to escape, which took a while because the boiler room was pressurised and had air locks, and when you entered the air lock you had to close the door to the boiler room before opening the door to the upper deck. This was to keep the pressure from falling; if this procedure was not observed the chances were there could be a flash back. Once the watch was clear, the alarm was raised, fire, fire, fire, fire in the boiler room, crash stop ventilation, hands to emergency stations, damage control crews close up. By now fire crews where getting organised, boundary cooling was put in place, to prevent it spreading to compartments all round the fire, hoses and foam where mustered on the iron deck, this is the place where it was needed, brass deck glands were removed and hoses connected, foam was connected, and the mains water turned on. This should not take long!

Someone notices the side of the ship is blistering, very strange; the boiler room should be half full of foam by now and getting cooler? It was then the gearing room upper deck hatch opened and the Chief artificer, covered in foam appeared, saying, "What the hell is going on?" It seemed the foam had been pumped down the wrong deck gland, ooops! By now the fire was out of control, and the ship's foam supply was almost exhausted; there was nothing to do but call for the dockyard fire tugs. They arrived and the fire was eventually put out; truth is, there was bugger all left in the boiler room to burn. The ship's company spent the night clearing up. Next day, we were towed into Portsmouth dockyard and into dry dock (again). One thing we noticed was the fact that two brand new igniters were waiting for us on the jetty when we arrived. At last, after six months of waiting, a miracle, 24 hours too late. The ship's company would have loved to get hold of the incompetent bastard who wired up the boiler room fan; he cost us a trip to the 1964 Olympic Games in Tokyo. We spent months in dry dock getting the boiler room back to its original condition; the good thing was everything was new, so less chance of breaking down. I suppose we should have been grateful it happened when it did, and not in the middle of the Pacific.

After our refit we eventually sailed for the deployment in the Far East, Singas here we come! The ship called into Gibraltar, for fuel and stores, and our first foreign run ashore; this was the first time I got to wear my tropical gear since it was issued. We also picked up a Chinese laundry crew and tailor; they settled in and soon got to work setting up. Prices were sent round to everyone, and they were very popular, Your white fronts and shirts would arrive back as stiff as hell; you had to peel them apart, due to the fact they starched them with their left over rice water, and they marked all clothes with a laundry mark known only to them. With all the washing they did you always got your correct kit back, amazing! The tailor did a roaring trade in cheap lightweight cotton working shirts and shorts, ideal for sunny climes; he also sold tie up boxer shorts, easy to wash and dry. Our next stop was Malta, the land of bells smells and pregnant women, so the saying goes. It was my first introduction to Marsavin, the local wine; I recall Thursday was the best vintage, god, it was rough. I also found the famous Gut, a street renowned for its seedy bars, frequented by sailors over many years. The locals at that time were not over friendly, due to the fact HMS Eagle had recently passed through. Evidently, a royal marine had been filled in by some locals, and all his mates piled ashore and went down the Gut and wrecked the place, and laid out anyone who tried to stop them.

We sailed the next day, straight into a force 9 gale; it was too rough to refuel at sea so we had to wait till we got to Port Said. Once there, we anchored. The whole port was a hive of activity full of ships waiting to go through the canal, also fishing boats, tugs, and dhows. Then along came all the bum boats, full of Middle Eastern tourist souvenir crap. The one thing they loved to trade was the Navy sea jersey; we found it hard to comprehend why, when the heat was up in the hundreds, would they want a woolly pully? It wasn't till the night time did we realise why; it was bloody freezing. Many a pully was swapped for a bottle of Johnnie Walker filled with cold tea. These bloody Arabs are persistent buggers; they do like to try and get on board and help themselves to anything that moves, as well as try to sell their crap. Consequently, the Captain ordered hoses to be charged ready to open up if they got too close. Many a bum boat has been sent to the bottom filled with water hosed in by laughing Matelots. I heard that the Chief bosun's mate on HMS Hermes dropped a concrete dan buoy sinker from the flight deck straight through the middle of a bum boat; the fountain it caused was huge, and his stock of leather camels floated off in all directions. I bet that was some sight.

After we had refuelled, we waited for the North bound convoy to come through the canal. Once they were clear we led the South bound convoy through to the bitter lakes at the centre of the canal. This was a parking area while ships from the Red Sea came through, all very well organised, and once they were through we headed south again. It was nice to see the local Arabs trying out their English on us, shouting, "Marks and Spencers! Fish and chips!" and mooning us on the canal side, but they got a bit of a surprise when one of the old sea dogs produced a steel catapult and a handful of ball bearings. He'd been here before and vowed to get his revenge; you should have heard those bastards squeal when those half inch ball bearings hit them in the arse. I bet they've still got the scars to prove it.

Once through the Suez Canal (which, by the way, is 100 miles long), we enter the Red Sea and head for Aden, a British protectorate on the southwest corner of Arabia, and entrance of the Red Sea. The landscape is barren, and the temperature is in the hundreds. Some of the lads are sunbathing, and after half an hour they look like lobsters; the inside of the ship is also hot due to the fact air conditioning had obviously not been invented yet. Our system of keeping cool was to put wind scoops out of the scuttles (port holes to you). This worked well when the ship was bombing along at 25 knots, but not so clever when along side, or indeed when the skipper decides to do a starboard 35 and half the bloody ocean came in through the window.

We arrive in Aden, what a godforsaken place this is; why the British government would want this place is beyond me. Anyway, the Navy has a small contingent there, and the army has the Argyles, and they try and keep law and order against the local tribes and terrorists. Our watch is given shore leave, on the understanding we go in threes; if you went shopping one person had to keep an eye out outside. At this particular time I was nominated to keep watch outside a shop; I spotted a Navy Land Rover coming down the main street; I then heard this *whoosh*, and I turned to see this Arab with a bazooka on his shoulder, and he had just released a rocket at the Land Rover. I waited for it to detonate; instead it went through the windscreen and out the back; the driver swerved and crashed into a tree. I yelled for my mates and told them what had happened; we made sure the driver was OK. He headed back to his base a little shook up, and we three brave souls ran like hell back to the jetty to catch the liberty boat back to the ship.

The ship sailed the next day and headed into the Indian Ocean. The crossing the line ceremony was carried out and all us first timers were initiated by Neptune and his little helpers. After several days, we were getting low on fuel and the ship was riding high out of the water; consequently, she was rolling like a drunken sailor, the iron decks were constantly awash and care had to be taken when going on the upper deck. No bloody wind scoops this time, and it was hot. The engineering officer could have put sea water into the tanks to ballast the ship, but did not want to because it would have meant a tank clean when next in dock. Just as well, the sea was like glass, and the slightest swell would have had us over, I reckon.

This was the first and only time I've seen people being sea sick in a force one. We reached the island of Ghan to refuel, and anchored in a crystal clear bay; you could see the ocean floor from the deck; several hammerhead sharks appeared, which deterred swimming, however, fishing proved to be easy as you could see where to put your line, and the chefs had plenty of fish to cook at the end of the day. There was an RAF base there, and the starboard watch were allowed ashore. The lads popped into their canteen for a few beers before catching the liberty boat back to the ship. Once the fuel tanks were topped up, we left for our next port of call, Langkawi (meaning strong eagle in Malay) the Island is situated North West of the Malay peninsula and is the largest one of 104 islands, some of which are submerged at high tide. On the way we practice various drills and gunnery practice; the ship's condensers keep playing up, these devices turn sea water into fresh by boiling and condensing, at least that's what the Chief Stoker told me. So now we go on water rationing, which means limited washing facilities. Showers are switched on for only fifteen minutes during the day, and the same in the evening; the routine as laid down is, you turn the shower on, wet yourself, turn the shower off and soap yourself down, then switch on and rinse.

After many days at sea, we anchor in Langkawi harbour. This place is like paradise, the scenery and the blue sea are something to behold. Can't wait to get ashore and see what it's like. When my watch has its turn for shore leave, I put my white front, white shorts, stockings, and white blancoed canvas shoes on. I make sure I have my ID card and money, now I'm ready for a run ashore. I hand in my station card to the quarter master, the duty PO falls us in for the officer of the day inspection; we all pass muster and load into the Whaler. The engine is revved up, kicked into gear and we head for shore; a few of us have a long walk round taking it all in. The people are very friendly, especially the Malays, the Chinese not so much; surprisingly, most spoke English. We look round all the amazing shops and stalls before finding a bar; we relax and have a few Tiger beers.

We then went to a small backstreet eating place, and ordered a variety of things from the menu; we all ordered something different, with the understanding that it all went in the middle and we would help ourselves. Well, when it arrived we where gobsmacked, as they must have brought twenty different plates of food, prawns, chicken, pork, vegetables, rice, fruit, you name it, they supplied it. Christ, we thought, this is going to cost us a fortune. As it happened, it cost peanuts, and everything was superb; it was so cheap we nearly left the same again as a tip, you would have thought we were royalty, they treated us so well.

The ship stayed for five days, and on the last evening of the visit the ship had a tragedy. One of the crew got drunk and couldn't wait half an hour for the liberty boat, and decided to swim for the ship. He didn't make it, and his body was recovered the next morning by local fishermen. His body was brought on board and placed in the ship's freezer till we got to Singapore, our next port of call.

I forgot to mention earlier that I got married when I was on the Maidstone. I was eighteen and a half at the time, and my baby snatching wife was twenty. The reason we got married so early was, I was to be away for a year and we thought the marriage allowance paid in those days would help us save more. A bit mercenary, I know, but money was not exactly coming out of our ears in '64; in fact, I was on £7.10sh, and my wife on the same, working at Fine Fare supermarket in the meat department, so the extra £3.10sh was a bonus. The priest at our wedding assumed the wife was pregnant and made some sly comment about it. The drunken bastard refused to come to the reception because we had no whisky. A certain Lt Commander David Eckersley-Maslin did come along to the wedding and the reception with his lovely wife, Ann, and two children, Nicola and Roger. My wife and I had been their baby sitters back in our courting days.

Now back to the trip, having left Langkawi, we headed south for Singapore, an uneventful trip apart from the usual machinery breakdowns of steering motors, brine pumps, and other magical bits and bobs which keep the ship running. We enter harbour, ship dressed overall, ship's company in full number sixes, that's our posh white uniforms; my, we do look impressive. Once alongside, the gangway is put down; shore supply is connected via cables from the jetty to the ship's junction box. This means the ship's generators can now be shut down for maintenance, and the ship's telephone cables are connected to shore lines, giving us access to the outside world. Post is sent and collected, a vital life line to home. The next few weeks are spent doing maintenance and repairing. My job during this time was ring main and generation, replacing lamps and working on motors and such, down in the machinery spaces.

One job I will never forget was changing the smoke light behind the boiler. It took four hours; the problem was not that it was difficult, but that it was hot, 180 F to be exact; one minute and my overalls were soaking. Out I came, two pints of water and half an hour later I was back down there for another go, and this carried on till the job was complete. At last, the ship is up to fighting readiness and we are ordered to sea to commence patrols. This consists of stopping communist insurgents coming from Indonesia to Malaya; some chap called Sukano has intentions of making Malaya communist. It was the equivalent of America's Vietnam, on a smaller scale; the difference was we (the British) had it under control. Our job was to stop and search fishing boats for commies and weapons. Boarding parties were sent to any suspect vessels, and any suspect fishermen were brought on board and interrogated by the Malay policemen, who we had carried on board. I've got to say they were mean bastards; human rights went out the window in those days. Policy on stop and search changed when one of our minesweepers went alongside a suspect empty boat and was blown up, killing three or four sailors, and damaging the front end of the sweeper.

After that incident, all suspect boats were hailed; if no one replied, the boat was sunk using gunfire; better safe than sorry, eh. During these patrols I was nominated as boarding party. I was given a Lanchester machine gun; it was a crude bit of kit, all it consisted of was a butt, trigger, barrel, a spring, firing pin and a magazine. It was not at all accurate, and it was virtually impossible to fire just one shot off, its trigger was so sensitive. I had to sleep on a camp bed in B turret; the deck was always oily and smelt awful; when called for action we had to make our way from the turret along the upper deck to the small arms magazine aft. Just as well Johnny Commie didn't shoot at us before we got our ammo; we wouldn't have had a chance. You might be thinking, why did they not give the ammo before the trouble starts? Well, you obviously don't know, Matelots and guns don't mix. An example of this was when we were getting ready for a boarding search and the Officer ordered us to load our weapons. The twat next to me pulled his cocking lever back to insert the first round into the chamber and instead of hooking it ready to fire, he let go and the round nearly took my ear off.

Chapter Four

In January 1965 I was given a job change: stores and spare gear, an exciting job you might think; not so, it consisted of dishing out electrical stores to those greenies who required them, then re-ordering to keep stocks up to date. Another part of the job was to get spare gear boxes out and check them. These pieces of heavy electrical equipment are packed in heavy wooden crates and the lids screwed down with dozens of screws. You might think a box with a label stating it houses a motor inside might just be telling the truth. My pessimistic Chief electrician at the time obviously thought otherwise, which is why on this particular day we had every spare gear box out of the tiller flat on the iron deck. This deck on a battle class destroyer is about six foot off the sea level; we, by now had around five boxes open and were checking the contents. So far, so good.

At this time our ship is on an exercise, and we are line astern of twelve other ships belting along at twenty five knots; unfortunately, the ship ahead of us has an engine failure. Our Captain now does what he is best at, and orders a starboard thirty five; this prevents us from ramming the disabled ship in front. This now means our ship heels over heavily to the right. As this is an emergency manoeuvre, no warning is given and mess deck wind scoops are still out; they now become sea water scoops flooding compartments and mess decks. Anything loose and not bolted down becomes a flying missile. The galley is now redecorated in custard, gravy and veg, and chefs are heard shouting obscenities at the sailors steering the ship. More important to me and the Chief Electrician is the fact that the deck we are on is now under water, at forty five degrees and flowing past at twenty five knots. We both make a grab for the hand rail on the superstructure and hang on for dear life. After what seems a life time, the ship becomes vertical again and we inspect the damage. The guard rails on the ship's side have gone, due to the fact our heavy spare gear boxes have torn through them on their way over the side. It was a welcome sight seeing those heavy boxes disappearing in the distant wake of our ship, bloody good riddance. This meant we did not have to open or check them and stow them back in the tiller flat. I did, however, have to re-order everything.

Although the chance of getting anything from Naval stores in the UK this side of Christmas was remote, which was unfortunate as we would need a fair amount of spares before this trip was over.

After the exercise we resumed patrol. The Captain stops the ship; 'hands to bathe' is piped, and most of the ship's company not on watch leaps over the side. As the ship appeared to be staying afloat, I remained on board and watched. After around ten minutes, someone on the safety boat spots a black triangle sticking out of the water. 'Shark, shark, shark,' he screams in a loud falsetto voice, and the sea turns into a frothy maelstrom as a hundred matelots break the hundred meter world record for the crawl. Bodies are climbing over one another to get onboard, no bravery there, I fear. Five minutes later the gunnery officer appears with a fist full of grenades, one at a time he removes the pins and drops them over the side. Five seconds and thirty fathoms later, they detonate; there is a dud thud and a few bubbles appear; that will teach those nasty sharks not to mess with the Royal Navy. The ship is ready to get under way, but this time the Captain is over the side with a length of line in his hand, and the other end is attached to the guard rails on the stern of the ship. What the hell is going on? The ship moves off, leaving the Captain in our wake, surely we're not going to tow him. Oh, yes, we are, once up to full speed the skipper appears to be standing on water; in fact, he is on a pair of skis swerving from side to side. We are now up to thirty six knots, flat out, what a novel way to travel, although I can't see it catching on.

Our patrol is now over. We are relieved by a frigate and head back to Singapore for a spot of well earned R and R. To get ashore you must travel through HMS Terror, the Navy's shore establishment. It has a massive NAAFI and canteen and wonderful sports fields. These fields are the mass graves of British service men, courtesy of the Japanese. Once out of the main gates, you head downhill to the village of Sambwang. This place is geared up for sailors, bars, souvenir shops, and local slappers. The first essential to buy is wanshi burbs; this is a bamboo and lacquer device which can loosely be described as an umbrella that kept you reasonably dry when the monsoons hit. Unfortunately, once it got wet and then dried out for further use, it stank of rotting fish which tended to upset people in the confines of a mess deck. Once you have had your fill of Tiger beer, the routine was to go to one of the food stalls, usually based over a monsoon ditch, which quite often had rats running through it. You ordered an egg banjo, a lovely fresh bread roll, with fried eggs and salad filling, then staggered back to your ship. The more adventurous would get a pirate taxi to Singapore; these were illegal and not licensed, but a quarter of the price of the legal ones. Looking back now, I realise they were death traps. The road into Singas was notoriously dangerous due to the fact it was built by prisoners of war, and they made the camber in the road the wrong way, which made cornering at speed a little hairy. Once in the city you were mesmerised at the diversity of cultures: Chinese, Malay, Indian, Brits, you name it, a bit like London today.

Back at sea on our next patrol, we did exercises with the RAF. They would fly out from Changi Air Base, and when they reached the target area would let out a drogue, a sort of wind sock on the end of thousands of feet of piano wire. Our job was to lock on with radar and proceed to try and shoot it down with TTB's – target triggered bursts, a shell that would only explode if it was within 50 feet of the target. This would indicate a hit at a real aircraft; our first few shots blew the drogue apart, and the radar locked onto the towing wire and our shooting continued to track up the wire with one TTB after another. With that, the aircraft sent us an emergency signal which read, "We are towing the target, not pushing it." Very droll. The Captain, keen to carry on shooting, asked the pilot to fly over low so he could see how much wire was left. If there was enough, he would order another run with a new drogue. The plane came in low, very low, and as it came in across the bow, you could hear a whistling noise of the wire; everybody forward hit the deck as the cable behind the aircraft lashed across the ship, the guard rails parted, and the wire put a score mark across a turret. Very funny, you Brylcreem boys, I guess that was pay back. The Captain sent them a signal: "If I knew you were coming in that low I would have got the cheese out."

A big enquiry was going on ashore at this time. The Master at arms on HMS Eagle had gone missing at sea; evidently he was piped on to the flight deck one night, and was never seen again. By all accounts he was a real nasty bastard, and got what was coming to him.

Ashore again, it was time for sport. I was on the ship's rugby team; we did really well and won the midi ships cup, and the Far East cup, beating frigates, destroyers and carriers. Our downfall came when a kiwi minesweeper came in. Considering it only had a very small crew and most of them were blacks, we were lucky to lose by only 40 points. I personally lasted only 10 minutes when this 17 stone Maori fell on me and fractured my ankle.

Due to this injury I was sent up to Fraser Hill, in the Cairngorm Mountains of Malaya for a well earned rest. We reached Kuala Lumpur by train, and a coach picked us up for the drive to the hill. I'm not saying the driver was a deranged formula one racing driver, but the speed he drove at was to say the least scary. It might have been the five hundred foot drop at the side of the road that caused people to scream. I don't know; I had my eyes shut in prayer.

Once there, it was a naturalist's dream: hundreds of butterflies, and bugs the size of golf balls, chit chats on every wall, which was OK till the night time when these monsters would bounce round the room keeping you awake. During the day we wandered round the place and came across soldiers doing patrols in the jungle looking for insurgents. They were invited back for a bath, something to eat, and a few beers, before setting off on their patrol again. After a week, we headed back to Singapore and our ship; spares were starting to get through and progress on breakdowns getting better. Inter-ship football matches were very popular, especially the evening matches when whole ships' companies would turn up. The norm was to go to the canteen and order a plastic bucket of Tiger beer and a glass, then make one's way to the pitch where the wooden stands would hold all the half drunk Matelots ready to watch their ship's team.

I competed in an athletics tournament in Terror; all ships and local athletics clubs were invited. I ran in the 100 yards in my bare feet and came second to the guy who had just competed in the Tokyo Olympics, albeit not very well. The Admiral at the time was obviously impressed because he sent a pair of spiked running shoes to the ship. As I had no intention of running again, I thought it a waste to keep them, so I sold them and had a run ashore on the proceeds, thank you sir, much appreciated. A little controversy came up when a guy living in married quarters went ashore; he had a few beers and asked a taxi driver to take him to a white woman for an evening's entertainment. Unfortunately, he took the guy to his own wife. What followed was an investigation which revealed many wives on the game, servicing rich, Chinese businessmen, a very lucrative trade. Mass departure followed, probably with mass divorce.

The ship now sailed for another exercise off the Philippines with the Yanks, Aussies and Canucks taking part. Afterwards, ships' companies are allowed ashore in the American PX for a few beers and a punch up; the Yankee Naval patrol were excellent in their use of baseball bats, as many a sore head will vouch for. Next we set sail for Hong Kong and a well earned rest. We entered harbour dressed overall; the ships saluting guns were fired in honour of the governor. We secured alongside and dozens of traders came aboard, selling watches, jewellery, clothes, and souvenirs; they would let you keep a watch for a few days to see if you liked it, very trusting these Chinese. The tailors offered a 24-hour service to make a suit. You were measured up in the morning, in the afternoon they came back for the final fitting, off they went, and next day your suit was delivered ready to wear, amazing. On the first Sunday the ship was woken up to what sounded like machine gun fire; in fact, it was 150 Chinese labourers with chipping hammers taking all the paint off the upper deck and superstructure. This, by all accounts, was normal for ships coming to Hong Kong. The work gang was run by a multi-millionaire Chinese lady called Jenny; her workers were known as Jenny's side party. The gang worked non stop; as one lot were chipping, the next lot were red leading, followed by the final paint job; all this was completed in one day. The ship looked as good as new. Admittedly, a lot of paint came off once we hit rough weather, but hey, what do you expect for the money. Jenny was paid cash for the job, and part of the agreement was that she was allowed the leftover food from the galley. She also provided highly a polished dustbin for jolly jack to ditch his leftovers from mealtimes.

What they didn't know was the so-called crap they were putting in the bin was taken away to the street stalls and transformed into Chinese cuisine with a few herbs, spices, and soy sauce. All slung on a bed of rice, and hey presto, a delicious meal fit for any drunken Matelot after his run ashore. The China Fleet club was the official Royal Navy club; it provided cheap shops, cheap beer, and the usual facilities, snooker, darts, magazines, etc. Huge tower blocks were going up at this time; it was amazing to see hundreds of Chinese labourers scampering over bamboo scaffolding which was all tied together with rope, no health and safety here then. The prices in Hong Kong were ridiculously cheap; we thought Singas was cheap, but it was even cheaper here, in fact, by half.

Seiko was in the process of taking over as the world's largest watch manufacturer; they made them so cheap that everyone was buying them. In fact, the Japanese were copying everything American at this time; it was commonly known as Jap crap. They eventually got it right as Honda, Mazda, Sanyo and a few others were to prove, a bit like the Chinese are doing today. The Red China store was out of bounds to Matelots, due to the fact the profits were used for insurgency against the British, probably for the bastards we're fighting against in Singas. We went in anyway, just for a look round, the place was lit up with 20 watt lamps, the most depressing place you could imagine; the brightest colour was probably soil brown, or pond green. Having said that, the craftsmanship on ivory was truly amazing; there was a riverboat made of ivory about 15 inches long in a glass case, one man's lifetime work only £95, ten weeks wages to me – not very PC, but probably worth thousands today. I don't wonder why elephants are becoming an endangered species with the amount of ivory there is in Hong Kong. I was nearly tempted to buy Chairman Mao's little red book in English, but common sense prevailed. The market stalls sold virtually everything; live animals, meat, fruit, veg, materials, herbs, spices, pots, pans.

The sights, smells and aromas were wonderful; the sheer hustle and bustle was like nowhere on earth, so many people, so little space.

It was time to head back to Singas and resume the Borneo patrol. After a week, we are ordered to take part in a multi-national exercise; we have three aircraft carriers, and twenty-odd frigates and destroyers. The Yanks, the Aussies, the Kiwis, and the Canadians provide the other fifty or sixty various ships. We are ordered to be the RED side (the enemy) and our job is to intercept the BLUE forces and sink and destroy (all pretend you understand). Anyway, the Captain has a cunning plan, the lighting on the ship is changed, necklace lighting is strung up, false steaming lights are placed into position, and a dummy mast is rigged up, all to alter the ships profile. At night we now look like a merchantman; at midnight the ship is brought to action stations, and we manoeuvre into the centre of the Blue convoy. We open fire with our two 4.5 inch guns, starting with a couple of star shells to light the place up, and then proceed to sink two Yankee destroyers, the Aussie carrier HMAS Melbourne, and a Canadian frigate before disappearing into the night. A highly successful exercise for us REDS. Although our Captain was a good sort, he did have a nasty habit of doing a starboard thirty round about supper time; I presume he ate his meal before he had his fun, as it's no joke peeling your supper off the bulkhead or your mate's head.

The ship was in two halves crew wise; the front end was separated from the arse end by the boiler room, engine room, and gearing room. There was a forward galley, and a separate after galley, these cooked the food to be taken down to the mess decks to be eaten at two tables. Consequently, meals were taken in shifts due to too many bodies and not enough seats. I recall doing rounds one night, checking for overheating equipment, fires, floods, etc. I poked my head into the galley, switched the lights on, and nothing happened for a few seconds. Suddenly there was a *whoosh* and the lights came on. I stood transfixed for a moment, trying to figure out what had happened. It was then I realised the place was infested with cockroaches, and turning the light on had scattered them. The next morning I reported the incident to the Supply Officer who ordered a fumigation of the ship when we got into harbour. This fumigation consisted of clearing the front end of the ship of all personnel, then using special smoke bombs to kill the roaches; the next day the after end of the ship was done, and in theory this was to clear the ship of these pests. Unfortunately, not so. On fumigating the front end, a hundred thousand refugee roaches headed aft via the machinery spaces; the next day when the after end was done, two hundred thousand roaches headed forward. Many of these roaches had become mascots of jolly Jack, they were painted various colours and let loose to see where they would end up; you'd be amazed how far these little buggers can travel.

On one particular run ashore, Gavin, a mess mate, bought a duckling in Sambaing market. He smuggled it on board in a shoe box which was to be its home. He kept it at the side of his bunk, and fed it on milk and cockroaches. At tot time he would hold it at one end of the table, and we would release roaches at the other end. The duckling (named Ugly) would be released, and it would tear down the table slipping and sliding, grabbing the bug, before being caught in a pillow as it went off the table. In the evening Gavin would take it to the bathroom, fill a bowl with warm water and let it paddle around, he would then take it for a walk on the upper deck to dry off. Unfortunately, one night on patrol we hit a bit of rough weather, and next morning Gavin woke up to find Ugly had fallen out of its box and onto his bunk, where Gavin, I'm sorry to say, had rolled on it. He cried his eyes out, and we gave it a proper Naval burial at sea, with full honours. Not so lucky was the monkey the seamen kept in the mess opposite ours; this abomination was kept on a long chain, and would screech like hell, and belt round the mess deck knocking everything over in its way, especially when the seamen fed it rum at tot time and got it pissed. One afternoon when everyone was having a siesta, someone decided enough was enough, and placed the half pissed monkey through the scuttle (porthole), chain and all, and unless it was a very strong swimmer I couldn't see it surviving. I don't condone cruelty, but I sure as hell was glad to see the back of that monkey.

All the time we spent on patrol we never broke down once. In fact, twice we were ordered to take over patrols for broken down ships. On one occasion, we were happily sailing along when RADAR spotted four Indonesian fast patrol boats heading towards us at thirty odd knots. No problem, except it was four o'clock in the morning, and when action stations is sounded when you are fast asleep, it does not go down too well with the crew. Once fully awake we were just in the mood to take these nocturnal commies out. As they near, the 4.5 inch guns are trained in their direction, and they appear on the horizon. Suddenly their signal lamps start flashing, and our signalman reads the message, "Doctor Sukano wishes you a good morning." Bastards, didn't they realise our chief elec has an anxiety problem and high blood pressure?

The week before we are due to sail home, the ship starts to fall to bits. First the steering motors fail, not one but two, then a generator wraps its hand in, followed closely by the water pumps. No problem, you might think; after all we carried spares. Well, yes, we used to, till they floated off into the sunset after our emergency starboard 35, a month or so previously. We now have to wait for the powers to be to decide how important our priority is, before the spares are flown or shipped out to us. While waiting for spares we managed to beg, steal, and borrow bits and pieces to get fresh water back; the spares from UK arrived within a week and were fitted. We had one last run ashore, to top up our rabbits (souvenirs). And the following morning we sailed on the morning tide for home; we all fell in on the upper deck in our number six suits, freshly starched by the Chinese laundry, you could cut bread with the seven creases in each leg.It looked very smart, but believe me it felt awful, not exactly washed in comfort.

After we sailed, I was given a job change, to Chiefs mess man, which consisted of cleaning up when the mess was cleared for work in the morning, and collecting the food from the galley at meal times. This proved a bit tricky when the after galley was out of commission and the food had to be brought from the forward galley. Trying to balance trays full of food along the iron deck in choppy weather was a bit dicey, so I tended to go the long way over the top catwalk. I did this job for a few weeks before going back to electrical duties. The lad who relieved me was collecting the Chiefs food one day from the forward galley, in a force 8 gale, when he decided to go along the iron deck with the trays. What he obviously did not hear was the broadcast that the iron deck was out of bounds, due to the fact the deck was under water most of the time as the ship went through the waves at 25 knots, and he was consequently washed overboard.

The lifebuoy ghost (watch keeper) on the quarterdeck spotted him in the water and pressed the man overboard alarm; he contacted the bridge to tell them what had happened, and the ship immediately did a starboard 30, nearly capsizing the ship in the force 8 gale. Everything not tied down was catapulted in the air, how nobody was killed I'll never know. A mayday was sent out, giving details of the emergency; we weren't expecting much help in the middle of the Indian Ocean, but within an hour, four merchantmen appeared and were searching with us. We searched till it got dark, with no luck; the search was then called off and we resumed our journey to Aden.

During the trip back, I passed my exam for leading rate. I now knew my next draft would be to Collingrad for course, and shore time with my wife.

We reach Aden, and the Captain orders the ship's company to attend a memorial service for the missing sailor. When it is over the master at arms organises an auction of the lad's kit; everyone is there, and the bidding is brisk, a collar goes for £50, a shirt for £75, a hat for £35, and so it went till the entire Navy kit was sold. His personal stuff was returned to his family along with a cheque for £1,350, the proceeds of the auction. This may not sound much today, but then it was probably the equivalent of at least

47

£10,000 in today's money; the guys' bids were taken out of their wages on a monthly basis till it was paid off. This was the normal procedure for the death of a sailor in the sixties, when the ship's company all joined at the same time and got to know each other, becoming lifelong friends, unlike today when sailors are joining and leaving on a weekly basis, and know one knows who the hell you are, let alone gives a toss if you happen to die.

Having fuelled, we head north for the Suez Canal. On our arrival, we have to wait for the south bound convoy to come through, and this takes half the day. Still, at least we get to push in to the front of the queue, and we now head for the Bitter lakes, the lay bye, in the middle of the canal. Once there, we pull over to let the Mediterranean traffic through; once they are clear, we sail for port Said, and the usual greetings by the Egyptian entrepreneurs in their bum boats: "Marks and Spencer's, fish and chips, Hey Jack, you wanna buy a nice carpet, or leather pouf?" We replied with, "Sod off, towel head, before we fill your boat up with seawater," and so the ritual goes on from ship to ship. The Supply Officer organises fresh fruit and veg to be delivered, and the remains of the stinking stuff left from Singapore is put in the gash barge.

We now head into the Med and hit a force 9. After several days of being thrown around and eating nothing but pot mess (this is a cauldron tied onto the galley range and constantly refilled with anything the chef cares to put in it, fruit, veg, meat, even the odd sponge pudding has been known to find its way in there, in other words a sort of stew), a bit like the ones they keep going for hundreds of years in some Pacific Islands. You would make your way to the galley with a bowl, and the chef would ladle the stew, between waves, into it, not exactly Cordon Bleu but welcomed, even if it was the same for breakfast, lunch, and supper. Eventually we enter grand harbour, Malta. Over the next two days leave is given to both watches; football and rugger matches are organised against the army and local teams. We are a bit rusty due to lack of fitness, and a lot of skin is lost on the grassless pitches. We lose all the games, but make up for it by out drinking the opposition in true Navy tradition.

Having recuperated and eaten something other than pot mess, we sailed for Gibraltar, and this was the ideal place to get our last minute rabbits (presents). For some of the crew, this was the first time for that pleasure, having spent most of their money on cigarettes, whiskey, and wild, wild prostitutes. This, for a few, became a problem, due to the fact their willies were still leaking after weeks of treatment. Not so bad for the single guys, but a bit of a problem for the few married guys, whose little heads took charge of their big heads, if you know what I mean.

Alf Pickup

At last we're sailing for home, through the Bay of Biscay and into the English Channel. We finally reach Portsmouth mid-July 1965, and hundreds of people are watching our arrival from Southsea front and old Portsmouth. Family and friends are lining up on the jetty; as usual, we're all dressed up in our number one blue uniforms. The ship is looking smart, mainly because we had spent the day before anchored out, painting over the rust and flaky paint so we could give the impression of having just come out of the showroom, instead of weeks of being battered by the sea.

While at anchor, the customs and excise boat pays us their customary visit; these Gestapo-like individuals want to see everything you have bought while out of the country; they then decide how much you paid for your watch, or camera, or silk Chong Sam you had made for the girl friend, and charge you duty accordingly. Personally, I took the cheap stuff up to show them and paid nothing; the good stuff I kept on the ship till days later when all the dockyard searches had quieted down. Family and friends are at last reunited and allowed on board, lots of hugging and kissing takes place; joy and happiness is the order of the day. For everyone that is, except the weeping willies.

Having taken summer leave, I join the ship again; we set sail for Rosyth on the Firth of Forth. The ship is due maintenance, and the ship's company is accommodated in HMS Cochrane while the ship is having her 50,000 mile service.

I receive my draft to HMS Collingwood for leading hands course; I am to join on the second of September. I say farewell to my mates, my kit is packed, one large kitbag, one canvas and leather suitcase, and a small brown weekend case. I catch the train from Rosyth station, and head over the Forth Road railway bridge into Edinburgh; the train fills up and we're off on our journey to the Smoke (London), Kings Cross to be exact. Rather than trying to hump my worldly possessions around on the underground, I invest in a taxi, and when I say invest I mean part buy it, at least that's what I thought when he told me the fare, the robbing bastard. Anyway, the train from Waterloo now stops at Havant, where I get off and head for Hayling Island by bus, where I am to be based shore side with my wife, Hermione, while on course.

Monday morning I wake at 5 o'clock, get into my number 2 uniform and head for the bus stop so I can catch the 5.45 bus to Havant, Once in Havant, I get the next bus to Fareham. Next is the bus to Collingwood, where I arrive at 7.30, with half an hour to spare. My joining routine is completed and I am assigned a class, the usual crap, morning divisions,

Catholics fall out (I must remember in future to be Church of England, save the legs and all that), then the march to the classroom.

Chapter Five

The first six weeks of the course consisted of maths, every day six hours solid; we started off with one times two, and finished with calculus and Einstein's theory of relativity (almost). It was hard going but I managed to get 80%. Next on the course was workshops, which consisted of getting a circuit board and a handful of components, and gluing them all together using a soldering iron to make an amplifier using a circuit diagram. The instructor would then test it, first by plugging it in to see if anything came out at the speaker, then by testing for dry joints. This basically tested the soldered joints, I think, by pulling the pins out of the valve base and breaking your amplifier. It was not a fair test, the ham fisted sod.

Next in the workshops was the making of a tap holder (thread making tool). We were given six inches of steel bar and from this we had to construct the holder. We were issued with metalwork tools, and after a little instruction, off we went. After two days of filing and measuring, I am near to perfecting my piece, when the expert instructor arrives and explains that I am filing incorrectly. He then proceeds to show me how to do it correctly by taking three thousandths of an inch of my piece that only required the removal of one thousandth of an inch; the swine buggered my piece, which normally I wouldn't have given a toss about, but as I was to be marked on it, I did. Only 71%.

My next lesson was Electronics; this involved loads of valve theory, capacitance, inductance, anodes, cathodes, neutrons, protons, all good old fashioned stuff – the only thing was, I did not envisage having to invent anything electronic, so why all the theory? Surely, the only thing I would have to do is diagnose a fault and then repair it, which is done with the aid of a BR (book of reference) or Haynes manual. Going through circuits component by component does not solve a short circuit in the control grid of a valve; using black molten wire, or an oscilloscope does. I got 63% on this one.

Next, internal communications, which consisted of all broadcasts, amplifiers, microphones, speakers, and the ship's internal telephone exchange – a 25-line for small ships and the 50/500 for larger ships (as used by the GPO). Unfortunately, our instructor for this had only just finished the course two weeks previously, before being drafted to instruct us, and his knowledge of the subject was embarrassing. Consequently, the only thing we could do was try and learn it from the manual at home and hope the exam was not too hard. I got 47% – one of the top marks.

Control engineering was next; this is electronics moving mechanical stuff, like guns, and missile systems, via computers and amplifiers. I got 70% this time. Stabilisers came next; these are used to keep the ship steady for the weapon systems, unlike the merchant navy that use them to keep the crew happy, wussies. I got 75%. Machine theory followed, boring, 59%. Management; proved I was able to organise a piss up in a brewery, just – 50%. Last thing on the course was Power; generators, switchboards, ring mains, switch gear, and all that sort of stuff. I got 62%.

In between all this they managed to fit in parade drill, shooting, and duties. The damn Catholic priest even managed to get hold of me and make me, yes, *make* me, do all that crap that was required for confirmation. I didn't have the bottle to tell him the Spanish inquisition was over; anyway, I was confirmed. I always assumed I already was, as I was married. During this time, I was able to get a married quarter overlooking the council estate at the top of Portsdown hill – independence at last. Not that I was ungrateful to my in-laws, my wife and I did manage to save a lot towards our deposit for a house, thanks to them putting up with us. On 1 January, 1966, I was made acting LEM (leading electrical mechanic), at last a pay rise from £7.10 shilling to £14.10 shilling a week, paid fortnightly.

My draft comes through; I am to join the reserve ships fleet which is under the name of HMS Bellerophen; the actual ship I am to join is HMS Belfast – she had just relieved her sister ship, HMS Sheffield, which would be towed away and scrapped in 1967.

I join on 21 May, 1966. The ship is berthed at the south side of Whale Island, the RN's gunnery school; now this looks like a war ship, bloody great guns everywhere. I do my joining routine; I'm given the job with high power and defect party. I was assigned to keep the ship's ventilation running; this is yet another 220 dc ship, so this consisted of replacing carbon brushes, and the odd bearing, mind you, some of these jobs consisted of taking half the bloody ship apart to get at them. These fans were obviously fitted in the ship before pipes and paneling. Fans on long brackets caused the fan to vibrate and the brushes to squeak; this was solved by rubbing a candle on the commutator, not exactly per the book, but it worked.

In 1966, Portsmouth Harbour was full of reserve ships, all cocooned in silver waterproof canvas, and ready for the next big one – war that is – and it made today's excuse for a Navy look a bit sick in numbers by comparison. One of these ships was HMS Rocket. A daily party was sent over to pump her tiller flat out, as lots of rivets were weeping and sea water was a problem. On one occasion some naughty boy forgot to go over, and by the evening the harbour master was on the phone asking why one of our frigates was sinking. By the time the boat was sent over, the arse end was only inches off sea level; fortunately, she was saved from a watery grave. One day I was assigned crane driver at the after end of the ship. A lighter came alongside with stores and I started unloading her; this was a delicate operation as the shore supply was prone to tripping if heavy loads were put on it. Consequently, each move on the cranes controls had to be done one click at a time so loads were kept to a minimum. You know what it's like when you're coming to the end of a job and you want to get home? Well, I finally admit when the crane's ponder ball (that's the heavy ball and hook on the end of the wire) was due to come up from the lighter for the last time, I rushed it. I whacked the control round to full speed, and consequently tripped the shore supply to HMS Belfast. The ponder ball stopped mid-flight, and got caught in the rigging of the lighter which was in the process of going full astern. Now, there were two options here: one, the lighter was going to pull me and the crane into the harbour, or two, the crane and me were about to capsize the lighter. Lucky for me, the skipper of the lighter spotted my frantic arm waving, and managed to change his full astern to full ahead, and prevent a disaster. The worst that happened was a couple of their crew pissed themselves. Questions were asked about the loss of shore supply but I was unable to help – till now.

While I was day running from my married quarter, the wife was having trouble with a persistent Marine in the flat above while I was at work. He and his wife were also using us to supply their groceries. This ever so slightly annoyed me, so we put a deposit down on a two bedroom bungalow in Portchester, and left the bootnick and his moneyless wife to starve. I expect their skeletons are still in the flat. During this time, my transport to work was a Mini. One morning the battery was flat, and I was three minutes late for work. The Commander at defaulters explained to me that he believed my story, *but* it was my duty to be on board on time, and if necessary crawl up the gangway, even if my legs were broken. I thought of asking him if there was morphine available in the event of this happening, but then thought better of it. I was stopped two days pay and a day's leave;

if I had known this was coming I would have stopped for a coffee on the way in, as the punishment was the same for being up to an hour late.

At this time I could not afford a new battery, so I learnt how to bump start the Mini. I would turn on the ignition, stick it in second gear, and push her along till the engine fired, then I would jump in and off we went; neighbours laughed at this, but it worked till I got my new battery. I bought a Haynes manual and did my own maintenance, due to lack of spare cash, and by the time I had taken it to bits a few times I knew it inside out.

While on Bellerophen, I applied for nuclear submarines – better pay, and modern living conditions. I received vetting forms to fill in for security reasons. There were loads of questions to answer, and I filled most of it in, but had to leave out information about relatives behind the iron curtain. For this I had to write and ask my Yugoslavian mother. She was now living in Austria with my sister, and all our relatives lived in Slovenia, part of Tito's communist regime.

Meanwhile, the Navy sends me on the submarine escape course in HMS Dolphin; this is a hundred-foot tall cylindrical tank, with chambers on the outside of it at thirty feet, sixty feet, and under the tank, the one hundred-foot compartment. The routine was to go into the thirty-foot compartment through a door, which was sealed; once inside there was a hatch half way up the tank wall.The compartment was flooded above this hatch, the hatch was opened into the main tank, and you then took a deep breath and ducked into the escape tank. Once in the tank you were told to breathe out on the way up to the surface. This was repeated at the sixty foot level.

The hundred foot ascent was slightly different; under the tank was a compartment, in the middle was the hatch into the tank above, and a ladder from the hatch went to the compartment floor. Half way down the ladder from the hatch was a steel sleeve; the compartment was flooded till it reached the sleeve, an instructor opened the hatch, and the tank was now open for the ascent. Same routine, you took a deep breath and ducked into the sleeve and climbed up the ladder into the escape tank, you then found yourself rising through the water, and on the way up you breathe out, because your lungs full of air at a hundred feet is the equivalent of five or six lungs full of air on the surface. If you don't breathe out you explode on the way up, and instructors are in position all the way up ready to punch you if needed.

Now I am not saying the ascent was slow, but the two guys behind me passed me at the sixty, then the thirty foot mark. I wonder what the hell is going on? I break the surface with hardly a ripple. I climb out of the tank, and ask the instructor why I took so long coming up, and he told me I was probably negative buoyancy, which could explain the trouble I had passing the floating bit of my swimming test. The next bit of the training was the hundred foot ascent with a survival suit on; this was more like it. We are now mustered at the bottom of the tank again, wearing a rubber suit with a hood. The suit was filled with air, via a valve on the sleeve, and totally enclosed; in other words, you could breathe in it on the way up. Once on the surface, you could blow up the suit, and it then acted as a self contained life raft, keeping you afloat and reasonably warm, hence the name survival suit. I presume the other ascents without a suit are done because it is not always convenient to be near a survival suit in the event of an emergency.

News comes through that I am to join the nuclear submarine HMS Renown; my draft will follow, as she is in the process of being built at Birkenhead. I am to join her there; my job on the sub is to be torpedoes and loading trolleys, presumably for the missiles. During this time, my mother in Austria sends me the names and addresses of my communist relatives, which I pass on to the security bods at Admiralty; I hear nothing for weeks, then my draft comes through, at last. I open it and strangely enough, its for the nuclear submarine HMS Aurora. Odd, I thought, I could swear she was a frigate. Could it be I am a security risk? Surely not because I have all these unknown relatives behind the iron curtain. Trying to find out proved a waste of time, as I was obviously not in the need to know category.

I'm now standing on the bow of HMS Belfast, looking at HMS Aurora across the harbour on fountain lake jetty; it's the fifth of April 1967, and I am to join her tomorrow morning, but find she is sailing today at 1200. I have finished my leaving routine, so everyone knows I'm going. I approach the regulating office and ask if I can join her this morning; bloody daft question, really. Of course you can't; your draft says the fifth, and the fifth it is. Jobs worth twats. They tell me I have to join her in Plymouth, and give me a one way ticket to that effect. I hump my kit bag and cases to Portsmouth town station, board the train, and head for Plymouth; once there I get a taxi to the dockyard, and the nice man on the gate tells me she sailed for...you've guessed it, Portsmouth. What is going on? This must be some sort of initiative test. I head for HMS Drake, Plymouth's equivalent of Victory in Portsmouth; I am issued with another railway warrant back to Portsmouth. I know I joined the Navy to see the world, but I stupidly thought it would be by ship, not British rail. On arrival in Pompey, I enquire at the main gate of the dockyard where Aurora is coming in, and I am told the Railway jetty. I head there and find I've beaten the ship back, congratulations, BR. The next six hours is spent sitting on my kit bag waiting.

The ship finally arrives and I join her. Card in hand, I go round all the departments, getting stamps and letting all and sundry know I am here. Quite a few of the lads from the Corunna are on board so I am feeling at home already. The divisional Chief assigns me to Port watch; I'm forward damage control party for action and emergency stations. I'm down in the Gyro room for special sea duty men (leaving and entering harbour) and my job is on the low power and internal communication section, which involves all broadcasts, comms boxes, telephones, and any generator or motor under 230 volts. The Petty officer in charge is a good egg, and I get to learn a lot of practical stuff over the next few months thanks to him. The ship sails for Chatham; over the next few weeks we store ship, and top up with ammunition, all the work ups and exercising to get the ship ready to go out to the Persian Gulf had been completed before I joined, thank god.

We managed a few weekends home, during which time I managed to implant my eldest daughter into my wife. Although I was delighted when I found out, I was a bit worried about being away while she was pregnant, none of this flying home crap in those days.

The ship sails from Chatham and heads through the English Channel to the Bay of Biscay; as per usual, it's rough and I take a day or so to get my sea legs; in other words, I feel nauseous with the ship rolling about so much. The weather calms down as we near Gibraltar, and once in the harbour, shore leave is given to the starboard watch. The Captain clears lower deck and gives us the entire lecture on how we are little diplomats and to act accordingly, show manners to the locals, respect their culture, but most of all don't get drunk and walk over their cars, as the local police take a dim view of this activity. Well, the Captain might as well have said get drunk and walk the cars, because once Jack gets drunk, a bell rings in his pea-like brain and he remembers something about walking and cars, and he puts the two together.

The next thing that happens is Main Street Gibraltar has twenty cars with dents in their roof and bonnets, where jolly Jack has gone for a midnight stroll. The local police arrive and arrest three sailors; they are placed in cells for the night. Unfortunately for them, the ship sailed at 8 o'clock the next morning, and the judge is not out of bed before nine. The court gives them seven days prison and a heavy fine; that's the civvies sorted, and the Navy now has them in HMS Rooke. Unfortunately, Gibair does not do Africa, so the sailors are given air tickets to Cape Town via Heathrow, meaning they first have to fly to the UK before catching another plane to SA where they have to wait for the ship; the fines and air fares will be taken from their pay, and then they will face the Captain's wrath.

The ship is now heading for the equator, down the West coast of Africa, and the first timers are due for the crossing the line initiation ceremony. A canvas pool is rigged on the flight deck, king Neptune gets ready to do his thing; daily orders got into the spirit of the occasion and offered leave to long distance swimmers, the black duty watch, etc. Neptune and his wife, Aphrodite, did the welcome bit, and it was noticed that Neptune only had two prongs on his trident; evidently, his wife had caught him paying too much attention to one of the mermaids. The clerk of the court now got on with the job of requestmen and defaulters; the Captain was awarded a medal for bravery in the face of the enemy (us), the first Lieutenant was awarded a medal for slave driving, and was given an iron cross with cluster; next he was charged with taking a red ball point pen without the owners consent, and with failing to give seven make and mends a week to the ship's company. He was ordered to sing the first verse of "Swing low sweet chariot" with the appropriate actions, much to the delight of the crew. Various other members of the crew were given punishments, and all ended up in the pool after a good ducking.

On completion of the ceremony, the certificates were awarded, much beer was consumed, and a good time was had by all. Obviously, now that we're at the equator the weather is rather warm on the upper deck, so what does jolly Jack do? He has a few beers, and then goes sunbathing, and of course falls asleep; four hours later he wakes up with a lobster coloured water bed attached to his back, e.g. second degree burns, and he is carried to the sick bay, where the attendant puts him on a drip to re-hydrate him. The fluid on his back bursts, his skin hurts like hell, he won't be doing that again in a hurry. Due to the fact this is a self inflicted injury, he is charged accordingly when he becomes fit for duty. Two weeks number 14's and a fine. Just as well it's not war time or they would be shot at dawn.

One night the ship's helicopter was out doing exercises with the ship, when it disappeared off the radar screen. Obviously it had gone out of range, no problem, apart from the fact it did not reappear. After half an hour, the operations room was getting anxious, and the ship was brought to emergency stations; the navigating officer was sent for, and he plotted a course for where it was last recorded on radar, and then estimated where it probably went down. The ship went full ahead, to 29 knots, and after an hour we stopped, and search lights were switched on, Within ten minutes we had located the downed helicopter; the navigator is the crew's hero. Only one of the helicopter's buoyancy bags had inflated, and it was on its side; the crew were safe in their life raft. The ship's whaler was launched and the crew picked up. The ship now manoeuvred till it was alongside the chopper, and divers went over the side to try and lash the aircraft to the ship; we did not have the lifting gear to get her on board, so this was the only way of saving it. Unfortunately, the bloody thing filled with water and sank. The Sonar department had a first, watching a helicopter sinking on their screens.

Time at sea was spent keeping the ship in tip top working order, and exercising various drills, including the man over board drill, fire exercises, damage control, nuclear fallout, chemical attack – we were ready for anything. Out of working hours, time was spent reading, watching movies (twice a week), playing cards and board games. A tot of grog was issued to us junior rates at lunch time, which was a measure of rum and two measures of water; for some reason the M.O.D. thought adding water diluted the rum so we would not get drunk, not so. We were also allowed two cans of beer a day, which some lads saved for a few days so they could have a bit of a bender at the weekends. This was all right, providing you didn't have a watch to do, God help anyone pissed on duty.

One of the favourite games in the mess was horse racing; this consisted of a canvas track lined out in sections, six coloured horses made of wood, and two huge dice. Bets were placed and the dice rolled, they're off, the problem rose when the horses got near the end; your horse could be two from the end, but if you rolled a four you went two forward crossing the finishing line, and two back, leaving your horse where you were, most frustrating.

Now that my wife was pregnant, I had to try and get promoted to make up the money lost when she finished work. I got the books out and spent time studying. Jesus, why didn't I go in for an interesting job, you know, formula one driver, Gigolo, stripper, that sort of thing?

Finally we arrive at Simonstown, just North of Cape Town, South Africa; this is the SA Navy's main base. Shore leave is given and we head for the railway station and get into a carriage, and the train is about to set off when this coloured guy leaps on and into our carriage. Nothing unusual about that you may think, only this carriage is for whites only; this guy was nearly in tears, fearing a heavy fine if he got caught by the local Gestapo. We reassured him he would be okay. A white guy explained why there was segregation between the carriages; he told us to look at the black only carriage when the train stopped. He said all the carriages were the same and brand new six months previously. When we got off the train we had a peek in the next carriage –every seat, light fitting, nut and bolt had gone. All this proved to me was the black people were living in poverty and took anything they could to improve their lot.

The City of Cape Town was a lovely place; the only thing was the signs everywhere, white only, black only, cape coloureds only. I'm surprised they stopped there, as they could have had signs like Jews only, Catholics only, Muslims only, black Jews only, White Jews only; they could have made the whole country out of signs. You might have had a bit of trouble if you were bursting for a piss looking for a sign which read, WHITE GINGER CATHOLIC DWARFS ONLY. From all this segregation, we could feel the resentment of the coloured population against the ruling class, the Whites. All apartheid seems to do is breed hate and resentment.

After a week, we sail for the Biara Patrol, off the east coast of Africa. Our aim is to stop oil tankers from supplying the now illegal government of Ian Smith's Rhodesia. Bloody waste of time, because the sympathetic white government of South Africa (the place we have just left) are supplying them by road. We did manage to stop one tanker by firing a 4.5 inch shell across her bow; this embargo-busting tanker was boarded, and its Captain was found to be our Captain's uncle, small world, eh! After bombing up and down the coast for six weeks with little or no luck, we were relieved by another frigate, whose name escapes me right now; what I do remember is that we did a nighttime replenishment at sea, and mail was exchanged. The other frigate's crew decided we needed potatoes (which we did, as we had run out) – the only problem was they came over as missiles, smashing into anything that got in the way. Now not wanting to take without giving something in return, our ship's painter popped up to his store and got a box full of small tins of damage control marking paint. These were launched at the potato throwers opposite. As far as I know nobody was killed, but the signal received next morning from their Captain was not a happy one. In the cold light of day he surveyed his multicoloured masterpiece, and had the cheek to complain. He obviously did not realise the work our lads had to put in to hose the spuds off our ship.

Next stop Mombasa, Kenya's main sea port, names are drawn and a lucky few are drawn out of the hat to go to Silversands, a beach resort just down the coast. It sounded great in the brochure; unfortunately, I was not one of the lucky few. Still, leave was relaxed; the ship's company only worked till midday, then leave was given to three out of four watches. Once in town, you could see where the colonial establishment had once been. The buildings, though run down and in disrepair, stood out against the local corrugated roofed huts of the Africans. The roads are full of pot holes; the whole place is run down and needs massive investment. I expect the government is spending the taxes on guns and the army, must get the priorities right if you want to avoid a coup, eh what! The local stores had plenty of goodies to buy, wood carvings of animals and tribesmen, animal skins, and African ethnic wear; they even had toys cleverly made out of Coke cans. The ex pats club invited us sailors for a few beers and a game of cricket, all very British. The black workers were always on hand, at our beck and call; I bet they resented us. I know I would have done in their place. It was not very nice seeing the local white trash snapping their fingers for service. I and a couple of lads went behind the pavilion to have a few beers with a couple of locals. They were a bit apprehensive to begin with, but soon realised Matelots are a different breed from these toffee-nosed twats.

After our local leave in Mombasa, we sailed for the Persian Gulf. I spent most of the time below decks in the air conditioning; consequently, I was one of the only white men left on board. The Captain in his wisdom decided to have Divisions in full number six tropical uniform. No problem, all was going well getting ready, the pipe was made "hands fall in on the upper deck for divisions." I made my way to the forward hatch, stuck my head out, a temperature change of 70 degrees hit me and I promptly fainted. Luckily, there were guys behind to catch me; by the time I had recovered divisions were over, which was a shame, really. I was looking forward to standing in 130 degrees of sunshine for an hour.   Our first stop in the gulf was a small inlet; the landscape looked like somewhere on Mars, and a shore party was dispatched with the weather experts. They recorded 145 degrees of heat. They also came across a group of people living there, whose main diet was fish; they were probably very brainy, but they had no fingernails or teeth, most bizarre.

Our Captain now decided to have a rounds inspection of the ship; this involved cleaning every compartment from top to bottom, and in some cases, painting. Not much fun, I can tell you. The Captain was a stickler; he would run his finger over the tops of doors and cupboards, and if you were found guilty of leaving a microdot of dust you would get a rescrub the following day. Now one particular seaman had spent the day cleaning and polishing the forward heads (toilets) and was rather proud of his efforts; the Captain arrived, and the seaman reported, "Forward heads ready for your inspection, sir." The Captain went round with his white gloves and got a small dirty mark on them; the lad got a rescrub. Now this pissed him off a little bit, after all his effort. The lad now spends hours re-polishing everything; its perfect at last, but to add a finishing touch he goes to the NAAFI and buys a bar of Cadbury's chocolate. He returns to the heads, and taking his lighter out, melts the chocolate down the back of one of the toilet pans. He now waits for the return of the Captain on his rounds. He reports the heads ready for inspection, and the Captain is impressed, that is, till he reaches the pan with the brown backing.

"My God, what the hell is that?" he screams. The lad bends over the pan and says. "It looks like shit, sir." With that he sticks his finger in it and tastes it, "Yes, it definitely is shit, sir."

The Captain is not amused, everyone else is pissing themselves, and the lad is taken to the regulating office and put on a charge. The next day he sees the First lieutenant and is given a week's number 14's punishment. Well worth it, he reckons; I agree – its now part of Naval folklore.

I take my written and oral exam for Petty Officer and pass; all that swatting pays off. It's 31 May, 1968. I now know my next draft will be Collingrad for the PO's course; can't wait, as it means I'll be home with my new baby and wife. Now that I am promoted, I move to the Petty Officers mess up at the front end of the ship; this is the bouncy end in rough weather. I am given a job change to the 4.5 inch gun; I have the electrics and another PO has the mechanicals; fortunately, this guy knows the whole system inside out and teaches me how to tune the amplifiers, check the firing circuits, and the manual shooting system. I would help him with the heavy stuff. One thing I could never work out was the fact the gun had hundreds of bent bits of iron of all shapes and sizes. These are lining up tools for various jobs; they arrived on the ship with cardboard labels attached and numbered for its particular job, and once it was used, the label invariably came off, and was then thrown in the tool bin along with all the others.

Next time it was needed it could not be identified, so a new one was ordered; over the years, ships must have had dozens of unmarked tools in their tool boxes, it must have been too easy to stamp the required information in the metal, rather than a cardboard tag. I did put a suggestion form in to do this but it was ignored; no doubt the guy at admiralty had shares in the tool making company. The same thing happened when I suggested using scaffold jacks instead of American shores in damage control. The American shore was a device that was used to prop up damaged hatches or buckled decks. It consisted of a square tube inside a larger one, lining up holes were drilled in both, the inside one had a flat plate welded on the top, and the large one also had a plate welded on the base. The idea was you extended it till it was at the nearest height to the damage. You then put steel pins through both, and next you wedged it in place with wooden wedges. All this took time, and if the compartment is flooding you don't want to be hanging about; my scaffold jack could automatically be wound up and locked into position in seconds.

I got no feedback on this one either, although many years later my idea was put on all new ships. I presume they had a surplus to get rid of first. I'm still waiting for my royalties. I digress; back to the gun. The 4.5 is a semi automatic, twin barrelled weapon. The radar picks up a target, the computer works out where the gun should be pointing by taking into account things like the roll and pitch of the ship, the ship's speed, the wind speed, the speed of the target, its height, the difference between the gun director and the gun. All these things are worked out by a computer the size of a tennis court; dozens of valve amplifiers are used, and these have to be tuned daily.

Stabilisation of the gun is controlled by a gyroscope on air bearings, which keeps the guns barrels pointing at the target whatever the ship is doing. The gun is also capable of being fired locally using a joystick; a small bullet-proof window on the top right of the gun enables a gunner to see the target; he has a seat and crossed wires over his joystick. Ammunition is brought into the turret via hoists from the magazines; the shells come up from a hoist at the front of the breech, and the cordite cases come up from a hoist at the back of the breech. Gunners load these by hand into the breech, and once in, the breech closes and the gun will automatically fire. The speed of firing is dependant on the speed of the loading gunners, both in the gun and in the magazines.

The noise of the gun going off is beyond description; if you didn't know it was coming you would crap yourself, the recoil could be felt throughout the ship, and the cordite smelt like a thousand vindaloos had been released all at once after a run ashore. Apart from the 4.5 gun, I also had two Bofors to maintain, one of which was giving the gunner an electric shock from the joystick every time he used it. I turned the power off and proceeded to remove the junction box cover, which involved taking forty-odd corroded bolts off, the lid was sealed and had to be prised off. As it came off I was covered in salt water, the box was half full; how it got in there and how the gun worked is a mystery. Anyway, much drying and cleaning later, the insulation was brought up to par, and the moaning, electrocuted gunner was happy.

While on the ship, I befriended a lad from Goa, he was a leading rate and an Officers chef. As I was now a Petty Officer, I was not allowed to invite him into the mess for a beer. So I would take a few beers into the Officers galley, which was close to the mess, where we would drink and eat the food left over from the evening's wardroom dinner. I became rather partial to steaks and lobster. How the other half live, eh! He promised to take me to a good restaurant when we reached Bahrain, and I couldn't wait. The ship finally berths in Bahrain, and fresh fruit and veg are loaded on board to replenish empty lockers. The ship's Mini Moke is unloaded; this is for the general use of the ship's company. Providing you booked it in the log it was yours; it had been given to the ship by British Leyland for trials. I'll give the thing its due; it never let us down, considering it was just lashed down on the upper deck and many a wave went over it, it was amazing it ever started. A quick squirt of WD40, a charged up battery, and *broom, broom,* you were away. You would not believe how many drunken Matelots that vehicle brought back to the ship in one go; it usually lost half a dozen on the last bend to the ship.

By now I was acclimatised to the heat, having the odd run ashore, and keeping fit by playing sport. I had a few games of football, and took up tennis. We had a really good barbeque on HMS Jufair; an American ship's company was invited, and they provided the T-bone steaks and Coca Cola; we provided the beer, as they couldn't be trusted to have alcohol on their ships; marijuana, no problem, beer no way. My Goanese friend and I go ashore into Bahrain, and after a few beers in the galley, we go off the beaten track away from the tourist area. He takes me into this Indian restaurant. I know it's Indian because apart from me, everyone is Indian; they all look at this piece of white trash, as if to say, what the hell is he doing here? I'm feeling a little self conscious.

My mate tells me not to worry and orders food for both of us; when it arrives there are at least ten dishes covering our marble table. Christ, I thought, I've only brought a fiver with me; well, I can always wash up, if they don't kill me first. Fortunately, we hadn't eaten all day so we got stuck in, boy what a feast, real curry with real herbs and spices, not like the crap in the Taj Mahal in the Guildhall Square, Pompey. The bill arrives, this bit I dreaded, I open it up. Bloody hell, how much – the equivalent of one pound ten shillings (£1.50) – the lads in town were paying that for a starter. See, it's not what you know.

The ship's new helicopter arrives; it's named Budgie, the name later stolen by HRH Fergie in her children's books. I thought about suing her for copyright, but was told to keep a low profile. The ship is now up to standard as repairs have been carried out and spares are topped up. We sail for the smuggling patrol; Bahrain is a major gold market and is swimming in the stuff, and a lot of this gold tends to find its way to India where there is a lucrative black market. The Indian authorities are keen to stop this trade as it affects their economy. Our job is to inform them of any suspect boats or ships that we search, that are heading their way from Bahrain. After three days at sea the most bizarre thing happened; we received a mayday from a dhow wallowing in the middle of the Persian Gulf. A boarding party was dispatched and found the crew in a state of dehydration and starvation. The Arab in charge begged us for food, water, and diesel, which considering what he was carrying, was a bit of a cheek since the boarding party found his cargo was one and a half million pounds worth of gold bullion. All we could do was supply his needs and let him go, as he was in international waters. Maritime rules state ships in distress must be given any assistance required. Our ship's company were all in favour of shooting the crew and sharing the loot; the skipper had other ideas and warned the authorities in India, and they call our system democratic. I daydreamed about maybe buying an ex-torpedo boat and some sailor uniforms when I left the navy. Then I'd head for the Gulf and do my own patrols, confiscating any gold found.

The ship anchored in some small inlet and the non duty ratings went ashore for a bar-b-q, an oil drum was cut in half and a stand made to hold it; meat, bread, and beer was shipped ashore. Unfortunately, we had no charcoal, so an old lag told us we had to half fill the drum with sand, pour diesel in it, then start the burn with petrol. Once the flames had subsided the sand was glowing enough to cook on; it worked a treat, although the taste was a bit different from the norm. After a few hours of steaks and beers, we emptied the oil drum (which now contained a lump of solid glass like material) and then we cleared the beach of litter before going back to the ship.

A good friend of mine, Punch Pullen, who was a leading rate, was having his birthday while we were at sea. He was a very popular guy, and was consequently offered much rum round the ship's various messes. I saw him in the morning and told him to come round for a tot of neaters the next day, as I thought he would have enough on that day. He went round the mess decks consuming glass after glass of grog; he eventually staggered back to his mess and turned in. At 1600, messmates went to check him and found him dead; the doctor was called and he was taken to the sick bay. It was estimated he had the equivalent of seven and a half pints of grog, and barring a stomach pump and complete blood change at two o'clock, he had signed his own death warrant. It was a sad day; one of the ship's true characters had left us; I must admit I had a good cry, as did many others. His kit was, as per the custom, auctioned off, and his widow received several thousand pounds from the crew, no doubt a lot of it was conscience money. I was only too happy not to have been a part of his demise. His wife and daughters were flown out within days; I don't recall whether the body was flown home for burial, or buried at sea. I do recall having a memorial service on the upper deck and the bugler breaking down half way through the playing of the last post.

Chapter Six

Back on patrol again after the enquiry, we settle down to routine. A canvas swimming pool is rigged up on the flight deck; it was very popular with chefs and stokers coming off watch after a hot day in the galley or engine room. A lot of the sailors liked fishing, you know the sort of thing, baby sharks, puffer fish, eels; now, to keep them nice and fresh they would put them in the pool. It was a rare sight to see a hairy-arsed stoker jump in the pool then spot a shark's fin, this was the nearest I've seen someone walk on water, and the language, well!

When we stopped at Kuwait, the British oil refinery guys were invited into the mess for a few beers. Later we were invited back to their canteen, but we didn't expect anything to drink as it was a dry Muslim country and alcohol was forbidden. However, they did manage to produce a liquor from potatoes, a sort of vodka they called Flash, which was tested for purity by the company's chemist; any bad brew could blind you, as one crew member found out by buying some crap off a local – it took six weeks before he got his sight back. The beer they produced was excellent. Asked how they managed to get it through the customs, they told us all spares from the UK were packed in hops. By all accounts it was quite a sight watching the local custom officers rummaging through the hops looking for booze.

There was a call for people on board to donate blood, as at this time the Israelis were hammering ten bells of shit out of the Arabs, and blood was needed. Although not many people were keen to give the towel heads blood, the incentive was the 21 dinars per pint; the odd greedy bugger went round twice and suffered accordingly – again, self inflicted injury – seven days 14's on recovery. It's bad enough being mercenary, but being greedy, you deserve everything you get.

Our next port of call was in Iran, or Persia as it was then. We anchored off, and the ship's football team and a few supporters including myself headed up the river. It seemed to take hours, but we eventually arrived in some God forsaken town. We are met at the jetty by some local dignitary who ushers us all into a dilapidated bus; this takes us to the local stadium.

The banner on the outside is written in Arabic and English, and states that the football match is England against the local side, most reassuring I'm sure. By now the stadium is packed with thousands of locals chanting for their team. The match gets under way and a two-all draw is the result; everyone is happy, not least me, I could see these buggers ripping us to bits if they lost against us infidels. We get back to the ship and western ways in one piece. The whole thing was one weird experience. I now know how Gordon must have felt at Khartoum when the Dervish attacked.

Back to sea and we head for Muscat, a walled city, and when we arrive we are told that no leave is to be given on our first day because there was to be a public execution. No doubt someone farted in the mosque and got caught. Matelots who went ashore were told that the city gates closed at midnight and that they must carry an all round light after dark, due to the curfew. Not many took up the offer as alcohol ashore was forbidden on pain of death (probably), and the women all looked the same – head to foot in black with just the eyes showing – how the hell you picked a wife is beyond me as I personally am not an eye man, bums for me every time.

However, good news came when a list went up to visit the oil refinery some way up the coast; I stuck my name down and was drawn out to go. We all piled into the motor whaler and headed off at lunch time; an hour and a half later we arrived, and proceeded to drink a few glasses of flash and home brewed beers. We swapped stories with the oil men and had a lovely feast at supper time, by the evening everyone had a nice glow and were well sated in food and drink. It was time to get back to the ship. The weather was now blowing up and the sea was getting choppy; we were all getting soaked to the skin. Half way back, the bloody engine cut out, and the sound of waves crashing on the rocky coastline was not a sound I wish to hear again. We drifted closer and closer, stokers were desperately trying to restart the engine; it coughed and spluttered, then fired, and off we went for another mile or two before it died again. The oars came out and we rowed like hell. I did not fancy this for the next twenty five miles, but we had no radio or means of contacting the ship about our dilemma. The engine was restarted, and then spluttered to a stop after ten minutes, oars out again. This nightmare went on till we got back to the ship at about three in the morning. It seems the engine on the whaler had a broken valve on one of the cylinders, no wonder it sounded so rough. We sailed next day, good job too.

After another spell on patrol, we headed on an uneventful trip to Bombay. On our arrival we cleared lower deck and manned the side in full whites, the saluting gun opened up to say hello. The colour of the sea can best be described as neat sewage with a hint of lime, e.g. bloody disgusting.

66

Mind you, the sight of half our navy's ex-battleships and cruisers was a sight to behold; they looked beautiful, with hundreds of Indian sailors painting and polishing. I don't think they actually had a navy, not one that went to sea anyway, the ships were just a means of accommodating a lot of people. Our ship anchored in the middle of the harbour; traders were allowed on board and set up shop on the flight deck; they did not have many takers on the first few days, as Jack wanted to get ashore and see what's what. Money changing was organised; the official rate was 15 rupees to the pound, however, we were soon to find out you could get 25 on the black market ashore. The PO writer in our mess took the mess funds ashore and changed them for 25; before the ship left he changed them back for 15 to the pound, giving the mess funds a healthy boost. Unfortunately, by the time the ship was due to sail there were more rupees than when the ship started. And a lot of the lads were refused the change back to pounds; consequently, they were stuck with the rupees, and this is where the traders made a killing as jolly Jack bought anything he could just to get rid of the worthless rupees.

Once ashore in Bombay, you get the impression of organised chaos as cars, lorries, buses, buffalo, tuk tuks, trishaws and even elephants all compete for road space; nobody seems to have the right of way, it's just a case of bullying your way to where you're going. The roads don't help either, as most are full of potholes. I believe the driving test in India consists of driving the vehicle ten feet forward, and six feet backwards; in other words, you have to be up to the standard of a three-year-old on drugs, scary huh!

The caste system of India is obvious, as the rich look rich, well fed, and in all their gold and silk, and the poor look poor, starving, and in rags. None of this coloured segregation crap here, it's all down to who your dad is – it's funny how the rest of the world seems to accept this form of apartheid. It's not unusual to see the odd dead body lying in the street; I heard they cleared them once a day, probably so as not to upset the tourists. You can see where all the gold goes to in India; people wear it instead of having tattoos on their heads saying, "look at me, every body, I'm loaded." This place is the capital of bling. The people are friendly, and most speak English and will talk to you. Almost anyone will change rupees into pounds, and give you a good rate to boot. The food from the stalls is cheap and authentic; you just have to hope the cook has washed his hands after his dump, otherwise, you will almost certainly get Delhi belly, which is guaranteed to lay you out for days.

After three days in Bombay we leave for Bangkok. The skipper keeps us on our toes doing drills and exercises. The weather is kind and we have a smooth run up to the river Chaos Phraya. We head north towards Bangkok, and going up the river we spot ex-naval Monitors, dozens of them: huge, flat-bottomed barges with a six inch gun mounted on the top; no doubt these were used for bombarding inland at some stage. They appeared to have people living on them, although they did not resemble sailors; I think they were just house boats for anyone who cared to use them. We finally reach Bangkok, and within hours we have to send divers down, as all the ship's intakes are clogged up with polythene bags. We need these clear because external water is needed to cool machinery, and the sea is our ship's radiator. The colour of the water is similar to Bombay, yuk. To see people swimming and washing in it is enough to make your stomach turn.

River traffic is like nowhere on earth: twenty-foot canoes stacked high with fruit and veg go by at thirty knots, powered by V-eight American muscle engines that just sit in the rear of the boat, the cooling pipes hanging over the side, sucking in cold water on one side and pumping hot water back via the engine on the other. The propeller end of a ten-foot prop shaft sits just below the surface of the water giving amazing forward speed; just like a big torpedo, they created huge tidal waves down the river bank, much to the annoyance of the local river dwellers. Bangkok City was modern, with high class clothing shops, and jewellers by the dozen selling gold, opals, emeralds, and of course their famous Siamese silver. The traffic in the city was more organised, and the roads half decent. On the other hand, there seemed to be a lot of poverty and people begging; on the outskirts of the city people lived in squalor.

A lot of the Matelots think they've struck lucky with the beautiful local talent, only to find the girly boys are not quite what they were expecting; mind you, I defy anyone to tell the difference without having a quick feel first. I bet there are a lot of disturbed men who leave Thailand.

Back on board ship, the air conditioning has gone kaput; the temperature is up in the 90s, and when you bear in mind the ship is full of hot running machinery, and the humidity is high, it's not much fun. Add to this problem the fact that there are no spares to repair it; we will have to wait till we get to Singapore, six days away, oh joy!

The ship is topped up with fresh fruit, veg, and victuals, we clear the poly bags for the last time, and off we go to Singapore. Most of the ship's company is sleeping on the upper deck at night on camp beds to keep cool; it's quite an experience sleeping under the stars. Instead of a mess deck full of drunken, smoking, sweating, farting, snoring Matelots, the fresh air takes some getting used to. To pass the time on the trip I give one of the engineers a hand stripping one of the diesel generators. I'm happy as a pig in shit; I'm thinking maybe I should have been a mechanical engineer instead of an electrical one, but too late now.

We arrive in Singapore and anchor mid-stream. Liberty boats are run for shore leave; I pop into HMS Terror for a few tiger beers then into Sambwang village to get a taxi. I hail a worn out Merc; the trip is hair raising as usual, the steering seems worn, as does the braking system, and the upholstery. The driver seems unaware he is driving a death trap. We eventually arrive safe, but not so sound. I pay the fare, a third of the price of a legal taxi. I wander down a few back streets and look for somewhere to eat, a priority after the ship's cuisine. A small Chinese cafe comes into view; the menu out side is in Mandarin, e.g. not English, but I'm ravenous, so I go in anyway.

I plonk myself down at a table laid with a plastic table cloth. An old lady comes over and speaks to me in Mandarin which, fortunately, I understand (I wish). I presume she is asking me what I want, so I point to a couple of things on the menu. She wanders off muttering. I just know she is pissed off with this foreign devil. After ten minutes she comes back with this huge plate of rice with prawns, crab, fish, and other stuff in it. I'm thinking I've got a good one here and start to tuck in. The little old lady starts giving me abuse; Jesus, what the hell have I done wrong now? Perhaps I'm not holding my chop sticks right, or perhaps I should say a prayer to Buddha first. She disappears and is back a minute later with a bowl full of shellfish and chicken in a sauce; evidently, the first dish was just the rice. She puts it down next to the rice, gives me a huge smile showing her two remaining teeth, and leaves me to it, which made me feel a lot better. I knew now she had not poisoned it, or put a contract on me with the Tongs. I finished the meal totally stuffed, and a hot, perfumed towel was brought to me, so refreshing in the humidity.

I asked for the bill expecting a fair price, and when it came, it was so cheap that I left the same as a tip. Even this was hard to explain to them, the fact that they provided me with such a superb meal deserved a good tip. I entered their shop a stranger, and left their best friend, handshakes and hugs all round. After the meal I went for a wander round. I saw Raffles and China town, and did a bit of shopping for presents. I then caught a taxi back to Terror, and got the liberty boat back to the ship.

During this time in Singas, the local government put out tenders for the King George the fifth dock to be filled in. I'm not saying it was a big dock, but you could get two aircraft carriers in it, and consequently it needed a lot of stuff to fill it. Obviously, it was going to cost the local government a lot of money to fill it in, and prices were given by various companies. But the one that was accepted was the one given by a Chinaman, which stated it would pay the government to fill it in. It worked like this: you are a builder on the Island, and the city is being demolished bit by bit to make way for skyscrapers. What do you do with all the rubble? Easy. You pay the Chinaman to dump it in the dock, he then pays the government a percentage, and everyone is happy.

Over the next few days, the air-conditioning parts arrive and are duly fitted, life gets back to normal and people stop snapping at each other. I had a few games of rugby in HMS Terror and watched the inter-ships' football matches with the customary bucket of Tiger beer. I got caught a few times in the monsoons; boy, does it come down, no wonder the ditches are so damn big. One consolation is the humidity is lower when it rains, and that means cooler conditions for a while.

Maintenance and repairs over, we sail for Hong Kong on an early morning tide, and we meet up with some Australian ships and HMS Eagle and Bulwark (British aircraft carriers). We are told to provide a towed target so the fleet air arm can practice low level attacks. This device is a metal strip that when towed provides a plume of water behind the ship, which the aircraft can spot and attack with machine gun fire. The ship's notice board has had a list up asking for volunteers to pilot the device; six young sailors volunteered, brave lads, and they realise their error when the shooting starts. Lightning aircraft come in and let rip; you see the shells leaving the aircraft and a few seconds later you hear the three second burst as a line of shells stream across the target. During the exercise, a Gannet aircraft falls off the flight deck of Eagle; the rescue helicopter is hovering over the wreck when it too loses power and crashes. The exercise comes to a halt as all ships help in the rescue – a bad day for the fleet air arm.

The exercise over, we head for Hong Kong. We enter harbour and do the usual dress ship and saluting cannon bit, all very ceremonial, I'm sure. Anything to keep the sailors busy, and the governor of Hong Kong thinking he is the big daddy. Things ashore have changed dramatically, all thanks to our American cousins on rest and recuperation from Vietnam. The R.N. China fleet club has now been taken over by them apart from two floors. Prices have trebled; when Mr. Chinaman asks for something in dollars you barter; you don't do what the Yanks do and pay the asking price, especially when he is talking in H.K. dollars worth 2/4p (11p), and the Yanks assume he is talking in American dollars worth 7/- (35p) and pays him accordingly. It's the typical over paid, and over here syndrome. It kills us poorly paid Matelots; our buying power is next to nothing now. Come on, you Gooks! Just joking.

Jenny's Chinese boys are on board with their shiny dust bins to collect our food leftovers so they can take it ashore, jazz it up with noodles and soy source then feed us and the Yanks later at their roadside stalls. The ship does not need painting so we're guaranteed a few days peace and quiet. We are alongside for a few days, so I leg it ashore to have a tattoo at the world famous Pinky's; his job is to go over a pathetic tattoo I had done in the arches by Portsmouth Harbour railway station. He gets halfway through it and is doing a good job when the ship's siren is sounded; this means a general recall for R.N. ships. I tell Pinky to chop, chop; he hurries the artwork, and finishes the masterpiece. I pay him and get a taxi back to the ship. Everyone is on full alert; what the hell is going on? Fortunately, we are not going to war with Russia or China; but rather a typhoon is heading for Hong Kong and we are to sail into it. This by all accounts is what the R.N. does. Once the ship has full steam and all the preps for sea are done, we sail. On the way out we pass several U.S. ships on their way in to what they consider is safety. What they don't seem to realise is, if the typhoon hits Hong Kong direct, they will end up in the main street, and will need more than a tug to get them floating again. Our ship is now catching the edge of the typhoon; the weather is force eight, and over the next few hours the weather eases as the front veers away and heads towards Japan. Good luck to them, they will need it.

One of the leading seamen has just passed his exam for Petty Officer, and as the PO's mess is full he has to stay in the junior rates mess for sleeping. To celebrate, he comes up to our mess and has a few beers; he has a couple too many and is staggering slightly as he heads back to his bunk in the junior rates mess. An eagle-eyed officer spots him and has the Master at arms arrest him for being drunk; the next day he is in front of the Captain who has no alterative but to disrate him back to leading hand. Fair enough you might think, after all he was drunk. Two days later, the engineering Officer and a few other Officers are having a champagne breakfast on the ship's bridge; the engineer has a few too many and is incapable of standing, and two stokers are sent for to carry him back to his cabin. The buzz gets round the ship, and the ship's company is eagerly waiting to see what the Captain is going to do. Well, the engineer is up and about the next day as if nothing has happened; we can only conclude that the Captain regarded his behaviour as high spirits and totally acceptable for an Officer, or he and the Captain were masons, or the skipper was being blackmailed; regardless, there were many pissed off Matelots on the ship, especially a certain ex-Petty Officer.

We spend the next week exercising with five other NATO Navies. Gunnery is a priority; we fire at targets and get good results along with the

Aussies, the Canadians, and the Kiwis; our American cousins tend to go for quantity rather than accuracy, and by the time they have finished shooting there is so much black cordite cloud around, it looks like Krakatoa has erupted, or else a busy day in a Los Angeles rush hour.

Exercise over, we head for Manila where shore leave is given and everyone makes for the American PX, that's their equivalent of our NAAFI. All hell breaks loose in the junior rates bar, probably caused by some stupid Matelots asking about the use of glass-bottomed boats in Pearl Harbour to see the wrecks of their fleet. The military police wade in with baseball bats and arrests are made. Over the next few days ships' Captains are kept busy working out how much to charge individuals for the wrecked PX, and how many days punishment to give. The chefs are well happy, with all those men under punishment doing their cleaning for them over the next few weeks. The war now over, we head for Albany, SW Australia; and after a few days at sea we find ourselves coming into a small cove surrounded by brown, barren hills and a jetty with a road disappearing into the distance. It's not the most cosmopolitan place I've ever seen, I have to say. The local dignitaries and their sheilas are there to meet meet us; the ship is secured alongside, and the Lord Mayor and his mates meet the captain, as they are invited on board for a few tinnies in the wardroom.

The ship's company are wondering, where the hell is Albany? We find out later that it's about two miles over the hill. From the top of the hill you look down into the town. It looks like Peyton Place, and the only greenery is in the town square, a small patch of lawn lovingly watered, probably ten times a day to stop it from shrivelling up. Anyway, the place looks neat and tidy and the natives are friendly. Jolly Jack smells out the local bars, all are air conditioned and strangely women-less; one gets the feeling Aussie men are either very macho or prefer male company, looking at Sydney (the gay capital of Australia) one might be inclined to think the latter.

Preparations are well under way for the big party, the ship is rigged with floodlights, and awnings are spread over the flight deck in case of rain, which was last reported six years ago – can't be too careful, eh.

The local paper has announced our arrival and invited the locals to have cocktails on board the following evening; the trouble is the wardroom and the senior rates messes can only cope with a hundred or so, and because considerably more turn up, the Captain has no alternative but to let the junior rates messes join in the party. The ship looks like an Indonesian ferry, bodies everywhere and ready to capsize. The locals are having a good time, drinks are flowing and new friendships are struck; sailors are invited to barbecues the following day. The party winds up at around midnight, and cars are seen weaving up the road back into town; as the headlights disappear into the night a strange calm settles over the ship – hard to believe it was throbbing an hour earlier.

The next morning is spent clearing the debris up from the previous night; heads are banging, black coffee is flowing like it's going out of fashion, and voices are kept low for fear of brains exploding, adding to the mess. By lunch time the world is nearly back to normal, and after his tot of rum and a few cans, Jack is ready to commence battle. The captain has given leave to everyone but the duty watch. The once deserted jetty now looks like a car park at ASDA, as the locals arrive to take an English sailor home for big eats and beer; this event is one of the highlight of the town's history. Nothing has been this exciting for them since the Lord Mayor's cat got stuck up a eucalyptus tree; it will keep the locals in things to talk about for years, especially the fact that we ran a few of the town's pubs out of beer.

Three mates and I got picked up by a local builder and his wife; they lived in a recently built bungalow on the outskirts of town, and about twenty minutes drive away from the ship. A bit disturbing were the fires blazing away on the nearby hills; we are told these are controlled burns done to prevent bush fires from reaching the town. Reassured, we tuck into steaks and ice cold beers till late evening. The builder's wife seemed to take a shine to me; I can't say she was my sort, but she insisted on having my home address. I don't think my wife was impressed when she wrote asking for my photograph. My wife wrote her back saying she was sorry but "piss off, you Aussie bitch, he's mine," or words to that effect. Anyway, barbie over, we're driven back to the ship. I've got to say it was a very enjoyable day and we were treated like royalty, no complaints with Australian hospitality.

I put my name down to go on a whaling trip, not very PC I know, but I had to try out what was to be a once in a lifetime experience. The next morning a lorry arrived to pick me and six others up, and we were taken to a shore-based whaling station up the coast. The last one on earth by all accounts, as all others are now run from factory ships. This particular whaling company consisted of a spotter plane, three old steam ships, and a slipway leading up to the processing factory. It was 7 o'clock when we sailed; the ship stank of fish oil, which took a bit of getting used to, and everything on the ship was steam driven: the fans, the huge reciprocating engines, the winches, and the generators. On the bow of the ship was the harpoon gun, a brutal looking thing, the harpoon itself was a solid, shell-shaped piece of steel with three flukes on the pointed end which ensured the thing stayed in the whale when it hit. The other end had a rope connected; this was coiled at the base of the gun, then leading up to the top of the mast and through block and tackles to eventually be secured to huge springs bolted to the ship's keel. The harpooner's job was to load the gun with a charge and place the harpoon into the barrel; he had to be wary of the coil of rope. One foot accidentally in the loop and your leg was in a tug of war with a whale and the ship; this was explained by the one-footed harpooner who ended half way up the mast when it happened to him.

The captain of the ship explained to us that the spotter plane would fly over the area looking for whales, and on locating a spout, would radio its position to the three ships. The nearest would go full steam ahead to secure the kill; on locating the whale the chase would begin, and, if lucky, the ship would harpoon the whale, the whole line would run out, and the whale would in effect be towing the ship via the mast and the ship's keel.

Once dead, it would be pulled alongside and the harpoon removed, a radio transmitter would be stuck in the whale; and it is then left to float while the ship goes for other kills. After completing the cull, the ships proceed to go alongside the whales, a loop of rope is passed through the ships casing and round the whale's tail. Three whales could be towed on either side of the ship in this way. One of the problems incurred was sharks; they would attack the dead whales in a feeding frenzy, concentrating on the tails for some reason, and this made the securing of the whales to the ship very difficult; men had to go over the side and get ropes round the whale's body.

Sharpshooters have to be in attendance to ward off the sharks. Once the whaling was complete, the ships would head back to the shore station, winches from the whaling sheds would pull the whales up the slipway where the blubber would be removed, boiled, and made into oil. Fortunately, I was not able to see this mass slaughter in action as we were unable to locate any whales on our particular trip, not much of a profitable day for the whalers. Once ashore we were taken round the factory, and they showed us lumps of ambergris taken from dead whales' stomachs. This substance evidently is made up of the undigested beaks of squid which form into lumps and is highly prized in the perfume industry, making it very, very expensive. No free samples, I'm afraid.

After a very interesting but tiring day, the lorry picks us up. Back in the mess, some of the guys are still entertaining; a lot of drunken locals are wandering about, they just don't know when to stop. I have a few pints and a whiskey; an early night is called for, I think; I have a hot shower and wash out my boxers and socks, and now the smell of fish has gone. I feel clean again. My bunk awaits; it's the top shelf of three, away from the mess square, which is heaving. It's noisy, but I soon drift off and dream of home.

After another three days, we prepare for sea and communications, navigation lights, compasses, telegraphs, and alarms are tested. The boilers are brought up to full power, generators are put on line, and special sea dutymen go to their respective duties ready for any emergencies, as the rest of the crew doll up ready for the final farewell on the upper deck. Berthing wires are pulled on board and the ship shudders as we go full astern. Sailors who have fallen in love have tears in their eyes as they wave farewell to recent acquisitions, some, no doubt, having left a few English seeds behind to develop into future famous Australians.

The ship soon gets back into routine as we set course for South Africa. Ironically — for me at least — five miles out the ship hits a whale and we lurch quite violently. The lifeboat sentry reports a mass of blood and gore flying in the air at the stern of the ship as the propellers cut through its body. More humane than harpooning I guess; it must have been a pretty quick death. Unfortunately, the ship's sonar was off at the time, so there was no chance of avoiding it.

The crew by now are well tanned and all looking like Pakistanis; I'm a bit worried about going to South Africa with a dark tan — what toilet do I use? Will I get thrown out of a white only restaurant? Worse still, will I be arrested for impersonating a white man, as the white trash, master race Gestapo there are very keen on enforcing the apartheid rule.

To pass the time away, the captain has the ship's company doing damage control exercises. The action stations alarm goes off, the pipe hands to action stations is broadcast, and everyone is running hell for leather to their respective positions. The ship is closed down to state one condition Zulu, which means every door and hatch on the ship is closed to make the ship watertight in the event of damage, and every one of the ship's company is in their place of action. The ship's company are all dressed in either overalls or number eight shirt and trousers; sleeves are down and trousers tucked into socks, DMS steel-toed, capped boots are worn, anti-flash gloves and hoods covering the head are donned, and gas respirators are carried in the event of a gas attack. A chemical injection kit is on hand in case of a chemical attack.

I'm in the forward damage control position with a tool bag and torch for when the lights go out. The power on the 4.5 inch gun has gone, along with all the lights, and my job is to organise my team to run cables (which are wrapped round brackets throughout the ship) to it, via connecting boards on each bulkhead from an emergency position in the nearest switchboard to the gun. Another electrical DC party is organising necklace lighting. While doing this, the stokers are running out hose pipes to fight imaginary fires, smoke bombs are set off, and everyone is shouting orders. Power is restored to the gun, and the system is tested and proved to work. This is organised chaos, but everything gets done and the ship is back to fighting mode and still afloat. Now comes the hard bit, clearing up – you would not believe the mess this little exercise produces. After the ship is brought back to normal, the usual wash up in the wardroom with heads of departments is convened. It transpires that we did a good job and are deemed capable of doing what we get paid for, which is reassuring.

Most of each working day in my department is used doing job cards, repairing faults, or doing planned maintenance. Job cards are forms which you fill in for departments to fix, e.g. leaking taps, duff telephones, duff radar, and duff anything really; when completed, these cards are sent off to a department in the dockyard. They are supposed to collate them and see if the fault is common to all ships, and then recommend a solution. I found out in later years that what actually happened to the cards was, they were put in boxes and sent over to Gosport and put in railway carriages for storage, no doubt to be held for ten years before being destroyed. Repairing faults is self explanatory; one of your motors blows up and you repair it. Planned maintenance is a system dreamed up by a civilian who has never been on a ship or worked out how long it would take to complete. For instance, the daily planned maintenance for the ship's telephone exchange, if done correctly, would take at least three hours. Add onto that the weekly, monthly, three-monthly, and the annual maintenance, and that doesn't leave much time in the day for fixing faults, or brushing your teeth. Let's face it – you would not get under your car every day to inspect the exhaust, the drive shafts, all rubber bushes, steering joints etc. It seems like the people who draw up these cards must get up at three in the morning to prepare themselves for work at nine o'clock, having checked the water in the toilet system is at the correct level, the voltage is correct at the fuse box, the milk from the fridge and the toast is at the correct temperature, etc. Or, do they try and make our lives a misery just to justify their jobs? Consequently, the minor maintenance cards are just signed off; the old adage "if it isn't broke, don't fix it" worked for me.

Chapter Seven

The long evenings sailing across the Indian Ocean were spent mainly reading. I could get through a book a day on average; the odd evening I would spend in the mess with my mates playing cards and listening to the ships DJ on the SRE (ships radio equipment). It almost made you wish you were in prison where there were no bouncy floors, and you had snooker and pool tables, darts, table tennis, television, gymnasium, a library, visit from loved ones, and best of all a whole room of your own. The strange thing is it cost four times our wages to keep the buggers in this sort of luxury, and here we were risking life and limb to keep them in a free society? You couldn't make it up.

After six days we arrive in East London on the south west coast of South Africa; they too seem to know we were coming as hundreds arrived to see us sail in. Berthing wires are passed ashore to dock workers who drop them onto the steel bollards, and the gangway is dropped into place by a shore crane. Shore cables and telephones are connected, lorries full of fresh fruit and vegetables are waiting for us, and the duty watch is summoned to unload them. Money changing is taking place in the ship's office, about two rand to the pound, no chance of making a few quid on the black market here. The usual dignitaries are invited on board, the big wigs to the captain's cabin, the rest to the wardroom for cocktails.

Shore leave is given from mid-day to non-duty watches. I decide I need a break from the lads in the mess; I just did not fancy going into the nearest bar ashore to get pissed, so I caught a bus and headed for the far side of town. I had no sooner got off the bus when I was nearly knocked over by a car. I stuck my hands up to apologise, half expecting to be called a stupid idiot. Instead, the car's window rolled down and this guy asks me if I wanted a lift. I told him no, as I was just going to have a look round.

"No problem," he says, "hop in and I'll show you the town." This guy turns out to be the head of Gestetner in South Africa, and introduces himself as Henry. He takes me home and I meet his lovely wife, Naomi, who he married after she nursed him back to health following a heart attack. You could not meet a more devoted couple. They invited me to dinner that evening in their luxurious home; I did the decent thing and invited them back to my steel box for a few drinks and they loved it; let's face it – only the elite few in this world get to drink in the Petty officers mess on an RN ship, one perk we have over them damn prisoners.

Over the next few evenings, Henry took me and some of the lads out to bars and nightclubs. He would not let us pay for anything; every time we tried, we were told it had been taken care of. Our last night ashore was spoilt by the dockyard Gestapo, who pulled Henry over for allegedly speeding and we all had to get out of the car. My mates and I started to give them a hard time till they unholstered their guns; after that we kept stum while they wrote out the speeding ticket. We gave them a nice Nazi salute as we drove off, and we advised Henry to take a different route home. I managed to get hold of a ship's crest for Henry as a small token of our appreciation; he was nearly in tears, the big softy. We sailed at eight the next morning, and who was there to wave us off – Henry and Naomi – I must admit I had a tear or two on that occasion.

Our next port of call was Gibraltar and Budgie was sent ahead to collect the mail, a welcome lift for the crew after weeks at sea. Once ashore, the usual suspects caused the usual trouble, and we left six behind this time – what is it with Matelots, cars, and Gibraltar? A big hoo-ha was going on ashore – a petty officer from another ship had gone to the local paper saying he had won the Spanish lottery; the news went round like wildfire. TV, radio, and the press all came down to his ship to interview him; they obviously did not know this was the same practical joker who only weeks previously had attended his ship's official cocktail party dressed as an Arab sheik. Having first hired an Arab outfit and a limousine, before being greeted by his captain for drinks, no one actually queried who he was, which was a bit alarming. He did, by all accounts, win a lot of money in bets, although I gather his captain was not too impressed when the buzz got round to him a week or so later.

Having spent our last few quid on rabbits (presents) in the Indian shops on Main Street, we set sail for the UK and home. When we get to the Bay of Biscay, we come across a container floating aimlessly. Obviously, this is a hazard to shipping so we have to sink it – the 4.5" gun crew is closed up and put to local hand control. The shooting starts, and after a dozen rounds it is split open, millions of cigarettes spill out and float around, and the container sinks, job done. We now get down to some serious steaming making up for lost time. After all, family and friends will be waiting.

Two days later, we are entering Portsmouth Harbour – it's the first of April 1969, and it's a year to the day since we left for the Far East; it just seems longer. Crowds are gathered from Southsea seafront, along old Portsmouth, and the Hard by the railway station; it certainly is some welcome. Everyone is shouting and waving, makes you proud to be British (even though they still have not given me a passport).

The ship eventually berths alongside South Railway Jetty, and I get my first glimpse of my gorgeous baby daughter, Helen, and my lovely wife, Hermione. She has two married friends with her, Hermi and Ron. Evidently, I am the proud owner of a two-year-old Mk 1 Cortina, a throbbing 1200cc of raw Ford power which they have sold us. The gangway is in place and families and friends are pouring on board. I do the normal thing and hug and kiss my loved ones. I take them into the mess where food and drinks have been laid on, and Hermi asks what the shelves round the mess are for. I explain that the shelves are in fact what we sleep on; she can't believe twenty-five of us live in such a small space, and wonders why they didn't just make the ships bigger.

I tried to explain that if they made them bigger we would not be a frigate, we would be a cruiser, and the conditions would still be as cramped. The ship builders tend to concentrate on putting in pipes, electrics, weapon systems, and propulsion before worrying about small details like where to put the crew's accommodation. Another small point is the fact that the admiralties like their ships to look sleek. Making the ship wider to make life comfortable, and a more stable weapon platform, although sensible, would be an innovation the old guys at their desks in London could not contemplate. It's a bloody wonder we're still not under sail. P and O we certainly are not.

The wife nearly kills me when I suggest we have another baby; I guess I didn't realise just how bad a time she had with Helen. After a few hours of talking and getting up to date with news and stuff, I gather my case full of goodies and clothes ready for leave. We head for home and I find that since being away, we are now the proud owners of a three piece suite, a TV, a washing machine, a new bed, a dining room suite, curtains and carpets. Christ, I thought we had won the lottery.

It seems my wife had used all her wages from Finefare supermarket to do a deal with Maynard's furnisher shop in Havant. Buy one thing at a time and pay it off in six months interest free. Luckily, since she finished work I got my promotion which covered her loss of wages. I was now on £21 a week as an acting Petty Officer, and we were scraping by very nicely, thank you. I spent my leave bonding with my new baby girl, e.g. feeding her and changing her nappies, which I managed to do without sticking the safety pins in her. Christ, you can't believe a sweet little thing like that could create such a smelly concoction from milk and pureed baby food. My wife left me to cope on my second night home; she popped out to see Engelbert Humperdinck at the Guild hall with a friend, while I sat wandering what the hell the smell was. I tracked it down to my little girl, and when I opened her terry nappy up, I was amazed how much crap she had produced. There was only one thing for it – baby under one arm, I ran a bath and proceeded to decontaminate her. The bath water changed colour to a light tan, and after a quick change of water I rinsed her off and put her in her cot, job done. I collapsed on our new settee in front of the Ferguson 17" black and white TV; boy, this is living.

After leave, my draft comes through to HMS Collingwood for a Petty officers course, and I am to join on the third of June. My relief arrives and I spend my last week showing him the ropes and where everything is. I pack up my kit and bits and pieces, as these will all be going home from where I will be commuting for the next eight months or so.

I join Collingrad on a bleak Monday morning; nothing has changed, and it's just as depressing as ever. Having completed my joining routine, I form up with my new classmates and we all fall in for divisions on the parade ground. The band marches on with the guard; the usual Roman Catholics fall out order is given. I choose to stay where I am, no more running to the drill shed listening to hail Mary and all that crap for me. Prayers over, the band flashes up, and we march down to White city for Instruction. We enter the classroom and are greeted by our new divisional officer; a young university graduate aged about 23, with two rings on his arm.

"Good morning, gentlemen. I am your new divisional officer. If you have any problems please feel free to discuss them with me."

With that, an elderly (late thirties) acting petty officer sticks his hand up and says, "Sir, I have a problem, my baby son has been crying all night keeping me and the missus awake; my fifteen-year-old daughter is going out with a thirty-year-old Arab; it's that time of month for the wife; the bloody car wouldn't start this morning; I was two minutes late for work this morning, so I'm on report, and about to lose two days leave and a day's pay; oh and by the way, I still masturbate, so I would be eternally grateful if you could sort things out for me."

By this time, everyone in the room is in hysterics, including our blushing lieutenant who says, "Point taken. I promise if I have a problem, you will be the first to know." Once the hilarity was over, he got stuck into

80

teaching us electronics – no more valve theory, we have moved on to transistors and circuit boards, two weeks solid – the old grey matter was in pain. Over the next eight months we cover measurements using ohmmeters, bridge meggers, oscilloscopes, ammeters, voltmeters, etc. Control engineering next, converting electrical signals into mechanical movement. Ships stabilisers next, used to keep the ship as even as possible for the weapon systems. General electrics, audio, management, surface weapons, sonar, and more electronics follow. I end up with a 74% average, getting better.

During this period we manage to sell our bungalow in Porchester for £6,500, a profit of £3,000. We purchase a massive, semi-detached house on Hayling Island for £7,500; it was a holiday home of a businessman who felt sorry for us and gave us a great deal. It's now February 1970; a draft comes through to join HMS Excellent, the Royal Navy gunnery school, and I'm wondering what the hell my job is going to be.

Monday the 28th of February, I drive down Stanley road in Stamshaw towards the bridge leading to Whale Island, a man-made island formed from the excavations of the building of the dry docks in the dockyard; it is held together with trees and wires which crisscross it, binding the whole place, to form HMS Excellent. Once over the bridge, I am stopped at the barrier and asked to produce my identity card and joining papers. I get out of my car and sign in; I am given a temporary car pass and told to report to the regulating office. I am given a joining card, the usual things, sick bay, pay office, petty officers mess, ship's office, and the workshops, which is where I am to be employed. I meet my new boss, Lieutenant Worth, a nice old guy, probably been passed over a dozen times and finishing his naval career in this job. I finish joining; I now have a full time car pass, a mess, and a job. I wander down to the workshops across the road from the drill shed, and inside the workshops are dozens of lathes, milling machines, and power drills.

At the far end is a small compartment with an engraving machine, and next to that is a naval store full of engineering spares, drills, bits, grease, oil, metal of all shapes and sizes, anything that may be required in manufacturing. The other end of the workshop is my domain – worktops, spares, and tools. At the back of this lot is the blacksmiths shop – welding gear, guillotine, and of course a forge. I enter my bit of workshop and meet the guy I am to relieve; he introduces me to six lads who are to be my maintenance team. My job is to keep the establishment lights on, also to keep the irons ironing, and heaters heating; the main job, I am told, is the officers' summer ball, and the annual families open day. The rest of the workshops, I am told, are there for the use of ships; anything that requires

81

making can be made here. It's just a shame nobody bothered to tell the ships that the facility existed; most ships automatically put a job card into the dockyard.

Consequently, the guys here have found ways of amusing themselves – they manufacture small brass cannons and mount them on oak with an inscribed plate reading, ORIGINAL OAK FROM HMS VICTORY. Made on an industrial scale, they were then sold to gift shops at a handsome profit. The guy in the engraving shop was doing a roaring trade and could have made a fortune, but for the fact he advertised in the evening news and got caught by an officer who wanted a name plate for his house. On the shoreline behind the workshops was another blacksmiths shop run by a civilian; his job description was gunnery target repairs. His true job was wrought ironwork manufacturer. I had a lovely set of gates made by him at a very reasonable price. The carpentry shop at the side of our workshop was also a hive of industry; the chief in charge covered himself by requesting to do private work using the navy's equipment. This request was granted. What the navy did not know was he was also using naval stores to make his private work; evidently, he had an order with Debenams to produce stools – dozens would be loaded onto his roof rack and in his boot. All the correct paperwork would be shown at the gate on the way out.

I soon got into the routine. The lads would muster at 8 o'clock and I would give each one a task for the day. I would stipulate: make sure the jobs are done properly and don't get caught loafing. I busied myself learning to weld in the blacksmiths shop; I knocked up a pair of car ramps, real heavy duty jobs, and consequently I had to weld up a roof rack to get them home. I also brought in a Triumph Herald to repair that belonged to my wife's aunty. I had driven it down from Carshalton over this particular weekend; the body work had come apart from the chassis and must have looked a rare sight from behind as I cornered. What I didn't realise was the bloody thing was so rusty, there was nowt to weld onto. I had to virtually make a new chassis, and after completing this I sprayed it and took it back to London. I think I charged her £75, and it probably worked out at a shilling an hour, with the time I spent on it.

The cheeky bitch had the cheek to say I had overcharged her; I felt like ramming it into a pylon and telling her to stuff her £75, bloody families. My next car job was my boss's; he had a Vauxhall Victor, these were made from bean cans and about the same gauge of steel, and consequently, they were rust buckets. This thing had holes everywhere and was always full of water. Anyway, the blacksmith and I are happily welding away under the car when we notice rather a lot of smoke coming from inside the car. The damn carpets had caught alight, and by the time we had put the fire out, the whole inside was a mess with burns and smoke damage. I was given the task of telling the boss. I'll give this bloke his due – he hardly batted an eyelid. We cleaned it up as best we could, and he covered the seats with some material and continued to drive it. He was more pleased with the fact he didn't get wet anymore when it rained, because we had filled all the holes in.

Things are ticking over at work, the lads have a game of football or sport once a week, along with the odd make and mend, and they manage to keep from getting caught loafing after doing their hour's work a day. July comes and things are starting to get busy; the main event of the year has arrived – the officer's summer ball. My team and I head for the store that houses all the lighting required for the outdoor event. Miles of necklaces, floodlights, spotlights, coloured lights, fuse boxes, switch boxes, and power cables. We are given a theme for the ball: this year it is to be HMS Victory – Nelson's time – this means chandeliers and lanterns and that sort of stuff. I meet with the boss, and because he is a mechanical engineer he hasn't a clue, and leaves the decisions up to me. The lads and I set about rigging the lights round the rose garden, situated just above the parade ground. The trees and the water garden are lit up with coloured lights and the walkways are lit with necklaces, it's all coming together; all we are waiting for now is the marquee, which arrives two days before the actual day of the ball, leaving us little time to rig it out.

We set about running a necklace round the inside perimeter, and lighting round the food and bar area, then the boss comes in and tells me that lights are required round the stage, and to rig six 300 watt standing lanterns round it. I explain we have no power outlets left, and he then comes up with a brilliant idea: connect them all together and put a bayonet fitting on the end, and plug it into a necklace socket. I try to explain that 18,000 watts replacing a 60 watt lamp might just overload the necklace a little. "Don't worry," he says, "it will be all right," and I confirm that this is what I must do.

I gang the lights together and plug them into the necklace as ordered. At lunch time I head for the mess, and I am half way through my cheese sandwich and pint of best when the main broadcast announces, *fire, fire, fire, fire* in the marquee. I have a little smile to myself, thinking, *I wonder what could have caused that?* It just happens on this particular lunch time the wind is blowing a gale, and by the time our fire fighting team and the local fire brigade arrive there is little left to put out. I head for the marquee; my boss spots me and comes running over.

"My god," he says, "do you think…?"

"Yes," I replied. "I do."

He is nearly in tears when he says, "What am I going to do? The commander wants a written report on his desk in the next hour!"

"Give me ten minutes," I tell him, and with that I head for the burnt out remains of stage lighting. I check that no one is looking and remove the bayonet fitting off the end of the offending cable. I put this in my pocket, head back to my boss, and tell him that due to the high wind, lighting cables must have gone taut and shorted out, causing the fire. The relief on that guy's face was a sight to behold; all he could see was his pension down the plughole, and now redemption. I thought he was going to kiss me, but fortunately, he restrained himself.

Luckily, the marquee company managed to send another one to replace the pile of ash on the playing field; my team worked till an hour or so before the ball started and managed to get some lighting organised, not quite to theme, but adequate and safe.

Our other big job was the summer fair. This meant the lads and I had to drag all swings and electric roundabouts and crap out to keep the kids happy, while the rest of the workshop staff had to get the stalls and games organised. One of my lads was given the job of running an electric roundabout; it was basically a motor driving a chain which turned the roundabout, controlled by a rheostat with a big brass handle, and this determined the speed of the ride. On this particular occasion, children had just been loaded onto it, and the lad in charge set it off at a modest speed by clicking the handle round a couple of notches. The camp commander's son was on the ride and had his dog on a lead trotting round beside the brat; the kids were shouting *faster, faster*! The commander thought it a good idea to tell the lad in charge to speed it up a bit, "come on, man, give it some stick." With that, the lad winged the handle round to full speed, and with such force it came away in his hand.

The roundabout was now at full speed without control. The kids started screaming, and the poor bloody dog was at the end of its lead parallel to the deck, flying round and slowly being hung. The lad in charge was desperately trying to replace the handle to no avail. Fortunately, half a dozen Matelots managed to fling themselves at the roundabout and grind it to a halt, burning the motor out as they did so. This little episode put a bit of a damper on the afternoon, to say the least. Still, we cleared up and put everything away for another year, and went back to our mundane existence changing lamps.

Next to the main gate was a chicken farm, which was run by a civilian who made a reasonable living flogging his free range eggs. Unfortunately, the chickens had a habit of hiding some of their eggs, and the guys going round every day would miss them for a week or two; consequently, the free range eggs became nostril-blowing stink bombs when opened. The guy was worried because sales were down, and people were boycotting his eggs as word got round. I popped down to the workshop and knocked up an aluminium box with six egg-shaped holes in the top and a 100 watt lamp inside. I got the idea from Lipton's grocery shop; I recalled them using such a device in the fifties when eggs were sold loose. The eggs were put on the box and any rotten ones would show dark while the good ones lit up. I took this device to the egg man to try; it worked a treat, and I was rewarded with two dozen of his finest. His trade picked up when people knew the eggs were now guaranteed fresh, and I was now his best friend in the world.

On the hill above the parade ground was a First World War Roly Poly tank. It weighed 27 tons, had two Vickers heavy machine guns, one either side; its top speed was 3.7 mph, with a range of 23 miles. It had a crew of eight, and was last used in the Second World War as an anti-aircraft gun. Unfortunately, on its first trip down Stanley Road it carved up the road so bad with its tracks that it remained on Whale Island throughout the war. Someone decided it needed renovating, so the engine was lifted out and taken down to the workshops. This huge engine was petrol-fuelled and made by Daimler; it had no valves, but sliding sleeves between piston and bore. Holes in the sleeve would line up with holes in the bore to either let in fuel for combustion, or exhaust the burnt gasses; it was ingenious for its time. Once in the workshop, a 10,000 pound press was rigged to free the piston, but this did not touch it, so welding gear was brought in to heat up the block, hoping to expand it away from the pistons – again no luck. Next, CO_2 was tried on the piston to try and shrink it, but after using all these ideas together, with wooden blocks and sledge hammers, we had to admit defeat. It was thought best to put the engine back in the tank, and give it to Bovington tank museum; after all, it is an Army thing.

In the good old days before Elf and safety, there used to be a thing called the field gun run; this was an event commemorating the navy's involvement in the relief of Ladysmith in the Boer war in 1900. Guns from HMS Powerful were hauled from Durban by the Navy brigade, to defend the town against the Boers. The first public display was in 1907.

Our Portsmouth crew trained at Whale Island and competed against Chatham, Plymouth, and of course, the Airy fairies (fleet air arm). The run consists of three sections, the first being the run out: the gun and limber are raced over a five foot wall, two 170lb spars are rigged and a wire run across a 28 foot chasm; two men take a 120lb wheel each across, and the carriage and 900lb barrel follow. Once over, all is reassembled and pulled over a second wall, and three rounds are then fired.

Next is the run back: men and gun return over the wall and across the chasm in one piece, the rig is collapsed, and three retreating rounds are fired. Lastly, the home run: a bugle sounds "G," wheels are removed, gun and limber are taken through a narrow gap in the wall, and once through, wheels are replaced and the run for the finishing line completes the task. A record was set in 1948 of four minutes; in 1962 a Pompey team did it in three minutes. The lads here are well capable of beating this; they do the run every day, and spend the rest of the day keeping fit. They all look like Charles Atlas, big buggers to say the least. They have steak for breakfast, and probably bricks and girders for tea.

During my time at Excellent I do a bit of private work ashore to subsidise the crappy Naval pay; this helps pay for a few luxuries like nappies, petrol, food, etc. My father in law got me a job down at the beach club on Hayling Island; I got £5.00 for working Friday night in the bar selling light ales for 10p and spirits for 15p; we used to take about £150 in the small bar – that's probably about two grand in today's money. At the end of the evening, the old sod would get us emptying all the glasses into a bucket; the manager would then filter this into the mild barrel ready for the next evening.

Obviously, while serving the lovely drunken public you would be offered drinks. I would say, "I will take for a light ale if that's OK." I would then put the bottles aside, and at the end of the evening I would have maybe 15 or 20 bottles. Old Fred, the owner, would come round and say, "What are those bottles doing there?"

I explained they had been bought by customers. He then says, you either drink them or put them back on the shelf to resell. Yeah, right, not being a drunk driver I put them back on the shelf. After that episode, I would work out in cash value the cost of the light ales and then convert them into spirits and bottle them in a babycham bottle before taking them home for Christmas. I also went in for Saturday morning cleaning, which consisted of un-sticking the dance floor after a heavy night's dancing on spilt beer and G and Ts, and general cleaning. The old bastard who owned the club would get me cleaning his car every now and then. I used to clean it then take it for a spin to dry it off; he came by one day when I was out, and he nearly had a bloody coronary, that "E" type was his pride and joy. Needless to say, my excuse did not wash, and I never got to clean his car again.

Alf Pickup

At that time, my father-in-law's health was going downhill rapidly; he had been diagnosed with bowel cancer, and he had gone down to six stone. A few months later I got a message while at work saying he had passed away. I cried all the way home. I loved the old feller; I thought of him as my dad. My real father died in the war while serving in the Luftwaffe as a doctor in 1944.

Chapter Eight

I've been at Excellent for twenty months when my draft comes through; I am to join HMS Zulu on the 13th of December 1971. I go to the regulating office, and they tell me I have to take my Christmas leave before I join the ship, bloody great, stuck on the ship over Christmas. In Rosyth of all places. I go on leave, and after two weeks at home I leave my family with a heavy heart, and set off in my luxurious limousine, a Morris 1100, and head for Rosyth.

It's one in the morning; the car is stuffed with my kit, a few civvies, a flask, and sandwiches. After leave, I have a few quid left for petrol to get me there; I head for the M6 motorway and put my foot down, the car gets up to 75 MPH, a bit slower when we reach a hill, the roads are clear and I make good time. The road between Carlisle and Edinburgh has dozens of rabbits on it, making driving a bit hazardous for me, and extremely so for the rabbits. I reach the outskirts of Edinburgh, and I now have to contend with thousands of rats on the road from the local land fill. I don't bother swerving to miss these; in fact, I make a point of running over as many as possible and boy, do they crunch well.

Once through the city I reach the Forth Road Bridge, only to find it's a toll bridge; oops, this is a bit awkward as I have spent nearly all my cash on petrol. I manage to take the car apart and find the required fare, I pay the man and head for Rosyth dockyard on the other side of the Firth of Forth. On arrival at the dockyard I show my ID card and joining papers to the dockyard police, and they show me where the Zulu is berthed. I park the limo at the end of the ship's gangway. The ship looks deserted. I march up the gangway with my kit bag and bits, salute the quarter deck, and am met by the officer of the day. "Good morning," he says, "can I help you?"

"I'm joining the ship," I tell him, and he then tells me everybody is on leave after just coming back from the Far East, so there is no chance of doing a joining routine. With that he tells me I might as well bugger off on leave till the New Year. I try and explain I was ordered to take leave before joining; he thinks that stinks, and suggests when I get home I pop into

HMS Excellent regulating office, and thank them for the extra two weeks leave. I dump my kit off and then realise I have no money. I go to this amiable officer again and explain the situation; no problem, he says, and with that we head to the ship's office, and he hands me £25 from the safe. Next month's pay will be a bit short, but what the hell, its Christmas.

I thank the officer and climb into my still warm car; I make for the nearest garage and top up with oil and petrol, it's now light and the rats and rabbits have all disappeared off the roads as I head home. My next fuel stop is a service station near Birmingham, and I decide to phone my wife. She asks where I am; I tell her Birmingham. "My god," she says, "have you broken down?" I tell her no, I'm on my way home on leave, and explain what has happened – joy all round. I tell her to expect me home early evening, but unfortunately, by the time I reach the Winchester bypass I am so tired that I am bouncing off either side of the road. I decide to have a nap, and wake up three hours later. I get home later than I said; my wife is frantic with worry, thinking that I had had an accident. I told her after driving nearly 700 miles with only a short break I was entitled to a nap.

Having spent another Christmas leave with my family, I was well up for joining my new ship in the New Year. My job on board was internal communications: eight broadcast systems, telephone exchange and associated phones, sound powered phones, helicopter comms, CCU's, plus all alarm systems and wind speed and direction units. I had a team of two leading hands and four electrical mechanics to keep the ship talking. The whole communication system was in dire need of revamping, and we set about ordering spares to get things up to par. I don't think the guy I relieved was over worried about maintenance; in fact, I would go so far as to call him a cowboy with the amount of botched jobs I came across – little things like taped up joints, stripped screws on watertight junction boxes, frayed phone cables – the list was endless.

I had a few runs ashore in Rosyth, a few beers in the local pub followed by a trip to the local chippy; this was a place that deep fried everything you ordered – pies, pizzas, black puddings, haggis – I tell you, there's nothing worse than trying to eat a meat pie full of oil when you are half pissed.

Most of my money was spent on petrol for the weekends, and on a good weekend I could get three passengers to come with me and share the petrol costs. One particular weekend, I was halfway down the M6 when my battery charge light came on. I pulled over on the hard shoulder and lifted the bonnet; the fan belt appeared to have gone. I waited till the engine had cooled down, then with the heater full on, limped to the next turn off and found a garage. I bought a new fan belt, but when I went to fit it I spotted the original; it had just come off the pulleys and was still in one piece. I thought, sod it, I've got a new one, I might as well fit it, so I cut the original one off and replaced it with the new one, big mistake.

Ten minutes back on the motorway doing a steady 70 mph, the red light comes on again – shit, what this time – I pull over again and find the belt has stretched, so I loosen the dynamo bolts and tighten up the belt and off we go again; an hour later we're back to square one. Again I find the belt has stretched, so I loosen the dynamo bolts and tighten up the belt and off we go again. An hour later we're back to square one, red light on, pull over, tighten belt – this happens another four times before we run out of adjustment, e.g. the belt is now too big to be of use. Fortunately, I manage to find another garage that will supply me with a belt that is not made out of rubber, and we get home three hours late, around midnight. I slept till one thirty the next afternoon. You've got to try and make the most of these weekends as we have to set off back on Sundays at 9pm to get back for 8am the next day; it's hardly worth the trouble for such a short time, but it's worth it just to be with the wife and daughter.

I recall driving back on my own one time, when I fell asleep at the wheel. I hit the hard shoulder and suddenly woke up; I jerked the wheel violently to get back on the road, and this in turn caused the throttle return spring to come off. The accelerator pedal flopped to the floor and the car picked up speed; by now the car was doing 82 mph. I tried braking to no avail, then I tried going into neutral on the next hill; it slowed a little but the engine was doing two thousand revs more than it was designed to. Then I had a brainwave – switch off the ignition, DER – this I did, but by now the engine was so hot it did not require spark plugs to keep going.

I slammed on the brakes and came to a halt. I leaped out of the car and lifted the bonnet; the engine was still revving at maximum, the manifold was glowing orange, at least I didn't need a torch it was so bright. All I could do now was wait for the carburettor to empty of fuel. After what seemed an eternity it stopped. I waited till it cooled down then got my torch out; I was debating what to replace the return spring with when I spotted it jammed behind the splash plate on the bulkhead behind the engine. The question now was how the hell do I get it out? Fortunately, I was taking some clean shirts back on board, and my dear wife had put them on wire coat hangers, the ideal tool for hooking things out with; after much poking, I managed to get the spring and put it back on the carburettor, but this time I bent the ends over so there was no chance of coming off. I set off on my journey once more; needless to say, by now I was wide awake. One thing I can recommend: if you need a decoke for your car, remove the throttle return spring for ten minutes, and let the engine run till it glows. I swear my old 1100 did an extra 4 mph after that little saga, not that I would want to repeat that episode.

During my time on the Zulu we stayed alongside, doing a mini refit, so no sea time there then. I managed to drive home and back eleven times over the next six months clocking up about 9,000 miles which is a lot for a clapped out 1100, good old British Leyland. I converted my railway warrants into petrol money to help pay for this expensive hobby. On the 3rd of June 1972, I join HMS Victory (Royal Naval Barracks). They send me to Whale Island for a leadership course; we do drills on the parade ground, and the assault course on the shoreline, followed by the usual initiative test. Here are four oil drums, six planks, and two lengths of rope: make yourselves a raft and retrieve the scientist on that buoy in the middle of the harbour.

Bearing in mind that four of us in a team had to make and float out on this contraption, you can imagine what fun was to be had. Two teams get half way to the buoy when their rafts come apart; eight oil drums, four bits of rope, and four planks are now on their way to becoming a shipping hazard. As the tide takes them out to sea, another team has the misfortune to have three leaky oil drums; sabotage is suspected, and as a result they sink. Now there are twelve Matelots bobbing about in Portsmouth Harbour.

Our team does not even get off the foreshore; one of the twats in another team has nicked one of our ropes, and trying to tie four oil drums and two planks together is not an option. Obviously, we did not win that particular event, but hey, we stayed dry. As far as I know, the scientist is still waiting to be rescued. After a few days we have a physical training instructor (PTI) teaching us unarmed combat. How to push a guy's nose into his brain with the heel of your hand, how to blow his brains out by cupping your hands and bringing them together over his ears, how to lift your arms overhead and drop to the floor when someone strangle holds you from behind, lots of dirty tricks. One guy in the class was about six foot six and built like the proverbial brick khazi. The PTI on the other hand was five foot six and about ten stone, of muscle I hasten to add. Now the PTI drags desperate Dan out in front of the class; he's been picking on him all week and the guy is really pissed off. The PTI now says to him, "I want you to strangle me."

The guy looks round at everyone, unsure what to do. The PTI repeats the order and assures him he will not be responsible if he dies. With that, the hulk puts his hands round his neck but before he can exert any force, the PTI spits in his face; the hulk lets go to wipe his face, and the PTI lays him out on the deck and stands with his boot over the hulk's throat, rendering him helpless. Over the rest of the day he keeps on at the big guy, trying to show us size does not matter. However, when it came to the two fingers in the eyes defence, he met his match.

Normally, if someone goes to poke your eyes they use the middle and forefinger on one hand and the defence is to just hold your hand up to split the two fingers, and save your eyes from being poked. When he called the big guy out to poke his eyes, he was not expecting the big guy to use a forefinger from each hand, and consequently, the PTI expecting the one-handed attack held his hand up to defend himself, and was rendered useless as the big guy's fingers found their target. That was the end of the self defence class – the PTI ended up in sickbay, and the big guy went home with a sly grin on his face almost as if he'd known what was going to happen, surely not!

Our next lecture was on drugs. This guy comes in with a suitcase, opens it, and it's full of drugs of every description: hash, opium, heroine, LSD tablets – I'm surprised he is even here; with this amount of drugs he could have disappeared and been set up for life. He lights a piece of hash, and it stinks like burnt rubber; how anyone could smoke this shit is beyond me. He proceeds to tell us what to look for in users, and what to do if we suspect anyone. The odd Matelots who got caught using heroin in the sixties and seventies usually got 90 days in DQs (detention quarters, a cell block at the rear of RNB) then a dishonourable discharge. This proved hard on them, as they were put on cold turkey till their 90 days were up.

Once the course was over, they sent us to the black mountains in Wales, dumped us off in the middle of nowhere, and gave us a map and a set of questions to answer. These involved touring Wales, looking for landmarks, what's the number of the local post office, how many houses are there in a particular valley, what is written on that sign post. No extra charge for the blisters, mind you, we did find a nice little pub to rest in for a while; trouble was we had to be back to base before it got dark. Base consisted of a broken down stone house situated above a reservoir – the accommodation was not exactly five star, bunks had been brought and fitted, and the next few days we spent renovating this place. Our job was making the roof watertight; it was good fun, far better than the walking about bit. After the weekend was over we all went back to our respective ships and shore bases.

My new job in RNB is to help supervise security of the establishment, on the main gate. At this time, the IRA was in full swing, blowing up anything that was British, so we had to be vigilant. We regularly had orange and red alerts, every vehicle was searched inside and out and top to bottom, and people were frisked, a wren for the women, and jolly Jack for the males. Strangely, there was always a junior rates dance on a Thursday night, and this was obviously the time the IRA was in bed because security was nonexistent – any bugger could walk in. You cannot search hundreds of people all arriving at roughly the same time to the eight o'clock dance.

Our watches were split between six petty Officers; they consisted of 8am-2pm, 2pm-8pm, and the all-nighter from 8pm-8am; we worked it so we had a few days off every week. One day I was on the gate and got talking to an officer, who used to be the supply officer from HMS Collingwood, and learned he was waiting for his court martial. Evidently, when he was drafted there, he was contacted by Fred Wain, the caterer, who supplied most RN ships and establishments. They came to an agreement – the officer would invoice the navy for six sides of beef, Fred would deliver four, and the value of the other two would be split between them. The only reason he got caught was the fact that he was being relieved of the job; he tried passing on the scam to his relief, who promptly reported him, hence the draft to RNB to await court martial.

I asked him if he was worried about his future, and he just laughed, telling me his house was paid for, he had thousands in the bank, and trust house forte had offered him a job when he finished his expected prison term. Their theory was, if you can feed an establishment of 6,000 on less than the navy gives you without anyone being any the wiser, then work for us and see how much you can save us. Mercenary bastards. I heard later he went to Winchester, the Army's glass house, followed by a dishonourable discharge. Fred Wain ended up in prison for fraud; strangely enough, his lorries could still be seen entering naval establishments and the dockyard, delivering stores. No doubt the navy was so reliant on him they had no alternative but to keep him in business. But before extensive investigations throughout the fleet were conducted, two or three ships had mysterious fires in the stores office, and by coincidence all paperwork regarding catering was destroyed. Makes you wonder how much was actually being taken from the mouths of poor Jack. One good thing, the quality of food improved throughout the fleet soon after.

One evening I was on the main gate when the Navy patrol came in with the meat wagon. In the back was this hysterical Arab from the Libyan navy sobbing his eyes out. "What the hell's up with him?" I asked, and was told he was caught smoking pot in a shop doorway. "Big deal," I said, but evidently it was a big deal. Colonel Gaddafi had ruled that any of his sailors caught taking drugs were to be sent home for execution. I guess I know now why he was crying – no human rights crap at this time.

Alf Pickup

The winter was a cold one in '72; our office at the side of the gate was kept warm by a pot belly stove, and this was kept topped up with anything that could be burnt once our coal ration ran out. The lads would go round the establishment and scavenge anything that was flammable: wood, paint, cardboard, etc. This stove used to glow orange, and more than once the flames reached well beyond the chimney and into the night sky, which caused startled civilians to call the fire brigade. We assured the brigade this was normal and not to worry, but they were not impressed at being called out at three o'clock in the morning; some people just have no sense of humour.

A few weeks after the fire brigade was called for our fire, they returned for a flood, but we were not guilty this time, as a water main had burst outside the main gate. Queen Street was under four feet of water; this happened at about five in the morning, and by eight o'clock Portsmouth was in chaos. It was quite a sight seeing cars floating by along with the local rubbish. I was panicking as my twelve hour shift on the gate was up and I wanted to get home; fortunately, someone remembered there was a gate at the back of the establishment into the dockyard, long forgotten keys were found, and escape was possible.

During my period of time in RNB, old buildings were being demolished to make way for new accommodation blocks. A constant stream of lorries took the rubble away to Chichester to become hardcore for a new building site. These lorry drivers were charging the contractors in RNB £6.50 a cubic yard to remove it and £7.50 to the Chichester contractors to dump it. These lorries were in and out six or seven times a day, and cleared around £500- £700 a day. Boy, talk about having your cake and eating it.

Tucked in the corner of the establishment was a civilian garage; the agreement with them was give us sailors a good deal, pay your rent, and everyone is happy. I got chatting to the chief gunnery instructor one day after seeing his Austin 1100 being towed to the garage. I asked him what the problem was, he said he could not get any gears, and the guys in the garage had told him he needed a new gearbox. I thought this a bit odd; normally you tend to have trouble getting one gear, not every gear.

That day I had the all night on, and decided to have a look at his car. I popped the bonnet and had a quick look, and sure enough the only problem was the gear lever; the connection to the gear box was a splined joint, and the nut and bolt clamping it together had come loose. Unfortunately, I did not have any tools with me, so I went back to the office and left the CGI a note on his desk explaining what I had found. I did not do a day duty for a few days so I did not see the CGI to speak to. When I did see him, I asked how he got on with his car's gear problem, and he told me they had replaced his gear box at a cost of £ 350. I asked him if he got my note. "What note?" he replied. I then told him what I had found. This guy went berserk, and within minutes was down at the garage having a go at the greasy mechanic. The mechanic assured him the gearbox had had it, that they'd had no choice but to replace it, and he came back to the office most disgruntled.

I suggested he get in contact with the gear box repair company, Platers in Gosport, to check his old gear box. This they did, and told him it was in good working order. Armed with this information, he headed back to the grease monkey back at the garage and assured the guy that unless he got his money back, he would inform the Captain of his problem and his little empire would come to an abrupt end. Within ten minutes he was back in the office with a cheque. I was then invited to the Chiefs mess for drinks with my new found best mate.

This security job on the gate seemed to be taking its toll on my health, as I started to get severe stomach pains. After an all-nighter on the gate doubled up in pain, I decided to see the camp doctor. I head for the sick bay and book an appointment. I get to see him at 10.30. I enter the office; a retired surgeon Captain of about 99 years old greets me with the words, "What's wrong with you?" I feel like saying, "You're the bloody doctor, you tell me." Anyway, I tell him my symptoms. I get the feeling he thinks he is superior to me as he does not even bother looking up, let alone doing anything physical like, checking pulse, blood pressure, or poking my belly. The good thing is, I may not be well, but I'll outlive this sanctimonious old bastard.

He hands me a prescription, Aspirin, wow, top of the range drugs for me. The pain appears to be getting worse over the next few weeks. Christmas day, I am on leave on Hayling Island and I end up on the floor in agony; my wife runs down the road to the phone box and calls a doctor. He arrives, not a happy bunny. He asks if I have been drinking. Chance would be a fine thing. I explain that I am under care of a naval doctor, and tell him I am on aspirin. The doctor said, "This guy obviously does not like you, as you have an ulcer and the Aspirin is making it worse, in fact it could kill you."

"Gee thanks, doc, that's most reassuring," I say and with that he prescribes me Tagamet, and gives me a dozen to keep me going till after Christmas. Within the hour my pain is subsiding and I am heading for normality after all these months. After leave I felt compelled to go and see

Rip Van Winkle in his surgery, and I booked another appointment. He calls me in, and without looking up he says, "Now what's wrong?" I explain that while I was on leave I saw a real doctor. With that he went a bright purple colour, and I quickly explained I had an ulcer and that he had nearly killed me with his Aspirin; his face went from red to white. Before he could say anything, I saluted and left. It certainly gave the old bugger something to chew over.

The third of November 1972, I'm in Saint Mary's hospital watching the birth of my second daughter, Theresa; she is a little beauty, even if she is covered in blood and guts. I tell you, what these women go through giving birth is beyond belief; I sure am pleased I was born a man. Thanks to the wife having a bad time with my first born, I am able to stay shoreside for eighteen months on her medical grounds.

In October and November of '73 I find myself back in Collingwood doing courses on ship installed radiac systems, ship installed chemical systems, telephone exchange, and communication boxes. Next, I'm off to HMS Phoenix, the fire fighting school; we do the usual chip pan fires, oil fires, and electrical fires, all this with breathing apparatus and fire proof suits. One has to be fairly competent when the ship catches alight in the middle of the Atlantic, no fire brigade out there. All this is gearing up to a draft in January. The draft arrives in December; I am to join HMS Devonshire, D02, a county class destroyer fitted with two 4.5" twin turrets and a sea slug missile system. Built in 1962, she is destined to do patrols in the gulf and Caribbean before being sunk by sea harriers in 1977. We are to sail to America and the West Indies, along with HMS Blake, really looking forward to it.

Monday the 7th of January, I arrive at South Railway Jetty, complete with kit bag and suitcase; the weather looks grey and dismal, not a good omen. I do my joining routine to let everyone know I am here; the guy I am to relieve has already gone on draft, so it's a case of find your own way round the ship. I decide to leave it till the following morning. I join number six petty officers mess, and I find my bunk is in the mess square, which is not funny when you are trying to get to sleep at night and the mess drunks want to rave it up till three in the morning. The mess square is topped up with beer barrels, lashed to anything that will hold them, bunks, pipes, even lockers; storage space is at a premium, especially on a long trip. I notice a fish tank has been fitted in the panelling on the ship's side, all very homely I'm sure.

Having settled in, I get my department together, three leading hands and four able rates; the ship is due to sail in two hours so I make sure they all know sea communications are to be checked, and phone lines are to be disconnected when ordered. My special sea duty station is in the Gyro room. I am there in case of an emergency, such as if the ship is closed down to condition Yankee. Most doors and hatches are locked down ready for sailing, berthing wires are taken in, phones disconnected, the engines rev up, the ship shudders as we move from the berth; family and friends are waving us off, as is normal on a long trip away from home. Once out on the open sea, the weather gets a bit choppy. I feel like shit, and get my head down; too much shore time makes you lose your sea legs, and it takes a while to overcome the dreaded nausea. I scrub round lunch and supper.

As we hit the Atlantic, the weather goes from bad to worse, by eleven that evening we are in the middle of a force 12 storm; you would think we were in a minesweeper rather than a destroyer the way the ship was bouncing about. By now, beer barrels have broken loose and are smashing about the mess, but nobody attempts to stop them from fear of getting killed by one. Everyone not on watch is lashed into their bunks; everyone on watch is lashed to their station; sleep at this point is impossible, and the fear factor creeps in – will we survive?

At 3.30 am, the ship's company come alive to the sound of the main broadcast alarm going off. Everybody leaps out of their bunks and heads for their emergency stations; no pipe has been made on the main broadcast for the reason of this, and the alarm is still going, which is a bit unusual as one has to keep one's finger on the push to activate it. I am sent for by the Captain, as this is my section. I suggest he contacts all the positions where the alarms are situated; this he does, and finds nobody is pressing the alarms.

The only ones not manned are on the upper deck! Oh! The only thing I can suggest is going down to the amplifier room and disconnecting the upper deck circuits to stop the damn noise. Does anyone know where the amplifier room is? The chief electrician takes me below and shows me my new domain; I find the junction box concerned and start disconnecting the upper deck circuits. After the third go, the damn alarm stops and the battered crew is informed that we are not sinking after all. The next day the weather has not improved, and the helicopter seems to have broken loose from her moorings in the hangar; you could here the damn thing smashing about as the ship rolled from side to side. I don't think there are many flying hours left in that bird.

By lunch time the old stomach is in need of sustenance, so I head for the dining hall. The chefs, bless them, have rustled up a pot mess, which is a huge pot filled with anything that can be cooked: tinned meat, tinned vegetables, tinned sponge, you name it. This pot is lashed onto the top burners of the stove and kept refilled over the period of rough weather; you'd be surprised how good this concoction tasted. I grabbed a stainless bowl and filled it with stew; I turned to get a spoon when the ship lurched violently, and the huge pot slopped over onto the deck. I slipped and in slow motion, my bowl of stew headed for the chief stoker. I tried to warn him, too late, he caught the lot smack in the middle of his chest. He let out an almighty scream as the hot gruel hit him; by now we were both on the deck in a crumpled heap. I didn't know whether to laugh or cry, but the chief stoker definitely wasn't laughing. The way he carried on you would have thought I had caused the problem, welsh tosser. After apologising to him for the umpteenth time I reloaded my bowl, jammed myself in a corner, and finished it without spilling another drop.

Work at this time was out of the question for the electrical branch, as survival was the top priority. The only people working were the stokers keeping the ship under way, the chefs keeping us fed, and the sailors steering the ship. At around the seventh day out, we were hit by a monster wave that towered over the ship. When it hit us on the port beam, it sent us over so far that HMS Blake, who was accompanying us, saw our sonar, propellers, and keel, assumed we had sunk. It was then reported that we had disappeared and a mayday was sent by her.

It appears when we righted, we and Blake were between troughs and she lost sight of us. Our mess at this time had beer barrels literally flying through the air; one of the lads in the mess suffered broken ribs and concussion, another ended up with a broken arm. Anything breakable broke; the hot water urn in the mess tipped out, the fish tank emptied onto the deck and all hell let loose; once we were upright again there was a frantic effort to get the bloody fish back in the tank – only problem was we had no water as the ship's water pumps had failed along with other machinery due to the hammering we had taken. Someone had the idea of emptying the remains of the hot water urn into the fish tank, someone else ran and got a bucket full of ice from the Scotsman ice maker, and this too was tipped into the tank followed by the fish. The amazing thing was out of thirty-two fish only one was missing, never to be seen again, all the others survived.

After a week of being hammered by rough seas and eating pot mess for breakfast, lunch, and dinner, we woke to find the weather had calmed down to a pleasant force six; sure, we were rolling a bit, but at least we could get on with repairing the damage wreaked on us by the storm. My team ventured onto the upper deck; to say there was total devastation is an understatement – every lifeboat and life raft had gone, the davits which held them were swinging in the wind, and the cause of the first night's broadcast alarm became apparent. The quarterdeck quartermaster's steel box, housing telephones, broadcast microphones, speakers, and alarms had completely disappeared, ripped off the superstructure by a wave; just bare wires were left sticking out of the deck glands. The other upper deck speakers on all systems had also disappeared; the ships superstructure had been stripped bare, this included navigation lights, and the wind speed and direction equipment.

Once we had assessed the damage we made a report to the weapons electrical officer, who told us to make good what we could from supplies in naval stores, then order what else we needed by signal, and these stores would be flown out ASAP. The fleet air arm boys had the hanger door open and were sweeping the remains of the helicopter up and placing them into dustbins; the biggest part left was the engine block, this was what was causing the noise in the rough weather, now they were able to lash the bloody thing down and give the ship a bit of peace at last. In the magazines, missiles and shells had broken loose, which caused a bit of a worry at first, but our sailor boys managed to make things safe – a few bits of armament were thrown over the side just to be sure. HMS Blake, our escort ship, also suffered. She was a helicopter cruiser carrying four sea kings, and Christ knows the noise they must have gone through with that lot rattling about.

We finally enter the harbour at Norfolk, Virginia – it is eighteen miles from the Atlantic and bordered by Chesapeake Bay and Hampton Roads Harbour, opposite Portsmouth, not quite home, but any port in a storm, eh what. This is one big Yankee naval base, in fact the biggest naval base in the world, spread over 4,600 acres; it houses thirteen piers which jut out from the harbour, each capable of berthing an aircraft carrier, and up to a hundred different ships are based here – it is truly awesome. We must have looked like some third world navy when we arrived, covered in peeling paint and rust, and half the upper deck missing. Anyway, we finally berth and connect up to fresh water, and electrical supplies, fresh fruit, vegetables, and stores are waiting for us. I'll give these yanks their due, they know their logistics. Free buses are available for going ashore and returning back to the ship – imagine this in our dockyard, I don't think so. It takes two weeks and a load of paperwork just to organise a van to pick something up from a naval store, let alone a free bus ashore.

Our mess deck looks like a bomb has hit it; I suppose a barrel of courage sparkling bitter travelling at speed can be classed as a missile; anyway, we tidy up as best we can, and fortunately, we are due to go into refit when we return home so all is not lost. The tiller flat is half full of water so the portable Rover gas turbine pump is brought into action;

amazingly, this bit of kit was one of the few things on the upper deck to survive. This monstrosity is supposed to be able to be handled by four men, making it portable, but it usually takes six, or a crane to move it. Once in position pipes are connected, one down the tiller flat to suck the water out, and one over the side to send it back to where it came from; a starting handle is turned, slowly at first, to turn the turbine, and once it gets up to speed the fuel is injected, ignition follows, and an almighty roar ensues, complete with a twenty foot flame out the arse end, pumping out commences at an astronomical rate.

I decide to go ashore to the PX, the equivalent of our NAAFI, only twenty times bigger, which is a bit like comparing WalMart with One Stop. I buy some presents for the kids and the wife, and a load of King Edward cigars, $6 a box as opposed to £30 a box in the UK. I don't smoke them, but I know a man who does, and I smell a small profit here. I get chatting to a couple of American petty officers, Elmer and Harvey J. Crocket the third; they invite me on their ship for brunch the next day, and I invite them for a few beers tonight. I get a bus back to the ship and have a siesta for an hour; around five, I have a shower and wash my nicks and socks, a week's worth. I go down to the low power machinery room to hang my smalls on the lines provided. As usual, drying space is at a premium, especially now after days at sea with no hot water and laundry facilities – the place looks like a Chinese wash house. I pull off the dry washing and put them in a pile by the door. Once back up at the mess, I bundle up the rest of my dirty clothes and take them down to the ship's laundry.

The poor buggers down there have washing piled up to the ceiling, and half way down the flat, I can see it being a week before we get it back. Back up at the mess I have a pint, and then head down to the dining hall for supper. There is a choice of five meals, all separate for a change; due to the heavy weather we senior rates have to eat off stainless trays till the new replacement plates arrive – this is one of our few perks. After dinner I chill out in the mess till the guests arrive, and at around 7.30 I am piped for on the main broadcast to go to the gangway.

I welcome Elmer and Harvey, and take them down to the mess. The problem on their ships is they are not allowed alcohol; I guess they can't be trusted like us Brits – they would rather be laid back in a war high on grass. Nelson got it right, eight pints of beer and a pint of rum a day, Christ; if that didn't make you want to fight I don't know what did. I digress, after four hours of swapping yarns, I am helping two drunken yanks up to the gangway so they can get back to their ship. I wave them farewell, and they tell me to arrive around eleven on their ship for brunch. The next day I step off the gangway and onto a bus. I ask the driver where the yanks' ship is, and am informed it is the third aircraft carrier down the jetty. Jesus, these are bloody big ships.

Anyway, up the gangway I go; I salute the quarterdeck, and the officer of the day, as is customary. "Can I help you sir?" asks the OOD, all very polite. "I've been invited to brunch by petty officers Elmer and Harvey," I tell him. They make a pipe for them, and I wait…nothing? Then one of their mess mates comes up and informs us that they were both arrested last night and are in cells after being picked up by the shore patrol for being drunk, can't imagine how. Great, no bloody lunch today, I was looking forward to a nice T-bone. I was about to go back to my ship when this mess mate says, "No problem, follow me," and with that, we head down four decks to the mess. Within half an hour I am eating food that the RN could be producing if it upped our allowance from £1.20 a day to £3.50. Anyway, the T-bone, hash browns, tomatoes, beans, bacon, and two eggs over easy went down very well, along with the fresh coffee. I invite this new friend for drinks, but he declines, saying he is a teetotaller; more like scared of getting pissed and ending up with his mates in cells. He gives me a tour of the ship and sends me on my way. Inter-navy relations are on an all-time high, with me at least.

Chapter Nine

My team and I are kept busy over the next two or three days, mainly doing repairs and replacing broken or missing equipment. Once we have run out of spares from the ship's naval stores, we are at the mercy of the British dockyard stores system; this consists of some civvies in an office who will decide whether the signals we send are of high enough priority to send us what we ask for.

The engineers have got most pumps and machinery working, the sailors have painted over the rust, and the chefs have the stores topped up, so after five days we're ready to sail. The brief rest was most welcome after our hectic voyage. We are now sailing south and heading for Fort Lauderdale, Florida, often called the Venice of America due to the amount of waterways round the city. After two days cruising we arrive. The lower deck is cleared for the ship's entry into the harbour; everyone not manning special sea duty is dressed in their number six uniform, and gleaming white Matelots cover the upper deck. I am down in the gyro room for the entry, but once we fall out I wander on the upper deck; Jesus Christ, half of the bloody city is on the jetty. Evidently, we are the first British ship to call in for over twenty years, and the yanks do like us English speaking sailors.

Within the hour, lists are going up on the notice board for golf, barbeques, and a general adopt-a-sailor for the weekend; leave is given to the non-duty watch, and as they step off the gangway a car is waiting to whisk them away – no transport problems here then. I am duty senior electrician, my job is to get the shore supply on and run our generators down, and first I have to parallel the generators with the shore supply. This consists of getting our generators running at the same speed as the shore supply; a meter with a rotating needle tells you when you achieve this: when the needle is at five to twelve, the supply breaker is closed and ship and shore are running in sequence, load is transferred via the voltage control, and once transferred, the breaker is open and the ship's generator is off load. It is now just a matter of getting the engineers to shut down the diesel and steam turbine generators. Once this is done, the duty watch are mustered; the officer of the day is a young arse hole of a seaman lieutenant. Out of the blue, he picks me out to give a lecture on breathing apparatus in half an hour's time; I rush down to the mess and grab my mate, whose department it is; he gives me a quick run down on pressures, times, and useful bits of info which I should know, but have forgot.

Now I can inform the duty watch who are mustered in the dining hall for my lecture. I give the talk with all the correct details, then hand the officer a gas mask, and inform the duty watch that he will be instructing them in its uses and limitations. The poor bugger knew even less than I did; he ended up being very embarrassed, and learnt a valuable lesson: have some respect, don't try and be clever, and don't fuck with your senior rates. He did call me afterwards to ask for an apology. I told him he started it, but I give him his due — he took my point and assured me he would give me at least 24 hours notice next time. That's all I ask.

The electrical department's job now is to do rounds of all electrical departments on a regular basis, to keep an eye out for fires, hazardous flammables lying about, floods, and any overheating of equipment. This is done every four hours and a log must be signed.

Tropical leave is given, work from 8-midday, and then leave to the non-duty watches till 8am. I've put my name down for a barbeque. I'm waiting at the end of the gangway and I am joined by eight other ratings when three huge American cars turn up on the dot. Three huge, over the top American couples pile out and greet us like long lost families. I'm debating going back on board, but my stomach urges me otherwise. Meanwhile, back at the ranch — well, it was a big house — the beers and barbie are going down a treat. The drunker I was getting, the more I liked these amiable yanks. I found the secret for liking these over the top foreigners —get pissed!

Next day, I stayed on board to recuperate. I got talking to a local contractor who had been invited into the mess for a few beers; seems like he had a local building development and was having trouble getting electricians to wire up the ceiling fans in the houses. Two of us volunteered, and next day at twelve o'clock we were picked up and taken to the site. The work was easy; all the houses were made of wood, so no concrete or hard stuff to drill through. We did three days work, and earned enough to keep us in beer for a week or two. Many of the guys went credit card crazy in Disneyland — okay if you have the kids with you, but grown men? Very childish, typical Matelots, I suppose.

After five days, we are back at sea heading for the Caribbean; our first stop is Virgin Gorda, a delightful little island with a few buildings seen in the distance. The ship anchors off, and ban yans are organised; these are beach rest and recuperation trips, (much needed after the hectic days in Lauderdale) or barbeque piss ups, for want of a better description. The non-duty electrical department chugged ashore in the whaler and claimed a good piece of the beach away from those drunken stokers down wind. One of the lads foolishly sat under a coconut tree, which showed its disapproval by dropping a nut on his shoulder, shattering it; luckily, it missed his head. With the boat, we sent him back on board to the sick bay. He was airlifted the following day to a hospital in San Juan, where he stayed for several weeks before being flown back to the UK.

Back at the barbie things are going better; the fire is well under way, and all is going well till someone realises there is no meat. Some prat forgot to load it in the boat, and we end up roasting some freshly caught fish, crabs, beans, eggs, bananas, and pineapples, which all added to the tropical theme along with the beers, of course. We also found out that if you can't open a coconut, just get some dumb greeny to throw it on a hot fire when no one is looking. It will of course ignite, and after a few minutes of heat, will explode into a thousand pieces of shrapnel and boiling milk. Even the drunken stokers came running to see what the bang was. This barbie was brought to a speedy conclusion as we packed up and took the wounded back to the ship; the sick bay was busy that day I can tell you. Don't try this at home, kids.

The ship up anchors and we set off for St Lucia, an island 606 square kilometres in size and independent of the UK since 1967. After two days we arrive in Castries, a natural harbour and capital of the island, and coming in it looks stunning. Unfortunately, the closer you get the shabbier it is; the place appears to be in decline since independence, paint seems to be nonexistent; what little there is peeling off, leaving wooden frames to rot in the tropical climate. We berth alongside the thriving jetty; a Fyfe's banana boat is loading up with the local produce, fishing boats are everywhere, and luxury yachts full of rich Americans fill the harbour.

The usual list of invites goes up; I plum for a local doctor who has asked for three senior rates to his house. Tropical routine is the order of the day; this means leave from noon, and the doctor arrives in his Land Rover to pick us up. The speed limit here is 30 MPH; I defy anyone to reach it, as the roads consist of thousands of potholes, up to three feet deep. Obviously, the local government are not into infrastructure repairs, you don't drive on the left here, or the right come to think of it. You drive to avoid the pot holes and the oncoming traffic. The doc had it weighed off to a T, and after twenty minutes we are out of the town and half way up the hill side overlooking the harbour, a truly beautiful sight. We pull into the doc's bungalow; his wife is there to greet us. I think she is Swedish, judging by her accent, and the doc is definitely English. Friends of the couple are introduced to us, we are led into the rear garden, and it is full of tropical flowers, landscaped, and well maintained. A local lad with a broad smile brings us all a beer and we get to chatting.

They ask us about the navy and the UK, we ask about local life. The doc tells us about the hospital where he works; mortality is high due to the inter-breeding, and people are constantly ill; the town people can't tell you who belongs to who, yet at the northern end of the Island where the so called uncivilised Caribs live, mortality is low and they can tell you the names of all their relatives for generations past. The local hospital is always crowded, yet the doc visits the Caribs only once a month, unless there is an emergency. Below where we are is a settlement, and this is where the poor whites, as the locals call them, live; these poor buggers are albinos: African looking, with pink eyes and white skin, they are treated like dirt by both black and white alike. The island's main economy is bananas, and evidently if you own four trees or more you qualify as a grower. When the banana boat comes in, the crop is picked and taken down to the harbour, where it is then weighed, and the going rate given to the producer. He will then go and buy enough rum and ganja till the next boat comes in.

After a damn fine feast and booze up, the doc takes us back to the ship, and the two chiefs invite him to their mess the next day. I don't mean to appear tight, but it saved me a few bob on my mess bill.

The next day, 10 gallon drums of battleship grey paint and coils of rope can be seen taken ashore by the duty watch; this is obviously going to spruce up the town. The Chief bosun's mate, a big man with a beard to match, can be seen taking money from a local business man, nothing suspicious there then. This guy had his own set of naval stores books for his own personal use, which I will talk about later in the story. One of my mates in the mess, a pinky, or radio guy, is turning into a Jehovah's Witness; the bible is out day and night, and is, quite frankly, getting on people's nerves.

I spend many an hour trying to dissuade him from ruining his career. I try and show him that the bible is just a load of fairy stories, Adam and Eve, talking snakes, Noah and his Ark, two by two, dead sea crossing? Get real, he wouldn't have it; everything in the bible is true, apparently. He has his request in to give eighteen months notice to leave the navy; his request is to be granted quicker than he thought, as he was told he could leave as soon as we got back to Portsmouth. Obviously, the navy did not want him converting any more sailors; no bible pushers, gays, or druggies in this man's navy, so he had to go. Shame really, as he was a real likable guy, apart from the bible bit.

I put in a suggestion, on the appropriate form, to convert an unused stainless steel coat locker into a drying cabinet, which would mean putting a black heater in the base, under a grill, and then rails to hang the clothes on, followed by connecting the top to the fresh air exhaust system to remove the steam. As there is no official way to dry your nicks and socks, I thought this a good idea, and evidently, so did the powers up high, as they sent me a cheque for twenty pounds. Nothing was ever done to implement the idea; I guess it's the thought that counts.

One of the chief artificers in the engineering department, invented a device to sense over heating in the engine gear boxes. This had been a problem when a gear box had seized up without warning, causing a major machinery failure, and his device would prevent this from happening. He sent the idea off and waited, and he heard nothing until Plessey sent the device to the ship as a modification. When the chief realised it was the exact device he had invented, he queried why he had not got anything for his troubles, as normally you get money for any invention, even though the navy retains the patent. He was told Plessey had developed it, so his exact idea was not wanted, lying bastards; it was clear it had been stolen and passed on to Plessey to manufacture. The guy who designed the sloping flight deck for extra lift for aircraft on carriers made £50,000; lucky for him, Plessey did not beat him to it.

After the weekend, we sail for exercises with our American cousins; gunnery, towing, sea rescues, and submarine detection are all put through their paces. We even let off a sea slug missile or two at radio-operated aircraft, PTA's, (pilotless target aircraft). You would have thought the title of the thing might have given a clue when some wag put up a list asking for volunteer pilots for it. Four morons signed up, and they were all fitted out with helmets and goggles and a set of driving instructions. They thought it would be something to tell their grandkids. They realized the error of their ways when one of them asked for a parachute in case he got hit; the resulting laughter from the ship's company gave it away.

The ship pulls into St. Lucia after a hectic five days of war games, and divers are sent down to blow up a reef; this is to clear the entrance to a brand new jetty so large ships can enter. We become the first ship to dock on this new facility, and are welcomed by the local dignitaries, any excuse for a cocktail party. More bloody work floodlighting the ship and making the flight deck area pretty with coloured lights. The red and white awnings are put up to cover the flight deck. The weather has turned dull and cloudy, and the wind is getting up; all the signs are for storms heading our way, and the ship is preparing for the worst, as everything is lashed down just in case. The cocktail party is moved to the wardroom due to the windy conditions, wouldn't want anyone to get blown away, would we? The duty watch is called out to remove the floodlighting and awnings.

The next morning, the sun is out and the weather normal, the front appears to have veered north, all that tying down for nothing, bugger. The local priest arrives to ask if we can put his church bell back; seems like it fell down in the last storm. A team of chippy's, sailors, and stokers are assembled and proceed to the church. The wooden framework which supports the bell has to be renewed, (the old one was rotten and full of worms, causing it to fail); this is done, and the bell is hoisted back up the tower, all half ton of it. The chippy carves the frame with the words, "If this bell should fall again, use the phone to ring our name, HMS Devonshire! 1974. Nice touch.

Our next port of call is New Orleans, south east Carolina, and after waiting a day for the fog to clear at the mouth of the Mississippi, we head up river. This is a strange city, situated below the river level; the dumb buggers who picked this place to settle must have had some sort of death wish, if you ask me. Anyway, leave is given and the usual entourages of keen Americans are there to greet us and whisk us off to their homes. I must admit the family and their friends I visited did themselves proud, as it was the best barbeque I've ever been to before or since; the variety of meats, sauces, dips, and marinades were out of this world.

The ship was docked a little way down a deserted jetty on the outside of town, which proved to be ideal pickings for a particular big, black guy with a Cadillac. He would pull past a couple of unsuspecting Matelots going ashore, they would run after the car thinking they were being offered a lift, and once they were alongside, the window would come down, and a huge pistol would be aimed at them. He then told them to strip to their pants and pass everything over, including their watches and rings. The order was then given to run for their lives.

After six Matelots had returned to the ship in their pants, it was decided to call the police; they arrived, and promised to patrol the area. It nearly worked. That night, the ship sent a naval patrol ashore, a petty officer and two ratings, and they were duly relieved of their uniforms and personal bits by the big, black guy in the caddie, most embarrassing. Everyone had a good laugh, everyone but me, that is; I was in charge of the following night's patrol. Fortunately, the following evening, a police car took me and the lads to the local police station. This huge building was closed, apart from the reception, and one policeman manned the desk. Me and the lads made ourselves comfortable. After ten minutes, a distraught woman ran into the building telling the desk guy she had been robbed by a guy with a gun who sat on the wall down the road.

We poked our heads out the door; sure enough there he was in the process of another mugging. After half an hour, there was a queue at the desk. Unfortunately, there were no police available to stop him, and after about six hundred dollars worth of cash, and who knows how many watches and jewelry, he decided to finish work for the evening and wandered off into the night. A police car finally arrived twenty minutes later; these guys must have been trained in the UK. The rest of the evening was spent listening to these poor unfortunates pouring out their problems to the desk officer. Luckily, our guys did not cause any trouble this night, so our patrol was not required. At midnight we were given a lift back to the ship, where there was much activity on board. Apparently, a sailor had come off shore a bit worse for wear. He had tried to climb over a barbed wire fence to take a short cut and slipped; the quarter master spotted him hanging upside down, and by the time he and the bosun's mate got to him he had stopped breathing.

The QM sent the bosun's mate for help, then proceeded to give the kiss of life, and by the time help arrived the guy was breathing again. Cutters were used to free him, and he was carried back on board, where he then stopped breathing again. The ship's doc gave him a jab of something and resuscitated him. He was taken down to the sick bay and kept under watch. The next morning he woke up with a hangover but was none the worse for his ordeal; he was a bit shocked when his mates told him what had happened. He told them he had taken the short cut to avoid getting mugged.

The next big job was the floodlighting of the ship and of course the cocktail party lighting for the wardroom. By evening, the ship was looking rather splendid. The cocktail party was going rather well, as the chefs and stewards supplied the food and drinks to the officers, their guests, and of course their mates below decks. A certain Irish Lieutenant rather let the side down by getting pissed out of his head, stripping off, and then doing a dance on the bridge top in front of all and sundry. I don't know what happened to him but I gather he was asked to resign when we returned to Portsmouth. After three days, we store ship and refuel, and the ship is now ready for sea.

At long last it's time to sail for home and refit, everyone is on a high, looking forward to getting back to friends and family and a bit of shore time. The days at sea seem to drag, all the films on board have been seen and most books read; a night of horse racing helps break the monotony. A canvas course is laid across the mess floor, six wooden horses line up, two dice, one coloured representing the horse, and one numbered are rolled; red five is rolled, and they are off. Previously, bets have been placed, winner takes all; six races and five pints later I find myself six pound up, not a bad night's work. I retire to my bunk and dream of home. I get my department clearing back logs of maintenance cards to keep them occupied over the next week or so. I get stuck into a major fault on a weapon broadcast system;

I've got the amplifiers out on the workshop bench, oscilloscopes, ohmmeters, and bridge meggers are all in use. I have the book of reference open and am happily doing my thing going through the circuits looking for faults, when the deputy weapons electrical officer (DWEO) comes in; now, this guy is about as nauseating as you can get. Before joining the ship he had spent three years teaching artificers at Collingrad, and now, being a teacher, and an expert at everything, he assumes everyone of his staff is an idiot, and proceeds to treat you as such.

"What is the problem?" he says. You tell him, and he suggests you try this; you tell him you have already tried this. "I want to see you do it again," he says, you do, and nothing. "Try that," he says. Done that. "Do it again." You do, and nothing, and this goes on and on. By now I am getting a little pissed off. I tell my assistant electrician to go and have a cup of tea. With that I slam the compartment door and become an astrologer, as I proceed to read this arsehole's horoscope. I politely tell him his job, per his terms of reference, is administration and technical expertise IF required. I explain the reason nobody likes him is because he tends to belittle everyone in the department, and comes over as a bit of a know it all. I suggest he chill out a bit, and show his senior rates a bit of respect, and with that, I hand him a screwdriver and leave him to it. I am expecting a call from the big boss over the incident, but hear nothing. A few days later we find a new DWEO has emerged from his cocoon, and everyone is amazed at his new attitude; I end up with an average write up on my employment record, his idea of pay back no doubt, and this probably sets my promotion to chief back a year.

Our arrival in Portsmouth is greeted by mass crowds of family and friends; the gangway goes down and the families are taken down to the messdecks where food and drinks have been prepared. You don't realise how much you miss them till you get to hug them again. After the ship has been secured, leave is given to the non-duty watch and everyone heads home to produce another baby boom in nine months time; having had a vasectomy, this does not apply to me. The next day we move the ship to

109

fountain lake jetty where preparations are being made to go into dry dock; the ship's company are to be moved into HMS Nelson (royal naval barracks), and consequently, all the messdecks are to be emptied of personal clothes and gear. I pack all my kit and belongings into suitcases and kit bags and throw them in my car. Lorries turn up to pick up the unmarried lads and take them to RNB accommodation. My mate, Alan, goes round all the messdecks bagging up all the left over clothes, shoes, cases, and anything else worth having, and dockyard workers are queuing by the hundred on the jetty, also waiting to scavenge anything worth having. Unfortunately for them, Alan beat them to it. He went ashore that night with eight big bags tied onto his bike; we all had a good laugh as he pushed it home, but the laugh was on us, as the next day he came in with £160 from his local second hand shop.

The chief gunnery instructor got one of his lads to put his suitcase in his Cortina, and an hour later, the ship's company was confined to the ship as there was a bomb scare on the jetty. The bomb squad arrived and got their remote controlled robot to head for a car; it could be seen pulling a case from the car, then using a controlled explosion to blow it up, and clothes and stuff were sent fifty feet in the air. It was at this point the CGI realised that the clothes were his. The lad had put his case in the wrong car, and the car's owner spotted the case and called the police, who in turn called the bomb squad.

Over the next two weeks, the ship is cold moved into a dry dock nearest the main gate; tugs push us in and we enter the dock, and then the gates are closed. Wooden beams are lowered by ropes along the ship's side, huge pumps are started, and the water in the dock is lowered. When the ship's keel bottoms on the dock floor the beams are jammed in place, wooden wedges are used as needed, and the ship is now upright in the dock, held in place by trees. The rest of the water is now pumped out and the dock is now dry.

Shore power supply lines are connected along with fresh water and telephones. Cooling water for the electronic equipment is supplied via a large tank on the jetty, and pipes are run and connected. On this particular evening a young stoker, just joined that morning, was given the job of watch keeping on the tank. He was told if the level goes down in the tank, open the tap and top it up. The young lad, keen to show enthusiasm, kept a sharp eye on the water level, and when it dropped an inch or so he topped it up; when it started dropping at a foot a minute he turned the tap on and left it on, thus keeping the level up as told. The next morning the chief artificer went down to the computer room to open up, finding himself having a bit of trouble opening the door. He resorts to getting a hammer to open the stubborn door clips, and as he hammers the last clip off, the door bursts open and thousands of gallons of water hit him in the chest smashing him against the far bulkhead. The flat immediately starts to fill up and water cascades through open hatches down the ladders to the decks below.

The scream of the chief is heard and someone pipes "hands to emergency stations, flood in the computer room!" Everyone blinks in amazement, what the hell is going on, we're in dry dock, for Christ sake. It transpires a pipe has come off on the connection to the computer cooling system; the pipe is still gushing water, and someone disconnects the pipe from the tank on the jetty, running what's left in the tank into the dock. The Rover gas turbine is dragged into position and run up to speed, and over the next few hours the compartments are pumped dry. The investigation starts immediately. Three duty electricians are on report for not doing electrical rounds every four hours, thus catching the problem early, and the chief stoker is reprimanded for not explaining to the young stokers on watch why water levels might drop, and what to do in the event of it happening. The young stokers are given a slap on the wrist and told to use a bit of common sense in future. I get down to the computer room to find some of my broadcast amplifiers have been under water, but fortunately, the water was fresh and the electrics should be all right once dried out, and all the removable units are taken to the dockyard for sonic cleaning.

You remember I mentioned the chief bosun's mate earlier; well, this guy had his own naval stores, not on the ship, but at home. Barring the bungalow he owned in the middle of the woods, everything in the place was government issue: the furnisher, carpets, pots, pans, grass seed, tools, and a warehouse full of anything you care to mention, he told me he would often go in the forest with his MK 1 escort estate and a chain saw and top his car up with logs for the winter. In fact, if you went down to the naval stores for an item and they did not have it, the chances are if you asked the CBM he would have it at home, and bring it back for you the following week. He used to take the gear out of the dockyard when the police were changing watch at six o'clock and not very interested in security.

I recall one Friday he asked me if I liked rabbit. I said no, but my wife and mother in law did. Monday morning he calls me over to his car on the jetty, and out of the boot he produces three freshly shot rabbits. Wondering what to do with them, I ask how do you skin them? No problem, he says, and with that he pulls out his sailor's knife and proceeds to slice them down the middle. Out come the guts and innards, and he then hacks off the head and feet before expertly peeling off the fur. Unfortunately, the first lieutenant was passing at the time and couldn't handle the gore; he could be heard spewing his heart out round the back of the gash bins. I hope I don't meet him in a battle.

During my time in refit, I placed my house on the market, as the wife was getting to be a nervous wreck with our schizophrenic neighbour, who one minute was normal, and the next an absolute bitch. I had the place up for £16,500, and I sold it to a lieutenant commander in the fleet air arm. I could see he was not over impressed having to buy a house off a measly petty officer; he probably thought I was a drug dealer supplementing my pathetic navy pay to buy such a house in the first place, as he had probably never heard of hard work to get what you want. I was not about to enlighten him. We moved to a detached three bedroom house in West Lane, Hayling Island; ironically, it was next door to the guy who sold us the last house. My wife hated it; still on the Valium, she was not getting over her depression.

After six weeks in dry dock, my amplifiers are returned from the dockyard. I plug them all in, switch on, and guess what? Nothing, nada, zilch, bugger all, seems like this sonic cleaning thing tends to blast capacitors to bits, and electronic gear in the seventies tended to have a lot of them in the circuitry; consequently, all the units sent to be dried out had to be replaced with new. Brilliant, just like having a new engine fitted in your car. All my stores ordered from the storm damage arrive and are fitted. I encounter a lot of trouble with the sound-powered phone systems; insulation is bad on the cable runs. The wire cable is a rubber covered with a cotton coating, and closer investigation reveals junction boxes full of green verdegris, which is causing leakage of the tiny current produced by speaking, making the system as good as useless.

I make several phone calls, and find the problem has been known about for decades. The problem is caused by the way the cable is manufactured; an oil on the copper cable reacts with the rubber sheathing when exposed to salt air. Considering this cable is in every ship in the royal navy, and replacing it would cost billions, and put the fleet out of commission for years, it obviously is thought best to ignore the problem, and make do. On several systems I found it easier to run new plastic covered cables, and this is a pain in the butt, trying to go through deck and bulkhead watertight glands. All this rather than try and get the old wiring to work.

Down in the dry dock, the ship's bottom is being de-scaled and painted, and huge zinc bars bolted on the ship's side are replaced. These are for degaussing or demagnetising the ship; a DC current is put through them to counteract the ship's natural magnetism made when the ship was built.

Zinc bars are also replaced at the ship's stern; these stop the steel hull from eroding; the bronze propellers, sea water, and steel create a battery effect, and the zinc blocks erode instead of the hull. The upper deck is starting to look the part as the sailors chip off the old paint and renew it with fresh. The ship's boats come back from the dockyard looking brand new, and replacement twenty-man life rafts are fitted after new davits and brackets are welded in place. In the hangar, the dockyard workers are removing the flight deck officer's relay box, which controls the communications to the pilot, ground crew, operations room, and captain, via switching on the Flight Deck Officers's belt.

Demarcation in jobs becomes obvious, as one guy unwires the cables, another unbolts the box from the bulkhead, and two guys take it away and dump it on the flight deck. The following day they bring the new box; a guy with a grinder removes the old studs, and a few days later a welder and his mate mark out the place for the new studs, and weld them in position. A painter red leads the bare metal, then undercoats and glosses, and the box bolter returns. Once in position, the electricians return to wire the new relay box, and after two days they leave without testing the system.

I stupidly assume all is in working order, but once I get round to testing the system I find nothing works. I send one of my lads into the dockyard to get the new circuit diagrams, and as per normal, none have been left for us maintainers. When they arrive, we check the box wiring, and find the wiring does not match the drawings. In fact, we find wires going in one terminal and nothing going out, e.g. big air gaps in the circuit. The chief in charge of the helicopter is now telling me it has to be working when we sail because he has harbour acceptance trails on the first day out. I inform the weapons electrical officer of the problem; he contacts the yard with no luck, as they are too busy to help, yeah, right.

He then informs me to get it working whatever it takes, as the new modified box cannot possibly work with our wiring. I can only assume they have given us the wrong box, so consequently I remove it and replace it with the old one salvaged from the pile of boxes on the upper deck. An hour later, the system is up and running, ready for HATS. The WEO asks if it is working, and I inform him it is. He seems to be happy. I did not bother to tell him how I got it going, as he did not bother to ask.

The mess is in the process of being refurbished by us residents; a ton of wooden framework has been ordered, along with forty meters of blue PVC, and blocks of foam. New seating and a bar are manufactured, new carpets are laid, and the usual suspects are missing from helping. All the usual excuses: too much work, my back is playing up, etc., etc. Arguments follow,

I'm getting pissed off with it all, and I request a mess change. There's a spare billet in six mess next door, and as there's only six in the mess I find it ideal.

I pack my kit and move in. There is a lot of work to be done, but the mess members are all willing to put in their two pounds of flesh to make it habitable. One night when I am duty senior electrician, I get my head down for the night, when around two in the morning the sound of the ship's running machinery stops. A power failure. I wake up in a pitch black mess, due to the fact the mess police lights,(night lights) and the emergency battery lights are disconnected because of the refit. I thrash my arms around, and being in the middle bunk start hitting the top bunk and the bulkhead. I panic, and go into "my god, I'm in a coffin" mode, which wakes up the guys in the mess. A lighter is lit and a torch found. Reassured all is well, I calm down, panic over. Shore supply is restored and I am down at the switchboard making supply breakers for lighting and ventilation. I return to my bunk, making sure I have a torch under my pillow; I drift off into an uneasy sleep, with my preference for cremation confirmed.

Once the ship is nailed back together, the crew is brought back on board from RNB, the dock is flooded, we cold move, and are towed through the basin and into the open harbour. Once secure alongside, the ship's diesel generators are flashed up and power is restored. The stokers set about flashing up the boilers and preparing the engines. My lads reconnect the shore phones. Over the next few days, harbour acceptance trials commence, and all systems are tested. The main broadcast blasts that someone requires my presence in the hanger. I leg it up there, and the guy who bought my house is standing there, hands on hips.

What could possibly be wrong? Surely, the roof hasn't come off? No, this fellow is doing the HATS for the helicopter; he wants an explanation as to why the new relay box has not been fitted, and I tell him the story. Over the next two hours, all hell lets loose, as top brass, dockyard officials, and my boss are trying to work out what has gone wrong. I am sent for, and show them that the new box and its wiring are not compatible with our ship's wiring. All agree, and the solution is to leave the old box in place till the problem is resolved by the design team. Meanwhile, the old box passes the trial.

After a week of harbour trials, we sail for sea trials, and once the testing of the ship is over, it is time to test the crew. This means two weeks at Portland under flag officer sea training (FOST), where everyone on board will be run ragged. Damage control exercises, fires, floods, chemical attack, nuclear attack, boarding parties, riot control ashore, you name it, we are tested for it, and all this under the close scrutiny of the Flag Officer Sea Training staff and their clip boards, marking us on our proficiency, or lack of it, as the case may be.

Chapter Ten

News comes through; the ship is going to do a goodwill tour of the Mediterranean, Spain, Italy, Malta, and Cyprus, to show the flag. I book the wife and kids a week's holiday in Malta, so they can meet me and the ship when we arrive. I load my locker up with toys and nappies ready for that week.

At last the ship is up to fighting efficiency, and after Portland we sail for Portsmouth to store ship and prepare for our trip; everyone is looking forward to this one.

Morale is high as we set sail for Gibraltar on that Monday morning, and family and friends are there to wave us off. The Bay of Biscay is kind to us for a change; things are looking good for the trip. We call into Gibraltar for our first visit. Four hours into the run ashore the ships siren rings out, donating a general re-call, and within four hours the ship's company is back on board and the ship is under way; this is the fastest general re-call since World War Two. The reason: the Turks have invaded Cyprus, and our job, should we choose to accept it, is to evacuate British citizens from the Island—this tape will self destruct in the next ten seconds, or words to that effect—more like just do it!

The ship is now heading for a war zone at thirty knots. The ministry of defence contacts our next of kin to let them know the situation, and holidays are cancelled, except for the rich officer class whose wives are already in Malta. We get to see them two days later as we refuel with a royal fleet auxiliary; they have been allowed to sail with her so they can wave at their husbands, big deal. The next big thing to happen is a signal which tells us to look for survivors from a Turkish destroyer off the port of Paphos; evidently, three of their ships, the Adatepe, Kocatepe, and the Tinaztepe had been attacked by Turkish star fighters, even though they were displaying Turkish battle ensigns. The Kocatepe had a direct hit in her magazine, killing eighty instantly. Forty-two were picked up by an Israeli freighter and taken to Haifa, hundreds more were still missing, and the other two ships just suffered structural damage from aircraft cannon fire. The reported

Greek ships in the area had long since left, and as both the navy's ships were ex-American, confusion ruled.

When we arrived some three days after the event, bodies found in the water were in a state of decay. The sea boats went to pick them up and retrieved six or seven men and a couple of women and children. Flesh fell off the bones as they were lifted into the boat, and they were then brought on board and left covered in the hangar. The Mae West American life jackets they were wearing were waterlogged and of little use. The captain had seen enough; he ordered any identification on the bodies to be removed and then 4.5" shell cases to be tied to the remaining bodies in the water so they could be sunk. Once it was established that there were no more bodies to be found, we sailed to Akrotiri. This is a British sovereign base, an area designated British soil and therefore out of bounds to Turks and Greeks. It was rumoured that service families were trapped in quarters outside the base for three days during the fighting; they lay on the floor while bullets flew through windows. The black watch were sent for, and led a convoy of lorries into town, bagpipes playing; the fighting allegedly stopped while the evacuation took place, then resumed soon after.

We anchored off, and ran boats ashore for stores and leave. I went ashore one evening with some of the lads; we were picked up by an RAF lorry and taken to the sergeants mess, and after consuming several pints of the local beer we decided to head back to the ship, only to find no transport available. This was a bit of a bummer as it was at least four miles back to the jetty. There was only one thing for it, and that was to borrow a lorry—this we did, much to the consternation of the RAF the next day. I don't know what their problem was; anyone we invited on the ship was offered a lift both ways, not left to their own devices as to how they got home.

During this time, I did a cartoon taking the piss out of the captain, and stuck it on the main notice board. I made the mistake of signing it PIX, and later that day I was piped for, and told to report to the captain's cabin. Shit, I'm in trouble now, I thought. I knocked on the cabin door and was told to enter; this I did, to be greeted by a grinning skipper asking me what I wanted to drink. Gobsmacked, I settled for a whisky. He then told me he thought the cartoon was brilliant, and I was to do one each day for the main notice board, and send him a copy. This evidently was his hobby, collecting cartoons relating to the navy; he showed me volumes of them collected over his career, and we sat for half an hour drinking his booze and laughing at them. Many of them were to be found in the navy news—no doubt this lot would be worth a fortune if it ever got to print. I thanked the skipper for the drink and left. I must admit I found it difficult at first, trying to find topics to do, but after a few days I found I could churn out a cartoon in minutes.

On the 23rd of July, we find ourselves anchored off Kyrenia, along with HMS Hermes, fleet auxiliaries, and other warships, and there on the beach are 1,630 holiday makers and ex-pats. Our orders are to evacuate them to the sovereign base in Akrotiri. Over the next few hours Wessex and Seaking helicopters are ferrying people off the beach; some have not eaten or had a drink for days, and they are taken down mess decks to be looked after, as only Jack knows how. Halfway through the evacuation, three Turkish M47 Patton tanks turn up, and they train their turrets towards us, as if to say stop evacuating or else.

Our Admiral in charge gets the ships to action stations, every weapon system is ordered to aim at the tanks, this included sea to air missiles as well as our big guns; the tank commander obviously thought discretion was the better part of valour, and his tanks roared off at full speed. One guy on board was seen crying his eyes out; we assumed he had lost a love one, but it transpired he had bought a Ferrari a week before, and Turkish troops could be seen thrashing it up and down the beach. Further down the coast a retired Major had been killed; outside his house on a hill he had placed a huge union jack. This seemed to have the same effect as the Turkish destroyers with their flag, inviting fighter aircraft to practice their bombing; he and his house disappeared in a cloud of dust. A total of 13,430 British citizens were eventually airlifted to Britain from Cyprus. Hercules, Belfast, Comets, Britannias, and VC10 aircraft, were all used for this operation.

Over the next few weeks our orders were to patrol the seas round Cyprus, protecting merchantmen, the Greeks, and the Turks were told any aircraft coming within twenty miles of our ship would be considered hostile and shot down. All went well till around five o'clock one morning when action stations was sounded: three aircraft were spotted on radar heading towards us. Signals were sent to the RAF control asking if they had any planes in the area; no, was the reply. Seaslug and seacat missiles were loaded, ready for launching, and the countdown started; I believe they got to minus seven, when the broadcast boomed, check, check, check. Half a minute later, three RAF Lightnings flew over us—Christ, that was a close one—not for us, you understand. During this period, American U2 spy planes could be seen regularly taking off from Akritiri air base, all very hush, hush—no doubt helping the Israelis in their battle against the Arab enemy.

Our stint in Cyprus over, our Med trip is out of the question now, so we sail for Malta, the land of bells smells and pregnant women—a bit of decent shore leave is most welcomed. Sport is organised against the army and local teams. The playing fields are like playing on concrete, e.g. grassless, a bit rough on the body, skinned knees and the odd broken bones seem to be the norm; we don't do that well due to the lack of training and fitness. Mind you, the third half always goes down well.

Jack unwinds down the Gut, with a few beers and bottles of Marsavin, the local wine—the June vintage seems to be the best, although Monday's vintage was not bad. The chance of any young lad dating a local is about as likely as the Pope becoming a Muslim, or the Queen becoming a pole dancer. Mind you, the way some of the lads carry on, I don't think I would want my daughters going out with one either, but I guess any bunch of young men in their situation would be the same. You only have to look at the Spanish holiday resorts today to prove that fact.

Having refuelled and stored ship, we sail for Gibraltar, our final port of call before heading for home; there, I hope to buy a few presents for the wife and kids, as they seem to be more geared up for the tourists than Malta. The weather is a bit on the rough side, force seven to eight, two of my lads have to take to their bunks—they've been so sick the doc sent for, and he is getting worried as they are dehydrated. He sets them up on a drip and gets their messmates to make sure they drink plenty of water. By the time we reach Gib, they are back to work and fully recovered.

Alongside, we connect the shore lines: one for the Captain, one for the quartermaster, and the combined technical office. The ship stays hot, staying on our own water and electric supplies. Shore leave and shopping over, we sail for Blighty and home. The Bay of Biscay is kind to us, fine weather all the way up to the English Channel. Some dumb yachtsman is in trouble off Portland; seems like he has lost his steering gear and is in danger of ending up on the rocks. The helicopter is scrambled and the guy and his wife are airlifted to Portland; the ship stands by as the local lifeboat attempts to reach the yacht for towing, but unfortunately, the tide beats them to it and it ends up getting smashed to pieces on the rocks. Let's hope he had full Comp insurance.

The usual customs and excise crew arrived at spit head, demanding to know what we had spent all our money on while patrolling Cyprus—funny sense of humour these clowns. We arrive in Pompy to the usual welcome, the ship berths on Fountain lake jetty, and leave was given to the non duty watch. My wife was waiting for me in our Mazda Estate, parked at the end of the gangway. We headed for the Dolphin pub in Havant for a couple of drinks and to catch up on the news.

My two girls were with the mother-in-law, waiting for dad's arrival; I couldn't wait to see them again, I had missed them so much. The ship was in for awhile for maintenance, so I had a chance to spend a bit more time with them.

During this period alongside, the IRA were in full flow, and regular bomb scares were common, none more than on our ship. Clearing the ship and accounting for everyone was a nightmare, as the bomb squad would arrive to check the ship from top to bottom for devices. None was ever found; this could take five or six hours and was a pain in the arse. It transpired a certain disgruntled sailor from the communication department was going to the Unicorn gate telephone kiosk and phoning the quartermaster up with a bomb threat. What he didn't know was the dockyard police had the phone bugged after suspecting it was the one used in the threats. The twat got 90 days in DQ's, and a dishonourable discharge; personally, I would have had him shot at dawn, then hung by the balls up the highest yardarm, for the trouble he caused.

During this period of shore time I got a job at Warners holiday camp in the evenings; my sister-in-law, Gillian, arranged it with the guy who had the cleaning contract. I was to start on the Monday along with another guy; the job was to scrub the dining hall out after all the happy campers had finished troughing their chips, peas, and whatever. I arrived at the dining hall sharp at 7.30, waited for 15 minutes for the other guy, and when he didn't turn up I proceeded to stack the chairs on the tables and swept the floor. Ten thousand peas and chips later, I mopped out and replaced the chairs. By now it was 10 o'clock, and I was knackered.

Three evenings later at around 8.15 this thing, fresh from his lobotomy and dressed like a tramp arrived; he told me he had been hired to help me in the dining hall. I proceeded to explain to him that my company would not tolerate people who were scruffy or late for work, which was true, my company the navy does not. I promptly fired him on the spot, and continued to do the dining hall. At the end of the week I received two pay packets, twenty five quid in each, job well done. I realised there was going to be a problem, every now and then, as I was down to do the odd duty on board the ship. The dining hall could not be done, so I consequently got a civvy mate to split the week with me, on the understanding if I was ever on duty he would swap, and this was the ideal solution.

One of the chefs at the camp trapped me one night and asked if I wanted to buy some cheap bacon and eggs. Always admiring entrepreneurial people I said yes; after all I would only be sweeping it up off the deck the following evening if I didn't take it home. This job lasted for six months before the company lost the contract, all down to the morons cleaning the dance hall, or should I say the lack of cleaning the dance hall. After this episode, I got a job collecting football coupons round Hayling; the reward was 12.5% of the takings. I would start at the council houses, two to five pounds a go, this accounted for a third of my money, next the private small houses, usually a pound or less. Lastly, the big houses, ten mile driveways and ten pence under a milk bottle, they couldn't even be bothered to open the door to the likes of me, snobby bastards.

One night I called at this old guy's house. He had been made redundant as a milkman, due to ill health; his wife was out at six in the morning doing a cleaning job to make ends meet. As I went up his drive he was at the front door waiting for me. "Just the man I want to see," he said. Uh oh, I thought, bet he has eight draws and hasn't heard from Littlewoods. "Come in, what are you having to drink?" he said. Gobsmacked, I ordered a whiskey. Evidently, he had won £14,000, thanks to my total honesty in handing his coupon in, not keeping his stake, as has happened with some collectors. He gave me £10, not over generous, but he needed it more than I did, and to see the joy on both their faces was worth it.

One week there was an abundance of draws on the coupon, and consequently a lot of claims had been made and pay outs were slow. The following week I was out collecting and people were waiting for me, demanding to know where their winnings were. Buggered if I know, I said, all I do is collect the bloody coupons; by now I was getting really pissed off. Some got nasty, and virtually accused me of pocketing their 25p; I made a mental note of these people for the following week. When I knocked on their doors they told me their £4.75 winnings had arrived. "Good," I said. "I hope you enjoy your winnings, because I won't be calling again, goodbye." Arseholes.

It was now April 1975, a new draft has come through, and I am to join MHS Fife on the seventh of June—another county class destroyer, same type of ship, different crew. During this time my wife was getting worse with her depression, and my daughter Theresa was playing up with her constant crying and clinging on to her. I decided to put in eighteen months notice to leave the Navy and be with them permanently. I put in my request to see the Captain; I was outside the Captain's cabin with all the request men and defaulters, when this voice called out, "Hello, Alf, how are you?"

I turned round to find this Captain facing me—it was David Eckersly-Maslin, the man who came to my wedding, and for whom my wife and I used to babysit. He shook my hand, "I hope you are not in trouble," he said jokingly, and fortunately, I was not. He chatted with me for a few minutes, and asked how the family was before going to see my Captain. When he came out he said goodbye, and said I must contact him sometime. Yeah, right.

Anyway, I saw my Captain and was told to take some time and think seriously about handing in my notice. I was still in the Captain's flat when this young midshipman approached me. "Petty officer Pickup? The Captain of HMS Fife wants to see you in his cabin right away."

Now, the Fife just happened to be tied up alongside. Christ, what the hell does the captain of my new draft want to see me for? I make my way to the gangway and board the Fife, and the officer of the day greets me with, "what do you want?" Not you, you snotty bugger, I thought. I explained that the Captain wanted to see me. "Very funny," he says, "Do you realise we are about to sail on a families day, and the Captain has his family, Admirals, lord mayors, and other dignitaries in his cabin, so why the hell would he want to see you?" Perhaps he wants advice on how to untie the ship before sailing, I thought. How the hell do I know?

I was adamant, and the poor officer was in a dilemma. He resorted to putting the onus on the Captain's steward; I proceeded to the Captain's quarters and met the Captain's steward, who was obviously waiting for me. He led me past all the departmental senior officers who were waiting to report the ship ready for sea—this was surreal. I heard the Captain's steward tell the Captain, "Petty Officer Pickup is here, sir." My sphincter muscle tightened up, then that familiar friendly voice called out, "Come in, Alf." It was Captain Eckersly-Maslin. I suppose I should have guessed, but it was the last thing on my mind. Ann, his gorgeous wife, came over and flung her arms round me and gave me a kiss, saying, "So nice to see you again, let me introduce you to my guests. Admiral, this is my very good friend, Alf, Lord Mayor meet Alf," etc., etc. This went on till the whole room had been introduced. David came over to me and apologised; I could not stay because the ship was about to sail, but I was to come and see him when they got back in. I explained I was to join his ship in a month or so, and with that he called in the Weapons Electrical officer waiting outside the cabin. "This is my friend, Alf. He is joining us next month, and I want you to look after him." I felt so embarrassed. I shook hands and said goodbye. On returning to Devonshire, I went in the mess and had a stiff drink. Bloody hell, what a day.

I went home that day and discussed my future in the RN with my wife; we decided I was to stay in and make a go of it. I withdrew my request form, and a month later I signed on to complete 22 years for pension.

Alf Pickup

I joined the Fife on the 6th of June 1975. By now, Captain Eckersly-Maslin had, if I remember, been appointed to NATO headquarters and made Commodore, so I was not about to serve under him, which was probably for the best, as I didn't want to be accused of any favouritism. I was a bit worried about the electrical officers after the family's day incident—look after some poxy petty officer when he joins, yeah, right! As it happened, the weapons electrical officer and his deputy were probably the best pair I had served under. The deputy, Dick Cooper, had advanced from the lower deck and had a real understanding of the lads, nothing was too much trouble; he was always ready to give advice and help when asked for, and we got on like a house on fire.

My job on board was internal communications, and navigation aids and lights, the 50/500 telephone exchange was in a hell of a state and the powers at be were not happy. Priority one was to get the system back to working order; my predecessor obviously did not have a clue. Relay contacts were bent out of all recognition, wiring was a mess, dry joints were everywhere, phones were falling to bits, and it took a good month to order spares and put things right. The next problem was the broadcasts; the main broadcast was run by a 300 watt valve amplifier, and having the equivalent of 500 watts of speakers connected did not help the noise output of each speaker.

I got the drawings out and sent the lads round to remove all the unauthorised rabbit speakers, wired in by our professional stokers, sailors, and chefs. The result was astounding; you could actually hear pipes being made. Even the skipper commented on it—more brownie points, or as they say, every little bit helps. I was sent on a refresher course for the latest Xerox machines, as new ones were to be fitted; the course lasted a day, and this guy went through all the circuitry, which totally confused me and the rest of the people on the course.

Big mouth stuck his hand up and said, "Excuse me, I don't suppose you could tell us how to repair it if it breaks." The short answer was no—brilliant, I thought, just like the bloody navy courses—they tell you how it's built, and how it works but not how to repair it, which is all we need to know. Back on board, the new machines are fitted, or rather placed in position, one in the ship's office for official use, one in the communication room for signals, and one in the after flat for general use. The next time we went to sea we hit a bit of rough weather; the one in the after flat slid off the bracket and bounced onto the deck into a million pieces. Obviously, the fitters from Xerox thought they were in some shore office and did not think to bolt it down; my lads swept it up and put it in a box, the damn toner was a pig to get up, and everyone was covered in black dust. When we got alongside, I phoned Xerox and asked them to replace the broken machine. I explained it had failed the drop test—confused, they asked what I meant. I politely explained what had happened, but don't worry, I told them, the other two machines were saved, and by the way, you owe my lads a few quid for their laundry bill. A new machine arrived within two days and was duly bolted down.

The ship is now in a maintenance period and this means some well-earned shore time. I am in the process of buying a new house, once again on Hayling Island, and this time it's a detached four bedroom job with a nice garden, only £18,000. I get a job with a local builder doing odd jobs for old dears; he pays me in kind by letting me run up a tab at the hardware shop. It worked out about £3,50p an hour. I ask one old dear what he charged her for the jobs I had done, and I nearly fell through the floor when she told me, £95 for two hours work—the bastard was ripping us both off. I consequently left her my phone number for any future jobs, and the work snowballed as word got round the old folks community. Pretty soon I was able to dump the builder and go on my own.

Back on the ship, the stokers are busy down in the boiler room with their chipping hammers and paper sacks. Their job is to hack the asbestos lagging off the steam pipes and bag it up, and then dump it in a skip on the jetty. They dress in overalls and a paper face mask. The ship is full of dust, no health and safety at this time—I wonder how many Matelots and their families have since died of asbestosis without realising what the cause was, all from these days of reckless work practice. Trouble is, some poor wife has to take these asbestos-covered overalls and wash them, putting herself and her children at risk.

My team is busy doing planned maintenance and job cards, keeping the comms in top order, an essential part of the ship's efficiency. One of my leading hands decided to test the wiring on a broadcast system using a 500 volt megger; unfortunately, he forgot to disconnect the diaphragms in the speakers, thus blowing the guts out of them and rendering the system useless. I smacked his wrist, or rather kicked his arse ten times round the room, and then sent him into the dockyard to beg steal or borrow some replacements—that was his work sorted for the next two weeks.

I received a phone call one afternoon from the local police station; my wife had had an accident in the car, and she and my daughter Theresa were both shook up but okay. I saw my boss and got permission to go to them, and when I got to the station, my wife was crying her eyes out—she kept on saying how sorry she was for crashing the car, as if that was important. I find out that she got caught in a sudden downpour, and she missed a junction with worn out give way road signs. Consequently, she had pulled out in front of a Morris Oxford, which hit the nearside wing and door at 30 mph; this pushed the car across the road, up a pavement, and into a council wall, demolishing ten foot of it. My wife's friend, Gill, who was with her, saw what was coming and swung round to save my daughter in the back seat, and in doing so she probably saved herself from serious injury, as the door ended up half way across her seat. My wife was charged with driving without due care and attention.

I was told the car was down at some local back street garage in Stamshaw. I arranged for a taxi to take my wife home, and made my way to Stamshaw. I found the garage and was asked by this grease ball if I wanted a quote for repairs and I said no, thank you.

"In that case," he said, "I will have to charge you storage."

"You can't do that," I said, "the car's in the street."

"Yes, but it's my responsibility."

Bollocks to that. I told him I would be back later in the afternoon. Sneering, he tells me I can't drive it as the wing is jammed in the wheel, the door is hanging off, and the headlights are hanging out. I made my way home, picked up a crow bar and sledge hammer, and a few bits and pieces, then caught a taxi back to the dead Triumph 2000. I spent twenty minutes levering and banging till the wing was clear and I could turn the steering wheel from side to side; next I pushed the door to as far as it would go, then tied it up with rope; the headlights I taped up. As I started the car up, the grease ball came out, a look of disbelief on his ugly face, and I gave him a cheery wave as I drove off.

Over the next week I frequented the local scrap yard, and I got a new door, lights and trim; the wing I beat out with a set of panel beating hammers and dollies—five pounds of fibre glass paste and twenty sheets of wet and dry later, she was looking like her old self. My wife was not over impressed when I painted HERS on the dented wing, and I eventually got round to spray painting and ended up with a fairly professional job. I went to the scene of the accident and found new give way lines had been painted on the road. Two weeks after the accident I arrived home to find my wife in tears. Portsmouth council had sent me a bill for the damaged wall—£450— I thought that a bit steep for two dozen bricks, so I returned to the scene, only to find the council had demolished 60 feet of wall and rebuilt it; bless, I'm surprised the buggers didn't charge me to repaint the bloody road.

I phoned the insurance company up and explained what was going on; they laughed and said the assessor would be round to check the damage of the wall and as there was nothing to assess, the council could squat. The guy in the other car involved in the accident was charged with speeding and dangerous driving; it appears he was doing at least 40mph, and could have avoided the crash had he been going at the correct speed.

My wife now had the car back, and I was going to work on a 150cc Puch scooter. I was driving on L plates. The kick start had broken, the spline had gone, and I always bump started it; to stop it I had to choke the carburettor air intake. I had put in for my motorcycle test and forgot about it, and when it came through I had two days to swot up on my highway code. I was to take it in North End, Portsmouth. The big day came. I met the examiner, and he told me to stop the engine, which I did in my usual way; it spluttered and died. I was questioned on the Highway Code. He then gave me directions where to go.

"Start your engine," he said. Oh, oh, I pretended to kick start it, and obviously nothing happened as the spline was stripped. I explained the problem.

"Can you start it any other way?" he said.

"Well, I can try and bump start it," I replied, and off I went. Unfortunately, I did not know the area and got lost, what with all the one way streets and things. Anyway, after ten minutes I found the examiner. "Where the hell have you been?" he says.

"Sorry, I got lost." He then makes me do the emergency stop. After all that, I pass the test, he starts writing out the pass certificate, and just then the back number plate falls off, and I cringe. As he hands me my pass, he leans over and in a very low voice suggests I get the scooter road worthy before I use it again. "Thank you sir, thank you very much."

About a month later, I am negotiating a bend on Hayling Island when the scooter goes into a slide on some loose gravel. Coming the other way is a Cortina; this I manage to clout on his off side wing before somersaulting over his boot and into a hedge. The guy in the Cortina pulls over and gives me a hand out of the hedge. He enquires about my health, and apart from a few bruises and scratches I am okay. He now gets down to the problem of his dented rear wing; it's not that bad, in fact it's hardly worth claiming on his insurance. I push my luck and tell him I am an expert in body repairs (well I have had a bit of practice on the old Triumph). I give him my address, and tell him to come round in the afternoon so I can fix it. I take the colour code from under his bonnet and head for Les Smiths in Havant for a couple of aerosols. I still have filler and wet and dry left over from my previous job so its not going to cost me a lot.

The guy, his wife, and three kids arrive at the house. I send them in, and my wife looks after them with tea and bickies. Meanwhile, I hammer out the dent, and, (if I say so myself), do a masterly job on the repair. Half an hour, and two cans of paint later, I call the family out to view the repair. All agree it's as good as new. I apologise for the inconvenience I had caused them, and they went happily on their way, crisis over. The scooter was involved in many more incidents over the next few months, including the time my brakes failed and I ended up jammed in the back of a motorcycle and side car, when he suddenly halted and I could not.

One of the things I pioneered, which is used today in modern cars, is the coloured bulb instead of red plastic reflector glass. This happened when someone smashed my rear light cluster. I resorted to painting the white bulb with red nail varnish. I guess someone at Ford spotted it and took the idea on; I'm still waiting for the royalties to this day. How I managed to survive going to work and back in that period I will never know.

One afternoon I was having an afternoon cup of tea in the mess when the Chief Electrical Artificer fell in the door; this guy was an alcoholic, but today he was totally legless. Hanging onto a stanchion, he called to me to do his duty watch for him. I told him no, and to come back when he was sober. The president of his mess was called for and he was carried back to his bunk to sleep it off. I thought nothing more of it till the ship's generator tripped and the ship was in darkness. The officer of the day sent the bosun's mate for the chief Artificer, and he told the bosun's mate I was now duty senior rate. He told the OOW who sent for me, I explained what had happened, and was then ordered to put the generator back on line and take over the duty, which I did.

The next day I was in front of the Commander on a charge of failing to do my duty—yeah, right, like I'm going down for a drunk. It's hard enough getting promotion without some twat dropping you in it and getting you demoted. I told my story and was let off, and the drunken Chief was sent for and charged with being drunk on duty. He got 30 days stoppage of beer and spirits, and a fine—like this will cure an alcoholic—two days later he was in the same drunken state as normal. I'll give the bloke his due, he could still parallel generators even when pissed; that is hard enough to do when you are sober. Get them out of sync and you have a good chance of the generators being ripped off their mountings and out the ship's side. I've only known generators being paralleled out of phase twice, and the thump it causes can be felt throughout the ship.

Over the leave period, all machinery, and non-essential electrical equipment is switched off, but the sewage tanks are in danger of becoming inoperative if they are not fed; evidently, the enzymes die through lack of crap, so the duty stoker has to feed them by dumping dried milk powder down the toilet bowls. When it comes to emptying the tanks, there is always a residue of peanuts and sweet corn in the bottom. Not like the old days when sewage was pumped straight over the side, which is not a problem at sea, but a few days alongside and low and behold, the poor bugger who has to go diving on the ship's bottom among the floating remains of Jack's vindaloo.

Chapter Eleven

The ship has now had its 100,000 mile service, and we are ready for harbour and sea trails. This, as usual, consists of testing everything from machinery and equipment to the crew's efficiency as a fighting unit. The engines are tested, full speed ahead, nought to 35 mph in five minutes, the steering is put on full lock, port thirty, followed by a sharp starboard thirty; everything on the ship is shaking to bits, and anything not secured ends up on the deck, and it either bounces or ends up in bits. Nice of the stokers to let us know beforehand—obviously a broadcast pipe telling everyone what was about to happen was just a bit too difficult—I've a mind to disconnect their broadcast systems and see how they manage, the bastards.

All radars and sonars are calibrated, weapon systems tested, the crew do every exercise, damage control, nuclear and chemical attacks, emergency stations, boarding parties, landing parties—you name it, we covered it. After several weeks of this we head for the dreaded Portland sea training. Flag officer sea training staff arrive at seven in the morning to test us on all aspects of what we have been doing over the last few weeks. These experts arrive with clip boards and mark us according to how they think things should be done; not necessarily the right way, but hey, they have the clip board. The next morning they arrive with report on what went right, and more to the point, what they consider went wrong. A meeting of departmental heads and senior ratings takes place in the wardroom; the FOST staff tells us how we can improve, and in their opinion be more efficient, and sometimes we disagree to no avail. The RN bible is gospel—after all, it was written in 1742, and being the King James Version it must be true. Shore leave is given each night; most lads stay on board, shattered after the day's events. Those that do venture outside the dockyard gate end up in the local pub for a few pints of scrumpy, that disgusting concoction of rotten apple cores, dead rats and yeast. This is usually followed by going to the local takeaway, a grease hole with an equally greasy bloke serving chips cooked in the finest crude oil from the Gulf—it is quite obvious the health and safety department know nothing of this place's existence; either that or someone is taking a huge back hander.

Weekend leave is given to one watch, and those that have them bring their cars back to use over the next four weeks. Night leave can be extended to Weymouth and beyond, and if you have a car you don't have to rely on the local three times a week bus. Towards the end of our sea training the weather cuts up rough. Now, trying to run damage control cables in calm weather is bad enough; running them in a force nine is damn near impossible, but you try telling that to these clowns, bloody good kids hanging onto their clip boards with one hand, and a water pipe with the other. Bloody well serves them right, they have to stay on board overnight because the weather is too rough for them to be picked up. I hope they managed to secure their camp beds down; I would hate to think they had a bad night's sleep being thrown about. The final day arrives and we pass the training tests—the ship is ready for whatever the admiralty throws at us.

Our first assignment is to go to Lehavre on a good will visit, and a list goes up to visit the Courvoisier brandy distillery. I put my name down and manage to beat 150 others to a place on the bus. The next morning, twenty-five of us got on the bus and headed to the Cognac region of France; the drive took hours. Once there, we were escorted round and shown how brandy is made—big deal: crush grapes, add sugar, and boil, put distilled solution in sherry barrels, leave for years, bottle, and then drink. The last bit was all us Matelots were interested in; this event happened after the tour and consisted of a glass of brandy with fresh orange juice, lovely. A French voice yells out, "Now if you would like to make your way back to the bus..."

"You mean we came all this bloody way for one drink?"

"No, Messieurs, here's a bottle each to take with you."

Fair do's, we climb into our seats on the bus. The officer with us warns us that we must put the brandy in bond when we get back to the ship, and then declare it to customs when we get back, yeah, right. Me and six others decide to have a drink from the bottle—the officer tells us we must dispose of the bottle before returning to the ship, as we can't put a partly-filled bottle in bond. No problem, we drank the lot, the trip back went in no time. When we arrived at the ship we fell off the bus, giggling like little girls. All but six of us declared their bottles to the officer of the watch. For some reason, he knew we were bottle-less, and legless; luckily, he was decent about it, and sent us away without trooping us for being drunk.

130

I woke up the next morning with a head like I'd just had a lobotomy, and a mouth like a geisha girl's gash bucket, never again—not for a long time, anyway. Back at work, I sent the troops out on various jobs, and resorted to doing a bit of paperwork myself. Five coffees and four panadol later, I was feeling better. I decided to have some lunch and get my head down; the skipper had given the ship a make and mend, so I stayed in my bunk till tea time. When I got up I had a bath and dhobi. I felt like a new man as I hung my nicks and socks up to dry in the conversion machinery room, while back in the mess the usual suspects are there drinking the bar dry.

I have a nice cup of tea and listen to the musings of drunken sailors; I'm trying to catch someone talking shop—the rule is, talk shop and you have to put a barrel on—same rule applies if you swear when women are in the mess, this keeps sailors clean and interesting in their conversation. Next day I go ashore and try my hand at tennis, and this proves to be a disaster. I go to do a McEnroe-type serve and my back goes twang. Four of my mess mates carry me back to the ship and tip me into my bunk, and there I stay for the next three days. Food is brought to me, but getting to the heads is a problem and causing a lot of pain.

The ship is in trouble; some of the lads have gone to a local nightclub and ordered drinks, and the gorilla behind the bar is trying to charge ten times the going price. Jack is not impressed and refuses to pay, an argument ensues, and the place becomes a battle zone; the place is wrecked. The police arrive and arrest everyone who remotely looks involved, this accounts for at least twenty sailors and thirty Frenchmen and women. The next day Embassy officials arrive to arrange bail, and work out with the nightclub owner how much of the damage is to be charged to the Navy. This will be deducted from pay over the next six months or so. The moral of this story is, if you go into a French nightclub, sneak in a bottle of cheap brandy from the supermarket and order a coke; this will cost the same as the bottle of brandy, but you'll be set for the night.

Our glorious French trip over, we set sail for exercises, which involves the RAF practice firing at our towed target. All goes well till some short-sighted pilot decides to strafe us between our masts. Talk about hitting the deck quick, fortunately no one was hurt with this so called friendly fire. Pity the pilot wasn't available for us to give him some friendly punches on the nose, the incompetent sod. I've got to say between the RAF and the fleet air arm; I definitely rate the flying of our guys. When they fly low, they fly low; I'm talking about clipping waves here, mad as hatters, but bloody good. After a few days we refuel at sea (RAS) with the Royal fleet auxiliary Tide Pool; the gun line is fired across, they connect this to a large rope which we can pull back, and the other end of the rope is connected to the fuel pipe, and a crane swings out with the fuel line and rope. The boom on the crane is fed across; we control the end of the pipe with the rope; once across, the end is connected to a deck gland, which in turn is connected to the fuel tanks down below decks, and pumping now starts at the rate of hundreds of gallons a minute. After two or three minutes, the deck connection fails and the fuel pipe parts gushing fuel everywhere—the order to stop pumping is given, and meanwhile, the crew, the ship, and sea are getting covered in fuel. After hundreds of gallons have been sprayed everywhere, the pumping stops. The next few days are spent cleaning the ship's superstructure, and everyone joins in—foam, froth, and hoses abound, jack is like a pig in shit, and everyone is soaked to the skin.

Back in harbour, a draft has come in, and I am to get a married accompanied to the Gibraltar refit group. I have a feeling my friend and boss, Dick Cooper, might have put a word in for me, salt of the earth, this guy. It is around this time I sell my present house. I was with three estate agents who supposedly tried to sell it with no luck, so I stuck an ad in the evening news, and a guy from IBM, just back from the states, buys it for the asking price of £16,000. We move into a four bedroom detached house three miles away, cost £18,500. My wife is still on depression tablets, and when I tell her we are going to Gibraltar, she is over the moon. At this point I get all her tablets and flush them down the toilet. Amazingly, from that day on she improves a hundred percent, surprising what a little incentive can do.

It is now November 1976; the days are spent packing crates, ready for shipping to Gibraltar, and also arranging for the letting of our new house. This is a must, to pay the mortgage while we're abroad, and we do it through Parkinson's estate agents. Christmas comes, and for some reason I don't recall, we invite family round—the kids ignore their presents and spend most of the day in our cardboard packing boxes. The grown ups make themselves at home and a good time was had by all. Parkinson's sends a guy round to do an inventory; he details every scratch, chip, and mark so the person renting doesn't get charged for something they are not responsible for; fair enough, I presume this works both ways? Life is hectic, arranging things for the trip; the kids are excited, and looking forward to the adventure ahead.

At last the day arrives for us to leave for Gibraltar; the keys to the house are handed over to the estate agent. Evidently, this sweet lady who runs a children's nursery in Havant is to rent it, and with loads of references we can't go wrong,(can we?) —at least the mortgage has been taken care of.

Alf Pickup

At Gatwick we board the plane—this is my second time in a plane, the first being the RAF Hercules from Gibraltar. This is different: proper seats and free food and stuff. The stewardess goes through the emergency and safety drill, which quite honestly is a load of bullshit. She starts, "Ladies and gentlemen, on take off your seat belt should be fastened securely across your lap, (she demonstrates with a bit of tatty belt), all loose bags must be stowed under your seat and folding tables up; this aircraft is non smoking."

I am thinking, why should the seat belt be fastened securely? It has no practical use, apart from cutting you in half in the event of a sharp stop. Please refer to a car seat belt for a more practical design; even this would have its limitations when hitting a mountain at 400 mph.

No smoking, bloody cheek, don't they realise how much crap comes out of their engines? Presumably that smoke doesn't affect anyone. Next she says, "under your seat is a life jacket, this must only be used in the event of an emergency landing (crash) in the sea." She demonstrates how to wear it, and she shows us the plastic whistle—is this is to call passing ships, or maybe to keep oneself amused with bird impressions during your last five minutes in the freezing sea?

Next is the 1.5 volt self-activating lamp—this half a candle power device is supposed to attract the rescuers? I suppose if 140 people form a circle in the sea someone might, just might, see you. She tells us not to inflate the life jacket till we leave the plane. This is all presuming we have a perfect landing and the plane stays afloat, but let's get real—the plane will probably cartwheel or nose dive into the sea to 20 fathoms, (where are the aqualungs kept?) a fire is raging, we're breaking up. A twenty stone American woman from ten rows back has landed on your lap and broken your arm, and your leg is in the next aisle with your foot stuck in a German's mouth. Water is pouring in, baggage from the lockers is everywhere, the floor lighting is lighting up the fountain pouring in alongside it, and it gives you a sense of security, until you realise there are fish going by the windows.

Time to don your life jacket and head for the chute; maybe not, time to have your last fag, more like. The stewardess continues with what to do in the event of cabin pressure failure, and tells us, "an oxygen mask will drop in front of you, place this over your nose and mouth and secure with the ties and breathe normally." Breathe normally, yeah, right, then act as if nothing is happening I suppose, apart from the fact the odd passenger and seat are flying through a hole in the fuselage at 30,000 feet, the plane is diving at an angle of 60 degrees, and the temperature has dropped to minus

60 degrees. I can think of a few more bodily functions that will precede breathing normally.

After the stewardess's bullshit was over I was expecting the aircraft intercom to come on and tell us the plane is being flown by a computer and that nothing can go wrong, can go wrong, can go wrong. Fortunately, the pilot came on and gave us the usual weather, speed and height spiel, and we settled down to a pleasant, crash-free flight.

We arrive at Gibraltar on a wet, miserable day; we are greeted by a civilian who leads me and the family, plus six suitcases, to a Royal Navy van. He then drives us across the runway, and on to HMS Rooke. I do a joining routine, to let everyone know we are here; there are no married quarters available, so the man and the van then transport us to the back of the Rock to a holiday complex called Both Worlds; it is built on the rock face and goes right down to the beach. We check in and are allotted a couple of rooms, with a bathroom and kitchen. At this point my wife is in tears, and does not want to unpack, and we are all soaking wet. I must admit, what with the rain and all, it was a bit depressing. We all pile into a taxi and head for Main Street looking for an estate agent. We find one and are shown some of the most decrepit hovels ever put up for rent: leaking roofs, cockroaches, stinking furnishings, you name it. We head back to Both Worlds and decide to leave it till the following day. I go to the onsite shop and get some food in for tea; the kids are bathed and put to bed, it's been a long day.

The next morning is glorious. I head into town looking for a place to rent, and after several hours with no luck, I head back to find my wife and kids on the beach. I join them and find they now want to stay. I think the sunshine might have something to do with it—the whole place is different from last night; holiday makers, local workmen, and fishermen are everywhere, the place has come to life. One thing you notice is the lack of cleanliness in Gib; at one time when the border was open, the Spanish would come over the border every day to work, and take anything recyclable back to Spain. Now that the border is closed, the Spanish have moved out and Moroccans have moved in, and the place resembles a rubbish tip.

Over the next few days, arrangements are made for the children to attend the local schools. We also find out about the doctors surgery, the dentist, and shopping in the NAAFI in Queensway, the main road running by HMS Rooke. I go into the dockyard to introduce myself to the department; my job is to be refitting Leander class frigates. I start work in four days time, after the family have all been settled in. I am shown the tunnel which leads from the dockyard through the rock to Both Worlds; this is going to save me a lot of time going to work in the mornings. By all accounts there are more roads inside the rock than round it—the place is a honeycomb of storerooms and secret passages.

Having topped the larder up with food and got all the cleaning gear to keep the place clean, we settle in. The kids are happy as Larry, on the beach every day—it's not hot weather but good for finding shells and building sand castles. A local man, Umberto, who is head of maintenance, drops in for a cup of tea and a chat, and over the next few months he becomes a good friend. He regularly drops in with toilet rolls and cleaning gear meant for the tourists. My first day at work is on HMS Scylla; in charge of the electrical bit is Charley Findlay, a big, rugby mad Chief Mech. I am designated to sort out the communications and navigation aids. I spend the next few months ripping out old knackered electronics and ordering new replacements. The system, as it was, meant a couple of months flat out work, then waiting for spares from the UK for the next four months, which left a few months of panic to nail it all back together, in time for it to be handed over to a new crew.

My wife, Hermione, is getting used to not being able to buy fresh milk or meat. The milk is either long life crap or powdered, and the meat is usually frozen Argentinean. Fruit and vegetables are brought over fresh from Morocco and cost a bloody fortune, robbing Arab bastards. Now and again the navy run an MFV over to Tangiers for a fruit and veg run, and wives and families are welcome. I took my clan over one weekend, and I was the only one who was ill on the way over—most embarrassing—at least the kids thought it was funny. I tried saying it must have been something I'd eaten, but they would have none of it. Once we got in the Kasbah we started to load up with provisions and souvenirs, the usual crap, camel leather poufs, bags, brass plates, genuine artifacts from Egyptian pharaohs. Half way through the afternoon, two Arabs are seen running out of a jewellers followed by the shop's owner shouting, "Stop them, they've stolen my watches!" I thought that odd at the time—surely he should have been shouting in Moroccan? After wandering around for an hour bartering, and listening to *Marks and Spencers, fish and chips*, from the locals practicing their English, I am approached by one of the guys who were seen legging it from the jewellers. "Psst, want to buy a gold watch?"

He shows me an Omega, hallmark and all, and not being one to pass a bargain I ask how much. "£100," he says. I have £15, and he says he will take this and my jacket, but I refuse. I like my jacket, and besides, it's cold on the boat going back. We do the deal for £15; my wife is worried in case customs are on the lookout when we get back. I stuff the watch in my sock, like they will never think of looking there, der.

We arrive back in Gib, the customs let us off without any hassle, and at home back at Both Worlds the groceries are unloaded, along with all the stinking leather stuff. Umberto calls with another dozen toilet rolls, more cups and saucers, I tell him what happened in Tangiers and show him the watch, and he admits it looks the real McCoy, but to be sure, he has a friend who is a local jeweller who will authenticate it. I give him the watch and wait for the result, and the next day he calls and tells me that without opening the watch the jeweller can't confirm either way. Meanwhile, a local fireman offers me £100 for it; he reckons he could sell it for three times that in Spain, but I refuse. I send Umberto off again to the jeweller, and he returns to tell me it's a fake, but a good one—no wonder those Arab bastards called out in English as the so called thieves ran away—and that was for our benefit, the perfect con for the greedy English tourist.

My mate Umberto gets me a job at Both Worlds painting the chalets out, and after three evenings painting I have completed three. On the fourth day, Umberto tells me he has a problem, the three Moroccans working for him have complained. Evidently, it was taking the three of them a week to do one chalet and I was doing them out of a job. I told him no problem, I would resign; he was sorry, but relieved the situation was sorted. At this time, the nice lady (bitch) back home was failing to pay the rent which should in turn pay my mortgage, leaving my bank account in arrears, which proved embarrassing for my wife when the NAAFI bounced a cheque. I was summoned to the pay office to explain myself to the pay officer, and this I did without getting into trouble with the navy. I telephoned Parkinson's estate agents to find out what the hell was going on, and they assured me it would be sorted.

Unbeknown to me, Umberto was taking Hermione and the kids shopping, and I would find boxes of fruit and veg and sweets for the girls. This guy was a saint, he even lent me his car one evening to get to a do in the mess. One Sunday we were all invited to his flat to meet his family; the food and wine flowed, it was one of the few times I actually enjoyed going to visit someone's home. After that we became part of the family, and still are to this day.

At this time I was without transport, and the usual thing was to buy your second-hand car from the guy you were relieving for £100; unfortunately, he sold it to one of his mates leaving me on shanks's pony, the rotten swine. It was only by luck one day, I happened to see the Padre from HMS Rooke at the side of the road down Queensway with his dead car, a lovely old Riley 4/44. One of the leaf springs had snapped on the back of the car and the axle was freely swinging about. I approached him asking what his problem was, although it was obvious, he told me he had just sold the car for £150 and was delivering it to its new owner when he came to a shuddering halt. I suggested the new owner might be a bit put off in its present state—he agreed—I said you go and tell them what has happened, and if they still want it, fair enough; if not, I'll give you £50 for it as it is. I waited half an hour till he returned, and I had my deal. I arranged for it to be towed into the dockyard, no problem, as it was still on the Padre's security pass.

Down at the back of our workshops I got the leaf spring out; the top hanger spring had snapped in half, clean as a whistle. The spring was taken to the engineering shop; I bribed a dockyard matey to drill the broken spring and the next one to it, so they could be riveted together—this was easier said than done—he managed to burn out four diamond-tipped drills before completing the task, and I slipped him an extra couple of quid for his trouble. The next day the spring was replaced and the car was as good as new. My next job over the following weeks was to re-spray it a nice chocolate brown colour. I even had an offer from the guy who had brought it to Gib from new; evidently, the car had been to South Africa, Australia, and back to Gib. When he sold it three years previously it had been round the clock twice with no major repairs to the engine. I'm not saying it would do nought to sixty in six seconds or anything, far from it, in fact I don't even know if it would do sixty. If it did, it would probably take six minutes, but it got me and the family to where we wanted to go in relative comfort.

After a few months at Both Worlds, we are offered a caravan by the navy, in a park by the married quarters, but we refuse it, and are prepared to wait till a quarter becomes available. Truth is we loved it where we were, beach on the doorstep, local friends, good neighbours. The girl next door was the wife of an RAF corporal, an arsehole who liked to give her a hiding every now and again; their son, Kevin, was a little bugger. Four years old and training to be the world champion at boxing. I know this because he just loved punching, preferably people. One day his mum came round for a cup of tea and a chat with my wife. Little Kevin started punching my daughter, Helen, so I picked him up and sat him on my knee. I then got hold of both his hands, and one after the other proceeded to use them to slap his face—after every stroke I would tell him that it was not nice to hit other people. Well, he screamed the house down. I checked with his mum that it was ok; she nodded approval, after a couple of minutes I released him, and he ran hell for leather back to his home crying his eyes out. I felt awful, but twenty minutes later he returned to me and flung his arms round my neck. "I'm sorry, Uncle Alf; I promise I won't hit anyone again."

Oddly enough, he never did, and we became good pals after that little episode. The neighbour on the other side asked us to babysit one night. She left a wet tea bag in the saucer, saying a NAAFI tea bag made two cups, and she had only used it once. Makes sense, I suppose. The next day I fished a dozen tea bags out of the rubbish bin and pegged them out on the line, and when people going by asked what they were for, I told them about my neighbour's money saving tip. Yes, I know, very childish, but a good laugh anyway.

My youngest daughter, Theresa, ended up in hospital after falling off the bed onto her head; the bump was the size of an egg. It was one of those moments in life when you think of God giving you a deal—make her OK and I'll do anything. Fortunately, she was all right after a night in hospital, and God did not ask for anything in return. School for the girls was very good in Gibraltar; they would start at 8.30 and finish at 12.00, giving them and their mum the rest of the day to spend on the beach or to go downtown shopping. My wife became the expert at bartering with the local Indian shop keepers; even our local friends would ask her if they wanted something cheap. After getting five radio clocks at virtually cost price for our friends, she was asked not to return. On one occasion she managed to get two gold ladies' watches for peanuts; I don't think the young Indian guy realised what he was selling at the time. A year or so later, she took one back because it had stopped, the young guy's father offered her five times what she had originally paid for it.

One of the big stores in Main Street was St. Michaels; it was really Marks and Sparks selling seconds, even though they charged the same as back home, crafty buggers, exploiting the locals who don't know any better. The NAAFI shop was our main source of food and toiletries, cleaning gear was supplied by my mate Umberto, and by the time we left Both Worlds we had enough toilet rolls to last us till we left the rock, two years later.

Many mornings in Gibraltar are dull to start with; a heavy mist known as the Levant would shroud the rock—the warm wind on the Mediterranean side meets with the cold Atlantic wind and forms this phenomenon. The weathered flat face of the back of the rock is covered from top to bottom in sheets of corrugated steel, which condenses the mist and the resulting water is collected to aid in the supply of water to Gibraltar. The rest of Gib's water is made in the desalination plant round by Catalan Bay. Normally, by eleven o'clock the mist has cleared as the hot sun burns through. By this time, the locals have already been down to the beach to lay out their towels, sun beds, and parasols (I now know where the Germans got the idea from)—Eastern beach and Catalan Bay being their favourites. Sandy Bay, below Both Worlds, was more for the tourists and forces families living there. On a Sunday, you could sit on a wall by the side of the road and watch the cars going by, and fifteen minutes later you would see the same cars going round again, and again, and again. This was because of the closed border, and people just love going for a drive on a Sunday—they even buy new cars, can you believe that?

By July 1977 we are informed we must move out of Both Worlds and into married quarters; my wife would rather stay, but orders is orders. We are allotted number 157, Edinburgh house, one of many blocks of married quarter flats situated next to HMS Rooke. It is a spacious, two bedroom flat on the first floor overlooking the caravan park and harbour; we have balconies front and rear. An inventory provides us with all we require, pots, pans, sheets, furnishings, etc., the place is gleaming. All our possessions are packed in boxes and loaded into the lorry provided by the RN, and we follow the lorry round the rock to our new home. The next few days are spent unpacking and settling in, then back at work in the dockyard—the work has virtually stopped due to the lack of spares, and the ship is in bits, all the old equipment is piled up ready for scrap. I am asked if I want to earn a few quid repairing washing machines in HMS Rooke. They have eight machines, of which only two are working; things are desperate for the poor single guys living in the establishment, and their washing is piling up. I accept the challenge; I manage to get a total of five in working order by cannibalising the other three. A shop in town is supposedly a dealer in spares, but they rarely have anything I want. In the end I convince the welfare fund to invest in some new machines; once they are all up and running I resign from the job, as the hassle is just too much. Every time some idiot overloads a machine and burns it out, it somehow becomes my fault, bugger that for a game of soldiers.

My mother-in-law comes out to stay with us for a week; she would like to go up the rock and see the Barbary apes, no problem. I get the old Riley out and we all pile in and head for the ape colony half way up the rock. Having got there, I park and we get out, and after ten minutes of watching these animals pinching tourists' sun glasses, cameras, and anything else their thieving little mitts can get hold of, we climb back in the car. I start her up and head down the hill back to the flat. Soon, I realise my brakes do not work—oops, this could be dodgy. I did not bother mentioning this at the time, no point in causing a panic. I went into second gear and hung onto the hand brake for dear life, and we slowly got two thirds down the hill. At that point, we reach the busy cross road, I had to crash it into first and turn the ignition off, stalling the car and fortunately stopping it before we end up in a multi car pileup. I applied the hand brake and told the family we had broken down, and we finished the journey on foot, fortunately, only a mile from home. I found the master cylinder seals had leaked all the brake fluid; a seal kit, some brake fluid, and a two hour roadside repair later and I was back in business.

I'm on my way to the dockyard one day, when I spot a neighbour from the block opposite looking at damage on his new car, a Fiat 124. The front wing has a nasty dent in it, and I offer to bang it out for him. "How much?" he asks. I tell him nothing, he accepts. That afternoon I get the required tools and materials together, and proceed to repair his beloved car. I charge him for the filler and spray cans, total £5.75, and he is over the moon. Then comes the shock, he gives me his old car, a little red Renault Dauphine, not a bad little car considering it is French. A few days later I sell the Riley 4/44 to the guy who first owned it; he offers me £150 for it, I accept.

While at work one day, I knelt on piece steel swarf. I thought little of it at the time, till a few days later when my knee comes up the size of a football. My wife calls the doctor out, I'm given antibiotics, and the steel shard is removed; a nurse comes in for the next two weeks, to ram thirty foot of wadding into my knee daily—you wouldn't believe the muck that came out of that little hole in my knee, yuk. Meanwhile, my daughter, Theresa, is at it again. She falls off the bed again, this time landing on the same bump which has not recovered from last time. She is unconscious as she goes back to the hospital, and stays overnight again. Fortunately, she is ok; I can see my wife and I getting done for child abuse at this rate. Please try and be careful in future, Theresa.

Word of my repairs to the Fiat gets round, and I have people asking if I can repair dents and scratches on their cars. I do a couple, when I am offered a job down at the car club on Coaling Island; this is the navy's small boat yard next to Rooke. The guy running the club is called Paul, a Chief mechanic; he and another guy are running a repair and spray shop and earning a handsome profit. Paul tells me the other guy has been drafted off the rock, and asks if I would like to take his place for half the earnings. I have to think about this, and ten microseconds later I give him my reply: yes, please. Over the next few days I familiarise myself with tools and equipment.

A compressor from the laundry of a frigate across the harbour was borrowed early one morning; it was not required on the ship as it was about to be used as target practice at a later date. This proved to be ideal for paint spraying, and I doubted anyone would miss it. Paul had a full set of panel beating hammers, dollies, and hydraulic dent removing equipment, complete with a full and comprehensive tool kit. The car club was for the use of any rating who wished to use it; guys would come down with their cars and ask to use the garage, no problem. We would take out any car we were working on, and they would drive their cars in. When they started using Paul's tools we stepped in—sorry mate, those are private, and you have to use your own. "But I haven't got any," was the normal reply. "Then I suggest you buy some; alternatively, we could do the job for you, at a reasonable rate for you, being a Matelot."

Over the years, three MK2 Jaguars found their way to Coaling Island— they had been abandoned due to lack of spares—during quiet spells we cannibalised two of them and got a 3.8 model up and running and re-sprayed; apart from the brakes, it was perfect. We would start her up once a week and hammer it down the jetty; a quick hand brake turn at the end usually stopped us falling off the end, although there were a few close calls.

As the work picked up, I employed a couple of my lads to rub down bodywork with wet and dry, and do any labouring as required. We would finish navy work at four, go home, have some tea, and leg it down to the garage and work till at least midnight with Saturdays and Sundays being full working days.

A main car dealer in Gibraltar called Basidoni got wind of our work, and he asked to meet us. I was at work in the yard the day Paul went to see him. He told Paul, "I don't know whether to put you out of business or give you work," and with that he took Paul down Queensway. Next to the cinema was a car park full of second hand cars, all part exchange jobs with Basidoni. He asks Paul to give him a price to re-spray every car, all seventy-seven of them. Paul gathered himself together and told him £75 each; on the condition we could do them at our convenience. "Done." The deal was struck. As we were having a quiet spell at that time, me and the lads picked up six cars and started work on them; most were in reasonable conditions and just required a quick rub down with wet and dry to key a cellulose top coat.

As we were not required to paint them in any particular colour, we used any leftovers from previous jobs, even mixing them to produce some horrendous tones. The Army camouflage department would have been proud of us. We delivered them back to Basidoni's car park, and several weeks later he paid us. He was chuffed to bits, as his original idea was to get his money back on the part exchanges, and he was actually selling them and making money on them.

My Renault Dauphine had a problem—it would start, but the engine was rough and rocking like a drunken sailor. I pulled a plug lead off, no difference. I tried another lead, no difference; the third lead was the same, and amazingly, the thing had started on one plug and was running, albeit a bit rough. It transpired that the head gasket had gone. I pushed it out of the way and forgot about it. Two weeks later, one of my lads asked if he could borrow a car for a week, as his girlfriend was coming out to Gib on holiday. There was none available at that time, so I told him if he got a new head gasket for the Renault he could use that. He duly bought the gasket and I fitted it. Because it was an aluminium head, I told him to take it easy for a day or so then come back and I would tighten it up.

Three days later, at around midnight, I have a knock on the door of my flat; two policemen are there.

"Are you the owner of a red Renault Dauphine registration G13679?"

"Yes, I am, what's the problem?"

"Well, sir, at the moment it's going up and down Sandy Beach on the tide."

"You mean it's in the sea," I replied.

"Yes, sir, that's about it."

"What do you want me to do?"

"Well, if you could sort it out in the morning, sir."

The next morning I head for Both Worlds and find out my little friend had stalled the car at the top of the road, and tried to bump start on the hill down to the beach, which obviously failed, and the car ended up on the beach. The incoming tide got hold of it and took it out to sea; all the people in Both Worlds had balcony seats watching the drama unfold. One thing that amused them was a doll belonging to my daughter, Helen, was in the back window waving to them. As there was nothing more I could do, I went home.

Four days later, the lad to whom I lent the car turned up.

"Hi, did you enjoy your leave?" I asked.

"Actually, I have something to tell you, it's about the car."

"Everything OK, I hope, where have you parked it?"

And with that he spills out the whole story. He was too scared to come and tell me earlier; he is so apologetic and offers to pay for another car. I tell him I couldn't give a toss about the car, but he must go and see my wife as all the beach gear was in the boot, and he should replace it. He was so relieved, two sun loungers and a parasol was a small price to pay for losing such a fine vehicle. Believe it or not, six months later I get another knock on my door, and this time it's the coastguard.

"Good evening, sir, are you the owner of a red Renault Dauphine?"

"Christ, now what?"

"Your car is bobbing up and down in the middle of the Med and is a shipping hazard; can we have your permission to sink it?"

"Please do, and don't come back telling me some submarine has run into it."

The security gate to Coaling Island was manned by a British policeman. If you wanted to get in, the normal practice was to show an identity card or some sort of pass. Fortunately for us, we had a tame copper known as Paddy, a five foot six Irishman, weighing no more than ten stone, and he was perfect for us. Not only did he let strangers in without a pass to get their cars done; he also went to the trouble of finding us abandoned cars. He would contact the owners and give them a warning, adding that he knew someone who could dispose of it for them at no charge; if they took up the offer, he would inform us, and we would tow them back to the yard and do them up before selling them on.

If they were beyond repair, we towed them up to Europa Point, which is a southern part of the rock; a wall runs by the side of the road with a huge pair of locked steel gates that opens up, so you can tip your scrap cars into the sea. Paddy would arrange the key for this operation. There must be hundreds of vehicles down there. I gather the practice has since ceased; someone must have finally realised that polluting the Atlantic was no longer acceptable. (It's just a pity no one told the German U-boat commanders about the pollution they were causing—where was Greenpeace when we needed them?)

I digress; Paddy was rewarded with a nice new twenty pound note for each transaction. One day Paddy put us onto a nice little mini. This lady, all twenty-two stone of her, realised that, bar removing the front seats of her car and sitting in the back, she was unable to drive it. We bought it for £75, painted it a nice chocolate colour, and sold it for £400. Another time, Paddy got us a VW beetle; it was parked half way up the rock by the prison, we managed to get it started and got three hundred yards down the hill, when the front offside wheel parted from the car. To see that wheel bouncing down the hill was a nightmare—you envisaged dead bodies everywhere—as it happened, no one was hurt, although the door of the shop it hit was a bit worse for wear.

Chapter Twelve

The Captain of Rooke brought his sports car down one day and asked us for a quote to re-spray it; we just charged him for the materials and he was happy, and he must have told all his mates, because before we knew it we were doing cheap re-sprays for the head of Gibraltar customs, the chief of police, and the top dog in the dockyard. This proved to be invaluable later, as Paddy had been moved to a security post round the back of the rock, and a new, over keen copper, fresh from the UK, took over on the Coaling Islands gate. For a few days it caused us a problem; he was stopping our civilian customers getting in without a pass, and he told us what we were doing was in some way illegal, and he was going to report us. We waited with bated breath. The next day Paddy was back on the gate, and he popped in the garage and told us the keen copper had indeed reported us to our Captain. He in turn contacted the Chief of Police, who promptly moved the trouble maker to a far distant outpost. You see, it's not what you know, it's who you know.

We had just finished spraying a Fiat sports car and giving it a final polish when the owner returned; he took the car and told us he would be back the following day with the money. We waited three days then popped round to his flat—he told us he could not afford the £150 at the moment, but would pay us later, yeah, right. We returned at midnight and put two jubilee clips round his drive shaft, and ball bearings in his petrol tank; we never got our money, but it was a joy to see him driving his pride and joy at 30 mph juddering along with his out of balance drive shaft, and his rattling petrol tank. Back down at the dockyard with the navy, the eight till four job was kicking in big time, with spares arriving and at long last we were able to get a move on. Over the next few months we rebuilt the operation room communications systems with new units, and new microphones and speakers were fitted throughout the ship. Once the ship was nailed back together and everything tested we handed over to the new crew. Their job was to take it to sea and make sure that everything was ship shape. When the ship sailed and disappeared out of the harbour our job was done—fingers crossed she didn't return in the next few hours. The next few weeks in the dockyard were spent waiting for the next floating scrap heap to arrive, so we could do its 50,000 mile service.

My family and I were due a holiday off the rock, so I hired the Navy welfare Land Rover; it cost £20 for a week. The ferry to Tangiers was booked, along with the Caravan in Rabat. The brief we were given before setting off was to stay away from the Atlas Mountains. The dodgy Moroccan Police had this little scam going. They would stop and search your vehicle, and plant a pile of hashish among your belongings. They would then let you go, and you would be free to drive off, only to be stopped and searched ten miles down the road by their accomplices, who would then find the hash, and fine you on the spot, and confiscate your vehicle, or threaten you with prison, nasty little bastards.

Once ashore in Tangiers, we find the coast road, and head for Rabat. What you notice is the hundreds of miles of golden, empty beaches. I guess the problem is the Atlantic, as the sea tends to be a little on the cold, nay, freezing side. The drive was a bit on the scary side, nothing to do with my driving of course, but the fact we were followed for about ten miles between Kenitra and Sal'e by four armed soldiers in an army jeep. You never know what to expect with these Arab types, but fortunately, they eventually peeled off and left us alone. When we arrived in Rabat we found the local charcoal maker and bought a bag for next to nothing. In the market we bought fresh fruit and vegetables. The local butchers left a bit to desire—sheep's heads and dead stuff hanging everywhere, complete with ten million flies—we bought some steaks and made a point of soaking them in Domestos before cooking, well almost. After loading up, I drove out of the market and we made our way to the Caravan site—my wife aired the van and prepared it for habitation, the kids ran off to play with some RAF family's kids, and I prepared the BBQ. Half a fifty gallon oil drum on a stand was what I had to get ready; I placed a load of old newspapers in the bottom, and put small pieces of charcoal over it; this I lit, and two minutes later the paper had all burnt away, but nothing had happened to the charcoal. I did this four times.

By now I was getting pissed off with this cheap Moroccan charcoal. In hindsight, I know I should not have resorted to using petrol, but, needs as must, the kids were getting hungry. I went to the spare jerry can and poured some petrol on the BBQ—I lit it, my arm, and half the bloody camp site, and this was not good. I eventually deflamed my arm, and found a fire extinguisher; this I was trained to use, and did a fine job of stopping the Caravan, the site, and Rabat from going up in flames. We decided to postpone the BBQ till the following day when I could purchase some fire lighters. Fortunately, the gas stove in the van worked quite well and we had hot food without the hassle.

My wife did an excellent job of bandaging my arm, and my kids, even to this day, cringe when they see me with a box of matches. I hate to think what psychological damage I have done them, although it does seems to have put them off smoking—every cloud of smoke has a silver lining, and all that. Over the next week we tour the area and take in the local culture: leatherworkers, brass workers, tradesmen, and beggars, all trying to scrape a living. My wife's bartering expertise comes in handy; she is getting the week's shopping for a third of what we have been paying in Gib. On our last day in Rabat, the caravan is cleaned, ready for the next holiday makers from Rooke. I attempt to hide the burnt grass and paintwork from the BBQ incident; we top the Rover up with petrol and groceries, and head for the ferry.

Back in Gib, the Rover is returned, along with all the other bits and pieces we had hired from the expedition store. The kids couldn't wait to get back to school; they had plenty to tell their mates about their holiday, and, of course, snitching on dad's misdemeanours.

The next day, my wife and Theresa are on the zebra crossing in Queensway when a speeding car narrowly misses them. A man rushes over after seeing the incident to make sure they are all right. He tells my wife he is a lawyer, he has the registration of the offending car, and knows the driver, a local police officer. He pleads with her to report it to the police station, and he offers to be a witness. She agrees, and after three weeks it goes to court. The policeman has all his family with him, and they are there to intimidate and look daggers at my wife. This ploy fails, as the policeman is fined heavily, and given the mother of all bollockings by the judge.

Back at Coaling Island, Paul and I are busy knocking out dents and re-spraying cars when guess what? Two weeks after driving the land Rover to Rabat and back, we are asked by the Captain of Rooke if we would like to pick it up at the ferry and repair it, as evidently it had been in an accident. We went down to have a look at what damage there was. Imagine our surprise when we saw it: four wheels on the ground and the bodywork at forty five degrees to the chassis; it had been rolled, the fifty beer bottles inside gave us a clue as to what had happened, bloody drunken Matelots. We commandeered a navy lorry and towed her to the workshops. After giving a quote for £750, which was accepted, we were asked to make the job a priority; people were relying on it for their holiday. The first thing we did was to park the Rover side on to a steel bollard on the jetty. We lashed both axles to the bollard with heavy ropes; we then tied ropes round the

147

roof and attached the ends to another land Rover. By gently pulling, we got the bodywork in roughly an upright position; fortunately, the Rover is made up of aluminium sheets riveted to steel frames. Once the rivets had been chiselled off, it was only a matter of straightening frames and replacing the aluminium panels. A new windscreen was fitted, and after five days work, she was ready for spraying. By the weekend she was on her way to Rabat.

A Moroccan restaurant owner called Mohamed popped in to see us one day. He explained he had bought a cheap Peugeot saloon from around the 1965 era; his problem was the engine had had its day, it was a none runner, and no spares were available for it. But, he assured us, he had managed to get another engine for it from his friend in Tangiers. Could we fit it, if he brought it, and the car down to us? I couldn't see a problem, so I said yes, £50. We ripped out the old lump, fitted the replacement, and now the trouble began. We tried starting the beast, nothing; we checked the fuel, followed by the electrics, still nothing. It transpired the timing on this French dustbin was out. We eventually got it started and it was returned to its owner. He came back a week later complaining it was only doing 10 mpg. All our fault, of course, we eventually tracked down the problem: the previous owner had put a ton of concrete, 4" thick, throughout the floor as it was full of rust. This made the power to weight ratio a little out of sync.

The summer ball in Rooke was one of the highlights in the social calendar; the event meant getting into tropical evening dress. This consisted of dress shirt and bow tie, white monkey jacket, cummerbund, black trousers, and shoes for the servicemen. For the ladies it meant dressing up in their best long dresses, although looking at some of them, you could be forgiven for thinking fancy dress was the order of the day. A band or group ensured the evening went with a swing, and the food was excellent, or so I am told. By the time my wife and I got to the table, the poor and starving had already filled their plates and handbags, it was embarrassing. I know the navy pay is not much, but to see these people in their best bib and tucker acting like hyenas was disgusting, talk about I'm all right, Jack.

Back down the dockyard, the process of stripping the next Leander class frigate gets under way, and another refit begins. As usual, the problem with spares remains the same, nothing in stock, and a four month waiting period for the UK dockyard to organise the piss up in the brewery, fat chance. At the garage, a local comes and tells us that the car businesses in the arches on Queensway are complaining about our business. Paul and I go down to see them; they assure us that far from complaining about us, they have in fact been sending people down to us, problem solved.

Alf Pickup

At the back of the boat shed lay a Royal navy, radio controlled, pilot-less target boat, its side blown out by some sharp shooting frigate. The chief shipwright and Paul manage to get the navy to let them have it for free, as it was a write off. The shipwright starts work cutting away the burnt fibreglass side and prepares the moulding for repair; we remove a 2.4 litre engine from one of our dead Jaguars and tune it. Enquiries are made about getting a marine Z drive and propeller, but this could be expensive. Mind you, this is going to be some speed boat. After two weeks working on the boat, a guy in a suit comes to see us; he tells us he will take the boat to his marina and repair it, bringing it to full specs, for free. The catch is we must agree that he can take a mould off its hull; no problem, but why is he doing this?

We find out the hull of the target boat is renowned for its speed, and a patented design exclusive to the RN. This guy's other business was smuggling from Morocco, and he needed a boat that could outrun Spanish patrol boats. How did he get to know about our boat? Well, his mate and ours, the head of Gibraltar customs told him. This man used to pop down to see us and ask us if we wanted anything brought back from Spain or Morocco. Three weeks after taking the boat to his marina for repair, we hear his marina had caught fire, along with our boat. Shit, anyone in need of a spare jag engine? Lovely runner.

Antonio, our local ice cream van man, was a regular caller round the married quarters in his old Bedford van; he loved my two girls, and regularly gave them a free ice cream. One day he broke down outside our flat, and I offered to fix his van. I got a tow rope and took it into Coaling Island; we got him going in ten minutes. After that he was a regular customer when things went wrong, and he always offered to pay. I just told him, "You start charging my girls for their ices and I'll start charging you" and we became good friends from that day on.

I was working on a car with Paul one day, when this guy pokes his head round the door and says, "Can you give me a quote on re-spraying my van, please?"

Paul whispers to me to get rid of him, as we are snowed under with work. I go outside and look at his van; Christ, the body was barely still on the chassis, it was that rusty. I pretend to go round it and price it up.

"I reckon about £500," I tell him.

"Good," he says, "when can you start?" I'm gobsmacked.

"I'll have a word with my colleague," I tell him. I tell Paul, and he comes outside.

"Would right away be all right sir?" he said. "What colour would you like it painted?"

He does not care, and this means we can use all our leftovers from previous jobs. Over the next four days we saw and grind out a good foot of bodywork from round the van, and replace it with steel plate; the welds are ground down; primer and three coats of greeny-blue cellulose are applied. So as not to feel too guilty, we panel out the inside with marine ply borrowed from the boat shed. We phone the guy up to tell him it's ready, and ten minutes later he arrives, a big smile on his face and says, "I honestly did not think it would be possible to do."

He looks round it, opens the back doors and looks inside; he is amazed we have boarded it out. "How much do I owe you?" he asks us and we tell him £500; he gives us an extra £50 and drives off more than happy. Later that day, a man drives in the yard, cowering over the steering wheel; the problem appears to be the roof is caved in. He gets out and tells us some Matelot has done the car, run down all the cars in Main Street. His insurance has given him £250 to get it repaired. I get in the car and tilt the front seat back; with both feet I kick the roof, and *boing*, hey presto, good as new, not even a crease in the paintwork. The man is speechless. "I've been driving this car for the last two weeks bent over the steering wheel; the dealer told me it was a write off, and you come along! How much do I owe you?" I tell him nothing, but he slips me £50 anyway, another happy customer. Even Lloyds bank would have trouble earning £50 in a micro second.

Every now and again I have a day off to go down the beach with the family. As I hate swimming and sunbathing, it is quite a sacrifice (especially when I could be earning money down at the workshop). Our local friends are usually already down there, and they have a place saved for us; the whole thing is very well organised with food, drink, sun cream, chairs, towels, you name it, they have it, every eventuality covered. It's just a pity they don't work for the dockyard stores department.

The local taxi firms are at each other's throats, and competition is fierce. There has been a succession of taxis mysteriously going up in flames. It starts with one firm's Mercedes being torched, and the following day the next firm's Mercedes disappears in a ball of flame. At the rate it's going, there won't be any taxis left in Gib. The police have a word with the owners of both companies before it gets out of hand and someone gets killed; the fires stop, and an uneasy piece prevails.

On the rock side of the runway is an empty canning warehouse; the story is the Argentineans were cooling their hot tins of cooked corned beef in the local river before exporting them, and typhoid, round the world. The problem was not the beef, but the cans; they had tiny holes in them, letting in contaminated water. There was a general recall worldwide, and a total ban on Argentinean corned beef. An entrepreneur bought all the contaminated cans he could get hold of for next to nothing. He then set up the factory in Gib and proceeded to empty the contents of all the cans into vats, re-cooked all the beef, killing all the contamination, then re-canned it and sold it at a huge profit, clever bugger.

On the first of January, 1978, my chief petty officer promotion came through, and I now had to go to slops and pick up my buttons and badges. I also had to buy new suits, as the taking off of the petty officers badges had left their mark. Bugger, more expense. I don't know who had the original idea of a CPO having three buttons on each sleeve, but to me it looked odd. Mind you, it was probably the same drunken design committee who designed jolly jack's outfit, you know, the silk, the collar, the lanyard, the milk churn lid, and earlier, the trousers with a flap instead of flies. Anyway, my wife did a fine job of removing and replacing buttons and badges to bring me up to the desired rank.

I got two lovely letters, one from Dick Cooper (my old boss), and another from David and Anne Eckersley-Maslin (now Admiral), congratulating me on my promotion. I felt truly honoured that these people had gone to the trouble: Dick, promoted from the lower deck and still in touch with the coal face, and David born an officer, and in touch with the whole navy, and indeed the world, as he was now a top defence adviser with NATO in Brussels.

Work on the cars carried on at a pace; the money was slowly piling up in the bank account. It should have been more, but Paul's wife did the money side, and being a greedy, stuck up, thieving bitch, tended to take more than their 50% share of the loot. She worked at a local restaurant and got friendly with her boss; after nine months she gave birth to a little boy who looked remarkably like her boss. Paul assumed it was his, but we knew different.

The Land Rover we repaired a year before was towed back to our workshop. The front had been caved in; evidently, the people who had hired it had run off the road in Marrakech. The navy had sent a tow truck over to pick it up and bring it back to us. We were asked to repair it, but considering the steering and suspension were a write off, we declined, as it was beyond repair, even for our skilled hands. A Rolls Royce was brought in one day, as the owner wanted to change its colour. I said thanks, but no thanks; Paul was all for it, but I won the day, and we passed him onto the garages down Queensway. Just as well, because the cellulose paint we and they used was not compatible with Roller paint. After several attempts to re-spray the beast, the corrugated finish was not what was required by the owner, and they ended up having to strip the thing down to bare metal and start from scratch. Not much profit in that job. MOT's in Gib were nonexistent at this time; it's a wonder there were not more accidents, some of the heaps we repaired were not fit for the scrap heap, let alone the road. One guy actually came in using a pair of mole grips as a steering wheel in his car; we managed to kit him out with a spare which we welded onto the column (and we kept the grips).

In the spring of 1978, I hired a brand new Sherpa motorhome form the navy welfare. Two of these vehicles were shipped out to Gibraltar to replace the land rovers and old caravans in Morocco. I booked the ferry to get to the other side of the harbour, via Tangiers (the border to Gib was still closed), as we had decided to tour Spain for a change. The girls and I spent the next few days loading up with clothes and food for the adventure ahead; I topped the petrol tank up, and fitted two full Calor gas bottles. We piled in and headed for the ferry, and once on board we settled down to our trip to Spain. We arrived early in the evening at Algeciras, and headed north towards Cadiz. As darkness fell, I pulled over into a lay-by, got the kids to bed – who slept in a double bunk over the cab – a bunk on either side of the cabin was made up for my wife and me. Lights out and a good night's rest followed.

Next morning at around seven, we all woke up to a freezing cold camper; the obvious thing to do was light the gas stove and generate a bit of heat. I stumbled out of my bunk and found my lighter, turned the knob on the hob, and a distinct lack of hiss suggested no gas. Bollocks, time to get dressed and check the gas bottles, the frost outside was not the most welcoming sight, and it was bloody cold to boot. I checked the bottles; both were on and full, what the hell was going on? The only thing I could think of was the pipe work, so I turned the gas off. Back inside, I proceeded to remove all our clothes and holiday gear from under the bunk, to give me access to the pipes. As luck would have it, I had packed a few tools in case of such an emergency. Fortunately, there was only one joint between the gas bottle and the hob; this I undid, and found the arsehole who put this lot together had used so much jointing compound it filled the pipe, blocking the gas. I cursed him and willed that his toilet would overflow, and that his exhaust would fall off on his way to his pipe connecting job.

I managed to straighten a wire coat hanger and clear the crap out of the pipe, and after re-assembly I turned the gas back on and lit the hob. I left the wife to re-pack all the clothes and stuff, which by now were strewn everywhere. After about fifteen minutes, it was warm enough for my shivering kids to get up and get dressed. We cooked up some eggs and bacon for breakfast, tea was without milk (well, I can't remember everything), and I made a note to get milk later. The sun was now a watery ball on the horizon, and the day was looking good. I checked the oil and water on the Sherpa, just in case the same prat who did the gas had been let loose on the engine. All seemed OK, so we set off for Cadiz and Seville. To say the Sherpa was a little under-powered was an understatement. It was the equivalent of a thirty five stone Sumo wrestler driving around on a 50cc NSU quickly moped; a race between him and us would have been a close call.

We passed through Cadiz and into Seville, and there we stopped to buy bread, and of course milk. The local yokels spoke as much English as I did Swahili, probably because I was the first foreigner they had seen since the revolution. As usual, the Matelots' sign language came to the fore, demonstrating the buttering of bread and the milking of my wife's breasts for the milk. I'm just grateful I didn't require any condoms. Our next destination was Granada; the old Sherpa struggled up the mountain roads, second gear was the favourite going up, and the brakes must have been glowing going down hill, what with all that extra weight, over and above the normal weight of a Sherpa van.

We now head into Granada on the edge of the Sierra Nevada Mountains, and situated high on a hill lies the Alhambra castle, a must see, as this is one of the ten wonders of the world. Built by Arabic dynasties over centuries, it appears to be the Arabs' attempt to produce heaven on earth, as described in the Koran, a Garden of Eden with running water. It is truly magnificent; even non-believers would find it inspiring. The one thing you notice is the architecture, with its mosaics, tiles, and carvings, all blending in with the gardens and water features. It was obviously all built to be easily defended, as well as to look good. On a hill opposite the castle lays Albiacin, the old Arab quarter, with its cobbled streets, and white-washed buildings. It is currently in a state of neglect, but it retains its Arabic feel despite the area being ethnically cleaned 500 years ago. The Catholics decided you either became part of their wonderful Christian religion or you were killed, or told to go, and this included Jews and any other religion.

I park and we head for the shops; we load up with fresh fruit, vegetables, meat, and of course fresh milk, a luxury after months of dried milk in Gib. The locals take a shine to the children with their sun bleached blond hair, and their pretty faces. After an hour or two, we pile into the camper and head for Malaga, a pretty city on the coast that is missed by most tourists as they get off the plane and head straight for the Costa del

Sol. We spend the evening in a small restaurant by the waterside, eating tapas and drinking sangria; boy, this is the living. I am seriously thinking of doing this for a living; you certainly don't need a lot to live on, if it wasn't for the wife, the kids, the navy, the mortgage, oh well, dream on Alf. That night we pull into a deserted caravan site, not a tourist in sight—see, it pays to come early, even if it is three months before the season starts. We bed the girls down, and settle down to read the English papers we bought; they are three days out of date, and cost a fortune, but needs as must, got to keep in touch with the old country, even if it is all doom and gloom. After a few more beers we crash for the night.

Next morning, we clear breakfast, and make a decision to go to a place called Mijas, which is inland in the mountains. It is a picturesque village with the usual white buildings and cobbled streets. It appears donkeys are the main form of transport round the village; most roads seem to be about one in four, bloody steep to say the least. Put it this way—you wouldn't want to buy a car from a local. My wife and the girls insist on a donkey ride, and they try to persuade me to go with them. Call me a coward, but there's no way you're getting me on one of those things. Anyway, I pay the fares, and wait for their return. After half an hour they return safe and sound, the girls loved it, the wife was a little anxious, but put on a brave face; I must admit they had guts going up and down those mountainous hills. I'll just stick to climbing masts.

We move on and drive through Ronda, on our way back to the coast, and Fuengirola; there we buy a couple of kilos of fresh prawns, and some bread for supper. We find a good spot to park, and it's getting dark, so the kids are changed into their pyjamas and sent to their bunks, out of the way, while dad cooks. I flash up the hob, oil is placed in the pan and heated up, and dad now takes a handful of wet prawns and throws them in the pan— guess what happened next. You got it, the whole bloody lot goes up in flames, the kids and the wife are screaming—I remember my naval training (again), and find a towel to cover the pad, the fire is out, with little or no damage, apart from the psychological damage to the wife and kids, they still cringe to this day if I'm doing a BBQ, as if I haven't learnt my lesson after two near disasters. Once the screaming is over, I set to work clearing the smoke, and cleaning the soot off the van walls, and after half an hour you would hardly know anything had happened, apart from three quivering females, that is. Anyway, I proceed to cook supper. First, I change the burnt oil in the pan, and then I thoroughly dry the prawns in a tea towel. I heat the new oil in the pan to room temperature before putting the prawns in one at a time. I had decided to cook them slowly this time, rather than the flambé method. By now the girls had got over feeling sick, and were ready for my gourmet meal. I bedded down that night with my daughters' whispered words to their mum ringing in my ears, "please don't let Daddy cook anymore." Bloody gratitude, first I save them from being cremated, then I cook them a lovely meal, I ask you.

After breakfast,(that mum cooks) we head for Marbella; the sun is up and all is well with the world. I seem to have pulled the perfect con to get out of cooking, a bit like dropping the best china to get out of washing up. The coast around Marbella consists of 27 kilometres of golden beaches, most of which are empty. I park the camper near to shops, some of which are actually open, despite the lack of tourists. We head for the beach with towels, sun tan cream, and picnic in tow; the temperature is a balmy 68 degrees, perfect for my delicate skin. After an hour, the kids are baying for an ice cream and my wife offers to go, so not being one to argue, I carry on relaxing with my book and a crossword from the out of date newspaper. An ice cream, fizzy drinks, and three sand castles later, we have our picnic, and after lunch it's back to sun bathing and swimming—not me of course, as I'm not in danger of drowning.

Late afternoon it starts getting chilly, so it's up bags and hammocks, to the warmth of the camper. The petrol tank is running low, so I drive to find a garage; we find one eventually and fill up. I hand over my Pesetas, a quick calculation tells me it cost £17—the bugger has ripped me off, but as he is twice my size I decide to let him off. As it's now dark, we decide to stay in Marbella; my wife de-sands the kids and washes them down, then changes them into clean clothes. Now in our best bib and tucker, we head for the night life; a nice little bar with Spanish music proves irresistible. We go in and are welcomed by what looks like a matador—obviously a local eccentric, or doing a dress rehearsal for the season ahead—anyway, he seems pleased to see us. I order drinks and a table full of tapas in my Spanish sounding English; he replies in perfect English sounding English— he must think what a prat. Three guys with guitars serenade us for the next hour; two jugs of wine and a few beers later I'm ready for my bunk, and the kids want to stay up all night. I compromise, and tell them we're going in half an hour. We depart the bar; they give us a fond farewell, as if they actually enjoyed our company, even though we told them we were Spanish enemies from Gibraltar? Back in the van I go for a pee, and remember the chemical toilet is nearly full; in my tipsy state I'm struggling to keep the thing upright as I carry it down the street looking for a drain. Job done. Back on board I replenish the chemicals, and settle down for the night .

Next day is our last, so after breakfast we head down the coast to Algeciras. After a few hours driving, Gibraltar looms in the distance, and as we get nearer we can see the border, twenty minutes and we could be home. Instead we end up at the ferry in Algeciras waiting to go on the round trip via Tangiers.

Back in Gibraltar, we head for our flat, and once everything is unloaded, the van is scrubbed inside and out and returned to HMS Rooke. Nobody mentions the smell of smoke, so I don't elaborate. I mention about the blocked gas pipe, guess what, the other van suffered the exact same problem; unfortunately, the chap hiring it was a seaman with little knowledge of anything mechanical, and it cost him a days holiday, and £50 to get it sorted out. If that original gas pipe fitter isn't dead by now I would be most surprised, with the amount of curses he has had placed on him.

Meanwhile back at the flat, the girls and I have a nice bath and freshen up; my wife gets stuck into a week's washing and ironing. I settle down to watch the bull fighting on Spanish television. I know it's a sick way of slaughtering beef, but it is exciting, in a sad sort of way.

A quick trip to the NAAFI follows, to load up on groceries for the weekend—no need for bread, meat and milk, as we loaded up at a Spanish supermarket before coming home. I pop down to the garage to see how things are going, and the good news was we had loads of work; the bad news was there were Captain's rounds in Coaling Island next Thursday. This means removing around twenty cars, and tidying up the garage and surrounding jetty. Over the weekend we spend the days towing, driving, and hiding cars. Fortunately, Basadoni the car dealer let us use his car park till after the event. The Captain asked how the business was going, and wondered where all the cars had gone—Mum's the word, eh.

Summer over, the weather cools, and the beach becomes less and less inviting. Heavy levant covers the rock on most mornings, and hangs around for most of the day; the good thing is this mist provides water for the population. The deck chairs and beach stuff are given to our local friends, as we will be leaving the rock in March. My draft comes through to join HMS Excellent in April 1979. I am to do courses and be available as a spare instructor. Christmas is spent at the flat; friends are invited round for food and drinks, and they reciprocate by inviting us to their homes, and having the girls for sleepovers.

By now I am getting a little worn, what with all these 16 hour days, so I decide to cut my working hours down at the garage, and spend a bit more time at home. Paul is not over pleased with my decision, but he is a robot with big plans of starting a garage when he gets home; he and his thieving dog of a wife are money mad. I am happy with my £4,000 savings in the bank, so I start taking life a bit easier. My wife and I decide to take our leave in Gib; this means we have to vacate the flat and pack our crates. The flat is cleaned from top to bottom; all bedding is sent to the laundry and the upholstery is cleaned; we wax the floors, and replace any missing or broken plates. The guy from the quarters department arrives with his check list and checks everything, and I mean everything. People's flights have been stopped just because cookers are not up to scratch; fortunately, we pass with flying colours. A lorry takes our crates to the docks ready for shipping home.

We've booked into the Bristol hotel for the second and third week in March; this gives us a week at home before I start my courses in Excellent. Our time is spent doing what tourists do, eating out, reading, shopping, drinking, touring the rock, and generally relaxing. It's now our final day in Gibraltar, and we're packed and waiting for our taxi; it arrives, and we pile in with our six cases; at the airport our local friends are there to see tip Off. There seems to be dozens of them—this is my wife's fault, she has this knack of befriending people—even now, she and her friend Gill cannot go abroad without meeting and befriending the bellboy, the waitress, or the local jeweller and his wife. Every year, Christmas cards arrive from wherever they have been; it cost me a bloody fortune in postage and cards.

We say our tearful goodbyes and board the plane, and the stewardess tells us the usual lies about what to do in the event of. The plane taxis down to the end of the short runway before applying full throttle, the brakes are released, and we shoot off into the air at an angle of forty five degrees, banking left so as not to encroach on Spanish air space. I am sat by the wing, and notice it is made up of many sections of folding bits; it looks like the damn thing is doing an origami lesson. I just hope the bits go back into one lump for the rest of the flight. I still find it hard to conceive that a tube full of human beings can be pushed into the sky with a couple of spinning dustbins on each wing.

The food arrives; well, I call it food, on the grounds of the fact it can be placed in your mouth and digested at a later stage, same as grass really, crap in, crap out. I go for a pee, then I get to thinking, do they dump my pee in the sea as they fly over it? If so, the bottled water I am drinking could be from a passenger of 1965. You know, the pee goes in the sea, it evaporates, it forms a cloud, and it rains; the bottle company bottles it, sends it to the airline, and here I am, bottle in hand, wondering. Then I notice this bottle is safe to drink because it comes from a two million-year-old glacier—my only problem now is that best before June date on it. Why?

The girls are marvelous during the journey, good as gold, and no trouble, as they are excited and looking forward to going home and seeing all their old friends. We arrive at Gatwick Airport; we head for the luggage carousel and start hucking out cases onto two trolleys. We notice the handle has been ripped off one, I go to the complaints department, they give me a form to fill in, and I leave it with them. Two weeks later I get a cheque for £35, not bad considering I only paid £25 for the set of four, result. Outside the airport arrivals, my brother in law, Sandy, is waiting for us; he greets us with a big smile, and loads our gear on a roof rack, and the boot of his car. We pile in and head down the A3 towards Hayling Island—after two hours we are back at our house.

At this point my wife starts crying; the garden looks like a jungle, and the back fence no longer exists, inside the place looks like squatters have just moved out (witch seemed pretty close to the truth). The furnisher is ripped, the carpet's fit for the bin, and the kitchen is full of broken crockery. In the bedrooms it is no better, blankets and sheets full of dog hairs. Our tenant, The Bitch from the kid's nursery, had been subletting, had dogs, and did virtually everything we had prohibited in our agreement. Time to pop in and see Parkinson's estate agent, you know, the guy who marked every scratch on the inventory and was looking after my interests while I was away. I enter the shop.

"Hello, could I see the manager please?"

"Who should I say is calling, sir?"

"Tell him it's the man from seven Seagrove."

The manager comes out, "Can I help you, sir?"

"Yes, I would like you to come round to my property, and have a look round."

He tells me he is very busy right now. No problem, perhaps later, I say. No, he is busy later. Perhaps this evening then, I suggest. Again the man is too busy. I turn to leave the shop; I tell him I am going home now, and then I add, "If you're not round my house in five minutes, I am coming back, and will drag you by the balls to view my house."

I left, and by the time I got home he had driven round and was waiting for me. "Now about this inventory from when we first let, as you can see from this item alone, there is a mark on the leather settee," I say as I take him down the side of the house where I have piled the contents of the house.

I show him the settee, now in three pieces, and ripped to shreds, and we go through the other items on the list, one at a time. By the time I've finished, he agrees they have not done a very good job, but it's not his fault;

apparently, Parkinson's had subcontracted the inventory out to a private firm.

"Oh well, that's all right then, so it wasn't your firm's job to keep an eye out for the dogs, the subletting, the upkeep of the garden, the house, etc., silly me, and there's me thinking that was what I was paying you 10% of my rent for." The guy left with his tail between his legs and a list as long as his arm.

Over the next few days my wife and I set about decontaminating the place, and bringing the jungle canopy rainforest down to ground level. The four grand I had saved refurnished the house and bought stuff for the garden, including new fence panels. These I repositioned to pinch an extra two foot from the field behind the house, every cloud and all that. Now the house was up to a high standard, we decided to do bed and breakfast, just to recoup some of our cash, you understand. .

My girls were booked into the local schools, and were settling in, making new friends and acquaintances; things were slowly getting back to normal. I joined HMS Excellent on the first of April 1979 to start my courses; the first course was at Phoenix, the navy's fire fighting school, and the week was spent doing theory and practical. This covered everything from fat fires to oil fires, electrical fires, how to use breathing apparatus, and how to contain fires by cooling all sides, and of course how to prevent fires in the first place. One has to know these things, as fire brigades are usually in short supply mid-Atlantic. The one thing I did notice, was the amount of wood that was being wasted by the dockyard; lorry loads would arrive to be burnt—not just scraps, but ten foot lengths of teak, oak, and mahogany. I could have kitted my house out like an Elizabethan castle with that lot.

Chapter Thirteen

Course over, I am now a fully qualified fire fighting instructor; typical navy, you do a quick course on something and you are now an expert. I return to Excellent to await my next course, which is at the Phoenix Nuclear, Biological, Chemical and Damage Control School, in a week's time. I potter round the workshops in Excellent; nothing much happening there. There does not appear to be a businessman in sight, nobody making any money, what is going on? I decide to take make and mends every day and do something useful at home.

Monday morning finds me at Phoenix NBCD School; the class goes through the usual damage control runs, plugging up leaking splinter holes with wooden wedges, shoring up hatches that are pouring with water, pumping out water from compartments full of smoke, all this in the dark, apart from the five candle power torch they give you. I must admit the simulator is pretty realistic, and pretty wet. Having passed that bit I am now an expert in damage control. Next on the agenda is the chemical bit; we are shown chemical suits, these are full protection to be worn over battle dress and respirators. They make you hot as hell and dehydrated; we are shown the pills to take in the event of a chemical attack, and the atropine injection kits, all made by the mad buggers at Porton Down.

They put us in a gas chamber to test our respirators, then for a bit of fun, they tell us to take them off and have a whiff of tear gas. This is such a hoot, everyone coughing their lungs up and crying their eyes out, the sick bastards. We are told about the ship's installed chemical system, SICS for short—these devices are fitted on the upper deck, and when operational give warning of a chemical attack. I will be doing a course at Collingwood as to the workings and use of the device later. We are lectured on biological warfare; this method seems to be only one we can do nothing about. So why scare the shit out of us by telling us about it? Evidently, it would only take a Russian trawler in the North Sea to pump a toxic strain of a deadly virus into the air, and with the right wind could contaminate half of England in days. Within a week the country would be open to invasion.

How cheap would that war be? Anyway, after two weeks I am now an expert in chemical and biological warfare.

My next week in the classroom is spent with commanders and captains doing nuclear warfare; a young lieutenant is the expert telling us all about it. It becomes blatantly obvious his teaching comes from a book. He gives us a scenario: our ship is in Portsmouth and low on fuel, and has to go to Plymouth to top up, but a nuclear cloud of fallout has covered the channel from France to Dorset. What action would we take when passing through the cloud? Various Officers give their opinions on how they would close the ship down, and then try and decontaminate once through the cloud. I am asked my thoughts on the subject; being a lateral thinker, I suggest we turn left out of Portsmouth and go round Britain to get to Plymouth, as this would save the ship from getting contaminated. The lieutenant says, "But the ship is low on fuel." I explain that as I understand it, RN ships never go less than 75% before refuelling, therefore, as no time scale was involved, it would be feasible. My fellow classmates agreed, much to the consternation of our instructor.

Two days later I was in his bad books again. We were going through the procedure of what to do in the event of a nuclear accident on the flight deck or hangar of a ship; if a device had been in a fire and exploded, (non nuclear) and its contents had spilled onto the deck, the correct routine is to draw a grid, then go round and mark every single piece of the exploded device onto the grid. This was after he told us some of the blue coloured bits scattered around were highly explosive, and only had to be touched to go off, thus rendering the markers of the grids legless. Big mouth suggested the ship was made to do a starboard 45 and hoses were used to get rid of the crap scattered round the deck over the side.

"That's all very well, but the book says it must be done this way."

"Could I suggest the writer of the book comes and shows us how?" I say to loud applause from my new friends."

Further instruction showed us how to decontaminate a ship after it had been through nuclear fall out. This is brilliant; all you do is dress up in the chemical suit, grab a radiac machine (for giving background radiation levels), a bucket of soap and water, a scrubbing brush, and a personal dosimeter (for reading your personal radiation levels, once up to your given level you come in). How strong the radiation dust is determines how long you can scrub for; five teams of three are sent out to clean a certain area of the upper deck each. After a given time they come in to be decontaminated in the cleansing station; this means the teams being stripped and scrubbed, and their suits bagged up for disposal. The next teams are then sent out to continue this futile business. The ship has a pre-wetting system, which if switched on in time can, in theory; wash most of the contamination over the side.

My NBCD course is now over. I am now qualified to be my next ship's NBCDI, the ship's expert on all things holy, God if you will—even the captain will be asking me for advice on what to do in certain situations. Good job I'm not the power hungry type, your life in my hands, eh what.

That summer my youngest daughter Theresa goes down with glandular fever and it's a worrying time. She ends up in St. Mary's hospital in an isolation ward, and after a week she is home again but very weak. She is so bad that she is off school for six months, and has a personal tutor. Playing on my sympathetic side, she cons me into buying a kitten. A little ginger shit that I despised; it was not so much the laying on the beds and settee, and bloody hairs everywhere that I hated. It was the dead seagulls and mice it brought into the conservatory at regular intervals that got up my nose. Not happy with just the cat, I am now coerced into buying six chickens, and my next job is to convert a perfectly good shed into a chicken coop and the usual: shelves to perch on, straw, a chicken flap, and a corral of wire to keep them within the coop. I hated the damn things, that is, till Helen and Theresa came running in the next morning with six wonderful eggs. I was all set to go and get another fifty chickens, and give Bernard Mathews a run for his money. But my wife, Hermione, would have none of it, no sense of adventure I guess.

Summer over, I am told my new draft is through: HMS Cardiff, a brand new type 42 destroyer. I am to join her on the first of October 1979 in Portsmouth.

First I have to go to Collingwood to do a course on ships installed chemical system (SICS) and ships installed radiac system (SIRS). I join a class of elderly Chief petty officers in a room down in White City. A civilian lecturer enters the class room and starts putting circuit diagrams up. He now starts going through them in the latest technical electronic theory. After five minutes I put my hand up, "Excuse me, what the hell are you talking about? I haven't a clue about this form of circuitry."

The poor instructor then asked the others if they could follow his instructions, and with that, the rest of the class all admitted that they too were at a loss. We spent the next two days going through the latest electronic theory. The rest of the week was used catching up on the course. After the course I asked the instructor how we repaired these consoles, and he replied, "You don't, you just replace the defective circuit board."

162

"Brilliant, you mean this course was actually for designers, not us board pullers, why in God's name do I need to know how the circuitry works if I can't repair it?"

"Because that's what I get paid to do." Touché.

I do my leaving routine in Excellent, and go on weekend leave; on Monday I join HMS Cardiff, registration number D108, at 4,820 tons, and armed with two sea dart missiles, a 4.5" mk8 gun, two triple torpedo tubes, two phalanx, and oerlicans—she is a formidable fighting ship. She has a top speed of 30 knots from her two gas turbine engines, and a Lynx helicopter for collecting our mail (and other stuff). I do my joining routine, and introduce myself to my new bosses, the Weapons electrical Officer, and the Deputy. I then go round and show my face to the electrical senior rates, a few of which are old mates. I get a pipe made for the junior rates to muster in their mess; I explain that I am their new divisional Chief, and I will be sorting out their jobs, watches, cleaning, action, and sea duty stations, and anything else pertaining to their welfare in the near future.

I assure them that I will be available for any problems in the technical office, my new place of work. Over the next week, I am sorting out a new watch and quarter bill, filing signals, learning how to use the new microfiche machine system—this is a system of viewing drawings on film strips instead of the old canvas drawings which took up a lot of space, modern technology, eh. I also have the job of making sure all the BRs, books of reference to you, are up to date with the latest amendments. Why the prats who write these books can't write them properly without bits missing in the first place is beyond me.

I spot my old mate, Dinga Bell; he is the chief Bosun's mate, and he greets me like a long lost brother. As usual, he has his own set of rates books, covering every navy item ever produced; it's always handy having an extra navel store on board. That weekend I hire a chain saw to take down four trees in my back garden, and I burn out two chains after felling just one tree. I guess I'm stuck with the other three. That is, till I told Dinga, who told me to leave it with him.

The following Monday he brings back the biggest chain saw you've ever seen, Government Issue, of course. I phone the wife up and tell her Dinga will be coming for tea, and I explain he has a big appetite. We arrive at the house, and straight away he flashes the beast up and starts felling the remaining trees as if they were butter; not content with felling them, he proceeds to hack them up into logs. This is good as we have an open fire and this will be perfect in the winter; the saw dust comes in handy for the chickens. My wife has prepared a roast beef dinner, and she puts Dinga's meal on a meat plate, piled high and near to overflowing. This is demolished, and then followed by a huge pudding and coffee. I offer to pay the man, and he acts like I have insulted him, saying, "That meal will more than pay for that little job." He returns back to the ship a happy man.

Being a newly commissioned ship, we have to do harbour and sea trails, and this is followed by work up in Portland. We do the usual damage control exercises, action station, boarding parties, and landing parties, etc. After passing our final assessment, Flag officer sea training comes into the Chiefs mess, and he asks us our opinion. Big mouth asks why they are still teaching 1945 damage control. He asks what I mean; I tried to give my view, explaining that modern weapons and missiles don't leave splinter holes in the ship's side that can be plugged with wooden wedges, as taught here; they leave bloody big holes for which there are no wedges big enough. At this point I saw him give his aid the nod, and he then started changing the subject, telling a story of when he was a captain and ordered to sink a barge full of oil, how he shot at it, and instead of sinking, it floated higher out of the water as the oil emptied. HA, HA, HA, went his entourage, very funny. I felt like saying, "You did not answer my question, you arrogant bastard," but thought better of it.

While at Portland, a camera crew came on board to make an instructional film on the ships installed chemical system. Muggings was nominated to show how the setting up was done. First a container was unclamped from under the unit; this was filled with chemical cocktail, and replaced. The next step was to turn a little brass handle fifty times to draw the mixture up; this primed an electric pump at the top of the unit. Once this was done it was switched on, and air is drawn into the unit from outside the ship. Any chemical from outside will react with the mixture in the unit and set off an alarm, and an emergency pipe is then made, GAS, GAS, GAS. The crew then react by putting on their respirators.

Filming over, I made a comment, "What idiot designed this piece of crap?"

"Actually, I did," was the reply from behind me; I turned to see one of the boffins walking over. Oh shit.

"What do you consider is wrong with it?" he said.

"Well, if you must know, it's the design of the chemical cup and pump, surely it would have been easier, quicker, and cheaper, to put the cup on the top of the unit, and have it gravity fed into the electric pump, rather than pissing about with that stupid little brass thing."

164

Gobsmacked, the boffin admitted he and his team had overlooked the obvious. I took him back to the mess for a drink, apologised for calling him an idiot, and it was accepted with good grace.

A lot of the problem with these designers is that they never go on a ship. Take, for instance, our ship's TV aerials fitted on either side of the ship—they look like a pair of huge ice cream cones. They work perfectly on a building high on a hill in Bath, where they were invented, but not alongside a dockyard full of cranes; our particular mess had a perfect picture with a broom handle and two wire coat hangers.

The electronic giant Plessey had a lucrative scam going on with the navy. The Cardiff's long range radar developed a fault, and a team was sent by the company to put a modification in to counteract it; unfortunately, all the other type 42's with no faults were sent the MOD, and consequently they all developed new faults caused by the MOD. Another Plessey team now develops a MOD to get rid of their faults; this MOD now makes our radar faulty, and a team is sent...well, you get the idea.

I go in the mess one day, and see Charlie Harper with this horrible red mark down his face. I said, "Bloody hell, Charlie, what the hell happened to you?" The mess goes quiet as Charlie appears from behind the bar and says, "Have you met my twin brother?" Shit, talk about feet first. I apologise profusely. Turns out the horrible red mark is a birth mark, oops.

After Portland, the ship and crew have an appointment with the ship's home city of Cardiff. We enter the dockside, it seems a hundred miles from anywhere, nothing but dereliction—it was obviously a thriving port a long time ago but now the heart has gone. In twenty years time developers will change it into a thriving waterside complex. Weekend leave is cancelled; and everyone is to attend the Lord Mayor's bash in the town hall; uniforms are the order of the day, and the city does us proud with plenty of food and drink.

On Sunday morning, an articulated lorry arrives at the end of the ship's gangway; the driver yells out to the quartermaster, "Can you pipe for chief Bell please?"

The QM obliges, and as Dinga gets to the gangway, the officer of the day is told to go and have a cup of tea, and this he does. Dinger now pipes for the duty watch to muster on the flight deck; he then details them off to his store. Twenty ratings are now in the process of loading an articulated lorry with various items from brass watering cans, chain hoists, to bales of rags. The full lorry then disappears through the docks (which by the way has no security,) to Dinger's bungalow in the forest, deep in the Devon countryside. The ship is probably now six inches higher out of the water, thanks to the de-storing exercise.

After our run ashore in Cardiff, the ship heads up the Irish Sea to Liverpool. Once up the Mersey, we park by the Liver Building. The gangway is no sooner down, than half the Liverpool police are on board—our mess entertains the CID, and these guys do like a drink, or two, or three, or ten. After four hours, these alcoholics invite us back to their gaff; silly us ask about ordering taxis. No problem, they tell us, they all have cars. We too have had a few, so the danger seems irrelevant, and we all pile into these unmarked police cars. The trip lasted for only a few minutes—let's face it—at 90 miles an hour, in the middle of Liverpool, going through red lights, with sirens blaring, it does not take long to travel five miles. This is the first time I have been rallying, and I can't say I enjoyed it; in fact, I nearly crapped myself. Most of our lads left the alkies to it after an hour and headed to the nearest Indian for some scran.

The next day the USS Bennington arrived in Liverpool; she is an old American aircraft carrier, and seems to be held together with rust. They send over an invite to our mess for brunch, and a few of our lads go over at around eleven. They are treated to T-bone steaks, hash browns, bacon, tomatoes, and a pair of eggs over easy (whatever that is), ketchup, and freshly cooked bread rolls, lucky buggers. I would have gone, but the secret committee, e.g. the mess president and his mates, kept it a secret till after the event. At around 12.30 they came back to our mess, with three American chiefs in tow. They even dressed up, bless; two of them had gold arms, more gold stripes on their jackets than sleeve, and of course the usual deluxe colour card of medal ribbons, most impressive I'm sure. The third guy was a lot younger and obviously had not been in four world wars and ten campaigns. He proved to be a real character.

The pints started flowing, and someone got the yard of ale glass down; not being a man of the world, the lad asked what it was. We told him it was a navy tradition for guests to drink a yard of ale as fast as possible. "No problem," he says, and we fill the glass. He tips it up to drink, the beer goes all over him, but he keeps going and downs the rest; we are impressed, then he says, "fill her up," and this time he drinks the yard without spilling a drop. This lad has got style, and by now he is getting a bit on the pissed side.

Charlie Harper suggests he upholds the tradition of the American navy by accepting a challenge from the Royal navy. "No problem," he says, and we explain the challenge. The two contestants kneel and face each other with a tablespoon in their mouths; the idea is to take it in turns to hit each other over the head with the spoon, and the one who lasts the longest is the winner. The young yank is the first to go; he tips his head back as far as he can and taps our guy on the head with the spoon, as our guy yells in pretend agony. It's now our guy's turn; he tips his head back to strike, and as his spoon is about to strike the yank's head, Charlie hits the yank full pelt with a heavy duty soup ladle.

"Jeeeeesus Christ, that hurt, you're for it this time, buddy," the yank says and with that, he attempts to knock our guy out with his next attempt, and our guy screams in pretend agony. After Charlie has hit the yank four or five times with the soup ladle, nearly decapitating him, the mess president decides he had better stop the game before a murder is committed. By now everyone in the mess is in hysterics; the two elder yanks think this is great, and cannot wait to get back to their ship and try it out on a certain mess member they don't particularly like. The boozing session now over, the yanks are escorted off the ship. The young one is a bit worse for wear, he has been sick, and is a little on the loud side; no doubt he will be in trouble when he gets back on board his ship. Still, so long as he enjoyed himself, eh.

After the Liverpool run ashore, we head back for Portsmouth and home. It's now the end of 1980. The ship is getting ready for a deployment to America, South America, and the West Indies in April of the next year. Storing ship is the order of the day, and everyone is involved; all the chiefs are piped to the gangway. Our beer has arrived from the Courage brewery, and we have to carry it from the lorry on the jetty, to various store rooms and spaces round the ship. Obviously, certain chiefs are on duty, and cannot carry out this duty. However, there are certain lazy bastards who choose to have very important jobs to do at this time, every time. One of them, a guy who drinks four times as much as anyone else (the mess alcoholic to be exact), but is never available to carry the barrels on board, is missing, again.

I go to the quartermaster's position and pipe for him; he arrives and starts shouting at me. I let him rant for a while, and when he has finished, I quietly tell him if he does not start carrying some barrels I will personally rip his head off his shoulders when we get back to the mess. He disappeared and I assumed he had gone below to help store the barrels; in fact, I found out after I had finished storing and gone down to the mess that he was in his cabin crying his eyes out. I think he must have taken me literally, the stupid big girl's blouse. I would not have thought a 16 stone muscle bosun would have reacted this way. It just goes to show, don't judge a book by its cover. Remind me not to be around him if we go to war.

167

The powers at be decide I have not enough to do, so they give me an extra job—explosive accountant. I have to go to Collingwood to do the course, and this means learning forty odd forms in a week. The forms cover every eventuality, ordering weapons, bullets, missiles, webbing, returning, transferring to other ships, forms for road, sea, and air, defective stores, permanent loan forms, temporary loan forms, you name it they have it covered. At the end of the week we are driven to the armament depot in Gosport to meet the civilians who deal with our forms. One particular dragon started to give us a hard time about filling in a particular form; she explained how we must fill it in properly. Big mouth asked her which forms she dealt with. "Just the one," was her reply. "And how long have you been doing this job?" I asked. Big smile told us, "Fifteen years."

"So you're quite used to it then."

"Oh yes."

"Well, let me tell you something. My job in the navy is administration, and taking charge of 30 odd, and I mean odd, sailors. My new job is filling in your form, and if necessary, every other person's form in this building, which by the way, we have just learnt in the last week, so please do not expect perfection." Gobsmacked, she apologised, the poor woman did not realise.

Back on board ship I organise a snap audit; I pull in all the temporary loan books and check gear against signatures, and any that are missing I re-order, and send the bill to the careless culprit. The officers of quarters are busy counting bullets, shells, missiles, torpedoes—not much missing on that side of things.

Back down at the mess things are getting heated; the alkies are moaning about the courage sparkling bitter, as it's coming out of the tap the colour of lager. The rep is sent for, he sees the problem, and has the cheek to tell us the caramel has settled to the bottom of the barrel. Caramel. What the hell is that doing in bitter? It appears the bitter is actually lager with caramel colouring. The reason, by all accounts, is bitter does not travel, especially on ships. Well, that's all right then; trading standards would have a ball with them today.

Picked up my monthly pay sheet today, £596.00 after tax, as a chief I am earning nearly as much as a police constable; it doesn't seem right somehow. I would not expect an able seaman to be earning as much as a police sergeant. Obviously, we sailors are not rated that highly by the government, a bit like the miners, I guess.

168

Alf Pickup

Someone high up in the admiralty has decided to reduce the crew. Five senior rates are to leave the ship and their jobs are to be handed over to those remaining. Around forty junior rates are also to leave the ship. The idea is they are supposed to be stationed in the dockyard as a standby work force for when we return from sea. The truth was, when we returned from our first trip all the men taken off the ship had been drafted. My boss told me I was to take over the hangar electrics, and I politely told him he would have to take on more of the admin, and he quickly scrubbed round the idea.

There is disquiet down in the junior rates mess; my office writer informs me that a big mouth lower deck lawyer in his mess is spreading discontent among the lads. I have a pipe made for all junior electrical rates to muster in their mess; the problem appears to be the painting of electrical compartments, not enough men and too many compartments, and Captain's rounds in two weeks time. I explain that senior rates will also be painting; the lower deck lawyer tells me that they don't have to do all this painting, as it's not in their job description. He has looked through Electrical standing orders—this gives everyone's job description—sure enough, painting is not actually mentioned, just cleaning.

"All right," I tell them, "no more painting." A big cheer goes up, and I then explain that their beer is a privilege, and from tomorrow will no longer be issued. Dead silence followed. I offer a compromise: "Your mouthpiece here will meet me in the hangar at 1600 hours. I will organise boxing gloves with the physical trainer, and we will fight to see who runs this department. If he wins, no painting and you keep your beer; if I win, you paint and get commended by the captain on your efforts, and keep your beer privilege. Is this agreed?"

Everyone seems to be for it, except for a certain surprised looking electrical mechanic. I return to the office, and at around 1530 a certain mechanic knocks the door. "Can I see you in private for a minute please, Chief?"

I meet him outside the office, as my boss goes by saying, "Everything all right, Chief?" "No problems, sir." The mechanic enters the office. "At least that's what I presume, am I right?" I ask.

"Yes, chief, I'm sorry, I didn't mean to be such a prat."

"Good. You won't mind going down to your mess and telling them then, will you?" From that day on, that lad became one of the best mechanics on the ship. During Captain's rounds, the department came through with flying colours. I got the senior rates to give me some cash, and I sent four crates of beer down to the junior rates mess. Harmony was restored.

Chapter Fourteen

Before we sail for the States, we have to ammunition ship. I've checked the accounts, and ordered enough ammo to make sure we will be topped up, ready for WW3. I also made a note on the order form: Dear Marge, hope the form is filled in to your satisfaction, love Alf. When the lighters (barges) arrived alongside, the officers of the quarters check the ammo off against an invoice as it is loaded. It can get embarrassing when a shell goes missing, but fortunately, it does not involve me, and so my head is safe. A final top up of fresh meat and vegetables and we're ready to sail.

An April Monday morning sees us leaving Portsmouth Harbour; as usual, family, friends, and holiday makers are there to wave us off, and from old Portsmouth to Southsea front they line the shore. The ship's company is dressed in their number ones and line the decks; I am down below at my special sea duty station, ready for the gyro to go tits up. Fortunately, we manage to get into the English Channel without mishap. Our next port of call is Bermuda, a series of small islands 21 miles long in the north Atlantic.

The weather holds well, and after three days at sea the first lieutenant organises a sods opera, which consists of anyone with a modicum of talent getting up on a makeshift stage and performing in front of the crew. The ship's comedians, the singers, the poets, and most worrying, the transvestites, all have a go. The worrying thing about the lady men is their outfits and make up, as they appear in lovely dresses, lipstick, and rouge? They claimed to have got their clothes from the bales of rags down in the engine room; the biggest rag I've ever got out of a bale was half a shirt, never a silk chiffon turquoise evening dress with sequins in mint condition. As for lipstick and rouge, well, the nearest you'll get to anything red on a ship is damage control paint. Now these guys are either professional actors disguised as Matelots with their own wardrobes, or dodgy, to say the least.

I organised a beard growing competition in aid of the ship's charity, which if I remember correctly, was for a blind dog. It was to last two weeks, each contestant put in £2.00, and bets were taken to add to the charity pot.

First prize was two crates of beer. After a week I was accused of match fixing, as I appeared to have the most fluff on my face. To save my reputation I shaved off, and I could not have been happier; how people can wear them things all the time is beyond me, what with all that itching and scratching, and combing soup and noodles out of it, yuk. As I recall, a stoker won the beer and nearly caused a riot down in his mess, he refused to share any of it, the selfish bastard. Fortunately, he had such a bad rash under his hedge he could not shave it off, so he was stuck with it till the weather cooled on the way back to the UK. That'll learn him.

While I was in my office one day I had one of my inventive moments. I was thinking, what chance would you have if you fell over the side? The truth is, not much; presumably you would be lucky enough to have a life jacket on and would stay afloat, but the chances of being spotted would be remote. The pathetic plastic whistle that is attached is fresh out of a Christmas cracker, and a 1.5 volt lamp is a bloody joke. I thought, how could a man overboard be spotted easily? The answer, I thought, would be a day glow orange, two foot diameter balloon with aluminium strips all round it, attached to a fifty foot line to the life jacket. The balloon would of course be deflated and velcro'ed to the life jacket to start with; a small hydrogen bottle with a ring pull would inflate it when required, like the new style life jackets. The day glow would make it visible in the daytime, while the aluminium strips would ensure a contact on radar at night.

I wandered down to the ship's office and got the appropriate invention and suggestion form and filled it in. I bandied my idea around for reactions; most thought it a brilliant idea, and the jealous ones suggested a bigger balloon so they could fly back to the ship, very funny, I'm sure. Having filled in the form I put it in my boss's intray, ready for him to forward it to the ship's office. They in turn would give it to the captain for approval; it would then be forwarded to admiralty for assessment, and hopefully a few quid for me. The Navy would then hold the patent if it were ever manufactured; they would get to keep the millions in royalties, and we mugs would get a few hundred quid for the idea—nobody said life was fair in the navy.

The trip to Bermuda was uneventful weather wise; our arrival in Hamilton Harbour was met with the usual local dignitaries dressed to kill, and ready to drink the wardroom dry. The crew had to dress up to impress as usual—there's nothing like British sailors in their number one uniforms lining the decks round a ship, pride bursting from every chest. Once the ship was secure alongside, the electrical department is mustered on the upper deck and detailed off to floodlight ship. This means aluminium booms round the ship are clipped into deck sockets and hung over the side parallel to the deck, and wire lines secure them. The outboard ends of the booms have fibre glass shades to deflect the light up the superstructure. Heavy duty cables run round the ship, and all the boom lights are plugged into them via waterproof plug and sockets; these cables are plugged into an upper deck socket on the superstructure which in turn goes direct to the main switchboard. Necklaces are also strung round in appropriate dark spots; the overall effect is fantastic. Walt Disney would have been proud.

Bermuda is a paradise unequalled anywhere, with pink coral beaches, golf courses, and spectacular scenery. All the houses and bungalows are painted in pastel colours with water tanks on their roofs; the gardens remind one of England in the spring. Roads here are very narrow, hence the speed limit of 20 mph. I was told residents are only allowed one car, which is a bit of a bummer if you are a billionaire. Still, I suppose you can only drive one vehicle at a time.

The other main form of transport is the scooter, of which jolly Jack takes a shine to; the hire company had five less to rent out at the end of our stay, and our sick bay attendant had his share of repairs to our budding Barry Sheens also. I had a wander round Hamilton and found everything very expensive, probably due to the fact everything is imported. On my pay, I could live here for half a day a week before running out of cash. The protocol here is to greet the locals with a good morning, or good whatever time of day it is, and you are considered very rude if you fail to do this. The resulting service you will get reflects this.

The visit over, we have no problem with drunken sailors, due to the fact no one could afford to get drunk. The floodlighting is taken down and stowed; fresh meat, fruit, and vegetables are loaded; and we are ready to sail to Belize, formerly British Honduras. The reason: terrorists from Guatemala are causing trouble and a show of strength by us Brits is required. Evidently, a British war ship will do the trick, like we're going to sail into the jungle and sort them out. We sail on the morning tide and head south for the Caribbean. On the way, we exercise with a couple of Yankee ships and a submarine, all good stuff, keeping us honed and ready for the Russian threat when, and if, required.

My pay slip shows I earned £596 after tax this particular month, and I hardly know what I will spend it on. My laundry bill is £6; this Chinese crew charges more than Chapman's, the robbing bastards. My bar bill is £11.50, so I suspect someone has been putting my bar number down instead of his own. Now, I will buy anyone a drink, but someone here is taking the piss.

Certain members of the mess, who appear to be in a constant state of alcoholic haze, seem to have unusually small bills. I approach the mess president and mention this. A mess meeting is called. I propose a barman is employed using the messmen, and I suggest they be paid from the mess funds. Their job will be to serve and mark down each individual drink served into a book, and in the event of the absence of a barman, individuals will get a witness to sign their chits. This is seconded and the motion carried; my next bill, along with the alkies', is much more realistic.

After several days at sea, we anchor off Belize—all you could see was jungle—Christ, what a godforsaken place, hot and humid, and a brown sea to boot. A boat comes out from shore; it's full of British soldiers and the NCO's come down our mess for a drink. Someone suggests they might want to have a shower first, due to the fact that someone heaved; it seemed like they had not bathed for a month or three. They jumped at the chance, but unfortunately, their clothes did not go in with them and the smell persisted—it reminded me of the pig farm in Collingwood. The following day we were invited to their camp, and while their mess was adequate with plenty of booze, the rest of their facilities were abysmal, and the local village was pretty third world, with little or no infrastructure. These army guys spent weeks in the jungle searching out the infiltrating neighbours from Guatemala, no wonder they stank.

The RAF had two Harriers jump jets stationed in Belize—why, I don't know—it's not as if they could see anything other than jungle or sea once they were airborne. Typical of the Bryllcreem boys, they made no attempt to fraternise with us lowly sailors; obviously nobody told them we were the senior service.

After a week in this hell hole, we sailed for Nassau, the capital city and commercial centre of the Bahamas. It is located on Providence Island; it became popular with the Yanks after their government banned travel to Cuba. Our ship was parked away from the cruise liner berths, as they obviously did not want us riff raff upsetting the rich yanks as they disembarked. One thing that was noticeable was the local black lads, dressed in smart suits, shoes, and fedora hats. They waited at the end of the cruise ships' gangways, ready to waltz the ugly, fat American women away to the local hotels—those guys deserved more than fifty bucks, they deserved a bloody medal.

The town centre was full of colonial architecture; the roads in the town seemed to be in reasonable repair for a change. A statue of Queen Victoria stood in the middle of the green—makes you proud to be British, even for us naturalized ones. The local drug dealers could be seen driving around in their blacked out Cadillacs, popping their heads out of the cars' windows now and again to offer ganja, or snow, whatever that is. All Jack wanted was a nice cool beer, or a rum and coke, both bottles of which cost the same by the way. Like today really, people moan about the price of petrol but are happy to pay the same price for a litre of water?

Sport was organised with the locals over the next few days. I had a game of rugby which we lost, and the cricket faired no better. The golfers, on the other hand, came back in their usual state, not remembering whether they had won or lost, but happy nonetheless. During our three day stay, six liners came in belching out fat Americans; those poor black lads must have had sore willies at the end of that particular week. They sowed their wild oats and planted enough seeds to colonise Wales, or a thousand acre field, all good for race relations I suppose.

Our next port of call was Santa Domingo, the capital of the Dominican Republic. Situated half way up the east coast of the country, the top half of this island of Hispaniola is Haiti. Santa Domingo is the oldest city in the new world; it has the oldest hospital and the oldest cathedral, and most of the buildings are of Spanish colonial architecture. The streets in the old quarters are cobbled; it's like going back in time to the sixteenth century. The city is open twenty-four hours a day. I went ashore and bought a few bits—amber seems to be popular so I got the wife a necklace and my mother in law a little something. I also bought five pounds of coffee. British influence here seemed to be nonexistent, as we were not required to do all the pomp and ceremony stuff. We just pulled in like any other vessel and parked aft of a huge merchantman. The harbour was one of the busiest I had come across after Hong Kong.

The next morning, a Roman Catholic priest came on board to see the captain; he requested that some of the crew should go with him to help build a school in the mountains. A notice was put up asking for volunteers, a hundred and twenty people signed on, and fifty were drawn out of the hat. I was fortunate to be selected. Meals and drinks were packed ready for the early morning trip the next day. The bus arrived, and we all piled on— this had also been bummed off the local bus company by the priest. This was his forte, getting people and companies to part with stuff for free, so he could help the villagers in his diocese. We set off and headed for the mountains, and outside town we passed a bridge over the river Ozama— the river was dry, and a whole village was based on its bed. The priest told us it was the only fertile place to grow crops, but when the river floods many of the villagers will be swept away to sea, along with all their belongs. Christ, what a way to make a living. Two miles down the road I spotted a melon stall; I stopped the bus and got off, the price was only a few Pesos' each, and so cheap I bought the lot. Back on the bus we cut them up and shared them, and there were still dozens left over to take up to our mountain village. The main road to our destination went from tarmac to gravel to mud; in fact, it got bloody dangerous the further we went. At one stage we had to disembark the bus and push it over a stream, and then we had to get off so we didn't end up down a four hundred foot chasm, as the wheels of the bus sent rocks flying over the edge. I can only guess this was not the local bus route to Tesco.

Our arrival at the village brought out the whole community who seemed to regard us as long lost friends, and everyone was smiling and cheering. Father Patrick did a speech and quick prayer in Spanish, followed by one in English for our benefit, basically saying we were here to help build the school. We started work pretty much straight away, as time was of the essence; the foundations had already been dug so we set to, doing the block work, and the shipwright and his team knocked up the windows and door frames. Pretty soon we were up to six courses, with frames in place, and the next job was to arrange a scaffold so we could go higher.

The amazing thing was all the materials and tools we needed were on hand. This priest had procured the lot from American firms; his main concern was the erosion of the land caused by the felling of trees for fuel. Up to the time we were there, he and his flock had re-planted a hundred and fifty thousand trees, all brought in as saplings from Canada. I wouldn't be surprised if the place was a rainforest by now. Lunch time arrived on the site and we downed tools for half an hour. Our bag meals and excess melons came out of the bus, and a lot of the villagers came out, not to join us, but to watch, confused. I asked the priest what was going on.

It appeared that food was a bit of a rarity in these parts. I consequently went round the lads asking who'd had breakfast. Those that did, I took their bag meals and gave them to the astonished villagers; in fact, all the Matelots donated their food in the end. At least we were certain of a meal when we got back on board, unlike these poor buggers. It might not have been as good as the bread and fishes story in the bible, but at least the locals thought of it as a small miracle.

We cracked on after our break and by mid-afternoon we were ready to put the joists and roof beams up. By tea time, the corrugated roof was on, and the floor inside was concreted over; a dozen Matelots were adding the finishing touches to the outside rendering. It may not have passed the building inspector's inspection, or regulations, but I bet it's still standing. Father Patrick and his flock were over the moon with our efforts. We told him to leave it for a few days before painting, or giving lessons to the kids. He told us he was expecting a diesel generator in the next few weeks, so he could light the place up—is there nothing that guy can't bum?

Alf Pickup

Most of our lads would have liked to have stayed and helped this guy; he was an inspiration to us all. We packed our gear and boarded the bus, and most of us were so knackered we fell asleep on the way back. Fortunately, the driver negotiated the road back without us having to get off and push, or going down a mountainside into a ravine. Back on board ship we showered and dragged the duty chef out to knock us up some tea and bacon butties; we were starving after all, or should I say very hungry.

Three days later we set sail for Puerto Rico, no fuss, no ceremony; we just pulled in the ropes and slid out of the harbour almost unnoticed. There on the last outcrop was our priest, Father Patrick, waving his arms and blowing us kisses, bless. A week or two later when the mail caught us up, we received a letter thanking us for our efforts, and a photograph of him and the kids by the school. These now take pride of place, on show in the Captain's flat.

Today, I am in need of a haircut. The ship's barber, a three badge able seaman, hacks away with his 1950 clippers which have probably gone through the equivalent of the Spanish armada's crews, and cut enough hair to fill a barn. Still, at sixty pence, who am I to complain? Back in the mess, the Chief shipwright is knitting a roll neck jumper to give his son when he gets back home—tight bugger, too mean to buy him a proper present. You can just imagine what his son has to go through when he gets to school. "What did your daddy bring you back from his travels? Oooh, a handmade jumper. I got a train set, a baseball glove, a bat and ball, and a Yankee sweat shirt."

The night before arriving at San Juan, we have a bit of a party; the nauseating chief steward takes the stage, and goes through his usual repertoire of sea shanties and dirty songs—this guy knows them all, but I doubt whether he even knows his four times tables. Mind you, from what I've heard, he serves a mean cup of coffee for the skipper. After a few beers and whiskies, I decide to get my head down; my cabin is a three berth and is nice and quiet, away from the noisy Chiefs lounge. I soon drift off and dream of home. At around two in the morning I am woken by the sound of a drunken brawl in my flat. I get up to see what is going on—two stokers are beating the shit out of each other, and the master at arms and I break them apart. It appears they were having a few beers and showing each other photographs of their girl friends. Guess what? Same photo, same girlfriend.

Next morning we tie up alongside San Juan, the walled city. This place reeks of history: castles, forts, pirates, and cobbled streets. Being American, there is a heavy military presence here, and consequently a PX shop, their equivalent of our NAAFI, only bigger, much, much bigger. I venture inside and get some toys and stuff for the kids and a few bits for my wife. I also buy six boxes of King Edward cigars—these sell at six dollars for a box of fifty, but back home they will bring £1.50 for each one, or I'll eat my hat.

On this trip I decided to stop smoking, and consequently, all the tight-fisted bastards in the mess offer me a cigarette, something that would have been unheard of previously. I accept their offers and crush them in the ashtray, and after this display, the offers strangely stop.

After a short sightseeing trip round the town, I head back to the ship, as I have work to do. The ship will de-ammunition when we return to Portsmouth and, consequently, this means loads of paperwork for me. I hate this administration crap—they have the cheek to call me a Chief electrician when the nearest I get to tools is putting a plug on my desk fan. Several of my young charges are studying to take their leading rate exams, so to help them, I organise a roster for senior ratings to instruct them. This does not go down well with all; fortunately, my boss sees the good side of my idea and makes it so. After a month of daily instruction, all the lads pass both the oral and written exams with flying colours. I am invited down the junior rates mess for a few tinnies to thank me, and to celebrate their achievement. My boss is so pleased with the result that he instructs me to organise training for all junior rates. He even had electrical standing orders rewritten to include this; normally it is up to individuals to study on their own to pass these exams, so the added help was a bonus.

News just in says that Bobby Sands has died; he was the IRA guy who went on hunger strike. This dead anorexic Irishman is now causing trouble, and we have gone to code red security. Now we have armed sailors on the gangway, which on its own is a worry, as sailors and guns do not mix. I often wonder how Ireland would be if someone came forward and said there had been a terrible mistake in history, and actually all the Protestants were in fact Catholics, and vice versa? Back in Bermuda there are riots at the airport, so it looks like we could be called back there at any time. Later in the day, the captain broadcasts that we will still be going home on schedule, which is a relief, as I can't wait to get home and see the family.

After five days alongside, we refuel and store ship and we sail the next morning for home. The weather is hot and the sea moderate—this will be the last chance to top up our tans, not that many will need it, as the crew already look like a Zulu raiding party. People keep busy over the next few days: the sailors painting over rust, the stokers keeping us on the move, the pinkies (radio department) and the greenies (electrical department) taking things apart and putting them back together again, as laid down in daily, monthly, and annual maintenance schedules, all this in between trying to fix faults. And just so we don't get too bored, the skipper has us doing damage control exercises, just in case we hit an iceberg, I suppose.

At tea time, four o'clockers are served up—this is a snack to have with a cup of tea after work; it may be a wagon wheel, or cake knocked up by the duty chef. In the evenings we have eight o'clockers—this is a suppertime treat, boiled eggs, cheese and bread, that sort of thing. Invariably, there is food left over, and any eggs left in our mess were quickly taken by one of the Mechs and pickled in vinegar; the bottle he kept in his cabin. This was all well and good till we hit a drop of roughers, and the jar and his eggs smashed on the deck. You would not believe the smell in that cabin, no amount of scrubbing or cleaning could get rid of it; it was still bad when I left the ship six months later.

The ship's quiz takes place each evening; all messes and the wardroom take part, and a crate of beer is the prize for the champions. The Chiefs mess wins, with the stokers mess runners up, the wardroom comes fifth, which does not bode well for confidence in our masters. We send the crate of beer down to the stokers, and it is much appreciated. I go through a book a day on the way home; I first check to see if the last few pages are there before I start to read, as a certain member of the mess thought it a good idea to remove them, then charge people a couple of pints so they could retrieve them to finish the book. He soon stopped the habit when the chief chippy removed the sleeves from his number eight working shirt, and demanded six gins for their return. He also loosened the stitches on the crotch of the guy's number one suit trousers. I can't wait for the next divisions; it should be quite a sight. I bet your life he has a sense of humour failure.

Our arrival in Portsmouth was met with a few people waving at us from Southsea front, and old Portsmouth; we berthed at South Railway Jetty. The usual dockyard mateys were there to tie us up, a few of the officer's wives had been allowed in, but no families had been invited due to the busy schedule over the next few days. The custom boys came on board and did their usual taxation of goods; these humourless bastards don't give an inch, and by the time they stick their ten Penarth on, you might just as well have gone into Marks and Sparks for your presents. I declared the kids' toys and a few bits for the wife—the cigars, well, I forgot. I won't be taking them home on the first night ashore that's for sure. The dockyard cops tend to be a bit keen on stop and search for the first few days after a ship comes in from an overseas trip.

Once the shore telephone lines and shore electricity supplies are connected, leave is granted. My wife meets me outside Unicorn gate; we

179

drive to the Dolphin Pub in Havant for a drink and a chat. My girls are at home with my mother in law, and I am keen to see them; it seems a life time since I last saw them. After a couple of swift halves in the pub, we head home. The girls seem as pleased to see me as I am to see them; they appear to have grown since I left a few months ago.

We are due to go into dry dock, so next day the ship is cold moved to Fountain Lake Jetty. Here we de-ammunition ship—all explosives, bullets, and missiles are lowered into barges, or lighters as they are known; these will then be towed into the middle of the harbour and parked till we come out of dry dock. A fuel barge comes alongside and the ship's fuel is pumped out into it. The ship is now ready to be towed into the basin, then dry dock. The dock gates open and we gently ease in; on either side of the ship are floating one foot square beams, which are held in position with ropes. They will hold the ship upright once the dock is pumped dry. The dock gates are closed once we are in position, and massive pumps start up, emptying the dock, as the ship's keel bottoms; dock workers hammer the beams into position, using wooden wedges as required. The gangway is craned into place, shore phones and power supplies are connected, and we are up and running again.

Chapter Fifteen

At home, my wife and I have set up for bed and breakfast. I head for a car number plate maker in Portsmouth, and he knocks me up two bed and breakfast signs; these highly reflective signs are hung outside the front of the house for passing cars to light up—cheaper than neons, eh what. The girls are shunted into the spare bedroom; my wife and I sleep downstairs, and the guests have two double rooms to choose from. In August, I purchase a four berth caravan for £250 from a mate on the ship. He kindly tows it down from Devon, and we manoeuvre it down the side of the house. This now becomes the girls', and their friends', full size Wendy house and sleeping berth. I now also have another bedroom to let.

My wife contacts David and Anne Eckersley-Maslin (he is by now an Admiral) for dinner. Christ, what was she thinking? Hard to believe, but they accepted. We laid on the usual 1980's meal: prawn cocktail, peppered steak, and some sickly sweet, and a couple of bottles of blue nun; how impressive was that? I know, not very. During the main course the front door opened, and the family who booked in earlier plodded in and up the stairs to their room. The look of amazement on David and Anne's face was a picture. "Ssorry, did I forget to tell you we do bed and breakfast?" I said. The rest of the evening went very well.

Now, I don't know many posh people, but those two are the most down to earth, nicest people you could wish to meet. They left at around ten, thanking us for a super meal, with the lovely Anne giving me a farewell hug and a kiss, and David a hand shake, telling me to keep in touch, yeah, right. I don't recall any Chiefs contacting admirals for a run ashore in my lifetime—still, nice of him to offer.

Meanwhile, back on the ship, things are moving a pace, new equipment is fitted, and modifications done. After a few months the ship is ready for harbour and sea trials, the dock is flooded, and we are pushed into the harbour. The ship is topped up with fuel, and the ammunition is brought back on board. The only snag is the dockyard has lost four of our Mk 46 torpedoes. I go through my paperwork and inform them to look in lighter number 45. They eventually find the lighter tied up alongside in Gosport—naughty, it should have been in the middle of the harbour, in case of an explosion. With harbour trials complete we set sail, and the ship is put through her paces; weapons, radar, and machinery are all tested to the max, and we are now ready for work up at Portland.

We arrive at Portland in a force eight gale, and anchor in the harbour, as it is too rough to go alongside. The flag officer sea training staff come out to us in a motor launch, and most are looking a bit green after the bouncy trip out. They start us off with a fire and flood exercise, not much fun when you are bouncing off the bulkheads. Didn't anyone tell these twats that navies don't fight in gales? At the end of day one, the clearing up is completed, the smoke is cleared, the water mopped up, and the damage control gear stowed away. It is time for the wash up in the wardroom, and it seems like we didn't do too badly considering. The poor FOST staff has now got to go ashore and write out a full report for our Captain in the morning. Considering it is now eight o'clock at night, and they have to be back on board at seven in the morning, I don't envy their job.

After two days, the weather calms down and we come alongside. At nine o'clock in the morning I receive an invitation card from the flag officer sea training, inviting me up to his mansion on the hill for lunch. I then realise it's my old mate, David. Chuffed to bits, I scribble a quick letter off to my wife and post the invite to show her. I now have to see my boss so I can have a make and mend to get ashore; he laughs and tells me not to take the piss, as nobody is allowed ashore. I explain the Admiral wants me to have lunch with him. "Of course he does, did he phone you, or send his butler?" he asks. I tell him I received an invitation card by messenger. "Fine," he says, "you won't mind me seeing it then, will you?" Well, actually, I've posted it to my wife.

I offer a compromise and say to him, "I will be on the gangway at twelve o'clock in my number one uniform; if the admiral's staff car arrives for me, can I have a make and mend?"

"No problem," he says. I am on the gangway at twelve; my boss is hanging over the bridge wings, watching me as I go down the gangway. Just then the staff car arrives. I step into the Admiral's car; I couldn't help but wave as we sped off. At the mansion I am greeted by my mate David (just joking Admiral, in case you ever read this). I salute him; he returns it, and shakes hands with me, "Hello, Alf, how are you?" "Very well, sir, and you?"

The conversation carries on; he asks about my family, and how things are going on the ship, and I feel strangely at ease with this great man. Once inside he offers me a drink, and we head for the dining room, where his

182

steward brings us soup and this is followed by the main course. I am not over impressed with what they are feeding my boss; this is reflected by the fact David apologises for it not being as good as the meal we served him at our house. I presume this is a compliment on my meal, rather than him casting dispersions on his chef. After the meal David apologises again, saying he has an appointment and we must leave; we both get in the staff car, which by now has his flag fluttering on the wing. As we go through the dockyard and pass the ships alongside, the shrill sound of the piping still can be heard, Matelots spring to attention, and officers salute as we pass.

At the end of our gangway, the car stops and I get out; I salute David and thank him for lunch. The car then speeds off to his next appointment. As I board the ship, the officer of the day comments how nice it was of the admiral to give me a lift, and I reply, "Not a lift, son, a lunch." He was a young lad after all. Just as I am about to go and get changed, the broadcast booms out my name, saying I must go to the Captain's cabin—bloody hell, now what? I arrive outside his cabin and knock on the door. "Enter," he calls out. Not come in, not who is it, not what the hell do you want, but "enter." I felt like saying, "entering now," but thought better of it. The nosy bugger wants to know what I was doing in the Admiral's car. I tell him the story, from when I used to babysit his children to the present day situation. He seemed a bit pissed off, due to the fact he had never been invited to dine with him. I felt like saying it's not what you know, it's who you know. I must say I left the captain feeling a bit smug.

After Portland sea training, the ship returned to Portsmouth and Christmas leave, and my new draft comes through—I am to join HMS Vernon in charge of the sonar workshop for the minesweeper squadron. I would not normally consider this a problem, but the fact I was not booked into Collingwood to do any pre-joining training was a worry. I'm supposed to take charge of something I know nothing about. After all, I'm not an MP—they are used to doing jobs without any knowledge.

The Christmas period arrives on board ship, and all the messes are decked out in decorations. The chefs are busy cooking the turkeys and plum duff for the single men, and those who are married but who don't live locally, commonly known as victualed in. We who live ashore get bugger all as we are known as victualed out. The petty officer chef is seen walking around the ship's passageways with what appears to be a twelve inch penis hanging out the front of his white trousers; it is, in fact, a turkey's neck with its heart stitched on the end, and it is most life like, even if the first lieutenant didn't appreciate it. No sense of humour, some people.

My mate, Alan, from way back on the Devonshire pops on board to see me, and wants to know if I am interested in selling copper-etched pictures of the Cardiff. Of course I agree, there is a £3 profit to be made on each one sold. I get permission and start advertising. Pretty soon I am ordering them by the dozen; everyone seems to want one or two. Alan tells me he has a rep on most ships, and four market stalls. One thing that confused me was the fact he was wearing a Petty Officer's uniform, when I knew for sure he was a Chief Mech, and I asked him about it. He explained he was on HMS Bristol which did frequent trips to the USA. While there he would go to the PX and spend a few thousand quid on King Edward cigars. He had a whole compartment filled with them, and once back in the UK he would sell them at a huge profit. Unfortunately, he sold some to a dockyard matey; this prick got searched going out of Unicorn gate, and ratted on Alan. He was arrested and got ninety days detention, and de-rated to PO. The regulating staff in DQ's hated him, mainly because he was a fitness freak and loved it. He lost his stock of cigars, but undeterred, he went out and bought himself a Mercedes convertible on what he had sold already.

Alan popped back to see me just a few weeks before Christmas; he had six bottles of perfume with him, and an airline brochure showing one of them priced at £25—this was the sweetener for the buying public. I was to buy them in packs of six for £4.50 off Alan, and sell them for a tenner. Now jolly Jack, being basically a lazy bugger and too idle to go shopping, found this a perfect way to buy Christmas presents for his girlfriend, his mother, his niece, and three other unfortunate females. The toilet water was probably just that, with a bit of added smell. Alan also brought me socket sets for £2.00, which I sold on for a fiver. My family and I had a very happy Christmas and so far, a prosperous new year.

I'm still waiting to hear from Admiralty about my life jacket balloon idea, as it's been six months since I put it in. My boss, a lieutenant commander, has gone on draft to his new appointment, so there is no point in asking the new guy what's going on. I head for the ship's office and ask to see the file on inventions and suggestions, and guess what? Nothing, the official form I filled in did not even reach the ship's office, let alone get seen by the Captain and posted off. I thought, that bastard has forgotten to put it in. Oh well, I'll just have to do it all over again.

Fate meanwhile played a strange trick. That very night on the BBC programme Tomorrow's World, the presenter was in the middle of London explaining to viewers that she was lost, and how easy it would be to locate her from the air using, guess what? That's right, my bloody balloon, right down to the same design. I thought about contacting the Mafia and putting a contract out on that thieving bastard. (Sue me if you dare, I have a Photostat copy of my invention, and it's dated.)

Instead I put a complaint in to see the Captain, and the next day I'm in front of the Commander, explaining why I want to see the Captain. He politely informs me not to bother, as it is probably all just a coincidence. I guess we mustn't cast dispersions on an officer and a gentleman. Personally, I think it warrants bloody court martial, as he not only stole from me, but the navy as well. I bet the swine has a villa in the south of France on the proceeds of his dastardly act. I just hope one day, while on his yacht, he falls over the side in the middle of the Mediterranean, and forgets his life jacket and balloon. That would be justice.

My commission on HMS Cardiff is coming to an end; my relief arrives and I hand over the job. I introduce him to the lads and the divisional chiefs. As he settles in, I clear my locker, and pack my kit bag and suitcase, ready for living ashore. I do my leaving routine, letting everyone know I am leaving. I pay my final mess bill. The junior rates invite me down to their mess for a farewell drink, and naturally they try to get me pissed, but I'm having none of it. After three cans I depart, thanking them for their support; evidently, I'm a jolly good fellow by all accounts, and so said all of them.

The third of February 1982, I join HMS Vernon. I find the regulating office and do the rounds; hello, I'm here, everybody. I eventually find my workshop, and introduce myself to two chiefs, a leading rate, and four mechanics. One of the chiefs, Ray, is an old shipmate of mine from the Fife, and two of the lads I know from Gibraltar. I'm feeling at home already. Ray takes me round and shows me the ropes. I tell him that, technically, he will be in charge, as I have no knowledge of minesweepers or their equipment. I told him that I will be hanging off his apron strings till I accumulate some knowledge—nothing like on job learning, it beats books. Our spare gear department seems to lack spares; I get the leading hand to get me a list of what we should have, and it seems like a lot has been used and not replaced. I make it a priority to top up, and next I check the tool boxes, again not well.

I send a lad over to naval stores with a demand note for new tools; he comes back saying the chief stores won't let him have any, because the store will be left empty. I tell my lad to type out a letter stating, "I, the Chief stores, take full responsibility if any mine sweeper cannot be repaired and made seaworthy due to lack of tools being issued from my stock." Get him to sign it. If he refuses give him letter two: "If the tools are not issued in the next half hour, a copy of letter number one will be sent to the Weapons engineering officer, and the stores officer, stating you would not sign it, or part with YOUR tools. With a supplement stating the tools being demanded are in your store, and available. Have a nice day!"

Within ten minutes of the lad going back to the store, I receive a phone call from the chief stores, and he is slightly irate to say the least. I explain my job is to repair minesweepers, and your job is to provide me with the tools to do it, so please can I have the tools? If it leaves you short in your stock, surely, all you have to do is re-order. It's called supply and demand, I demand and you supply. He eventually agrees, after I explained the letters I sent were just a joke (NOT).

After a few weeks I get into the swing of things; I quickly find the sweepers tend to come in for repairs at inopportune times, like two in the morning for instance, and consequently, we have to be available to be called in at a moment's notice. One day we get a call from the dockyard asking us to provide a sweep cable for an American Sweeper. Now this cable is a huge piece of kit that sits on a reel at the back of the boat. It is by its very nature a thick cable, an electrical wire surrounded by cork, so it will float when sweeping for mines. It is lowered over the stern and let out to form a loop; once let out, a huge current is passed through it, and this in turn provides a magnetic field which detonates any magnetic mines. Fortunately, we have a spare; I phone up and order a low loader lorry from the transport pool in the dockyard to pick it up; the crane on Vernon's jetty will load it on the lorry. The lorry arrives, the loading goes well, the cable reel is secured, no problems, till we reach the main gate that is. Traffic outside is halted as the cab of the lorry inches out into the main road, then, disaster—the reel gets jammed under the arch of the gate. Forcing it would probably bring the gate crashing down round our ears, time for a re-think. The only way that thing was going to get unstuck was to lower the cable reel; obviously, we had to let the tyres down on the loader to ease it out of the gate. The problem now was we had a lorry and trailer in the middle of a main road with flat tyres, oops.

Two hours later, the lorry's and the low loader's tyres are pumped up. And we're off—I'm riding shotgun in the lorry so I can oversee the job in hand. On arrival at Fountain Lake Jetty I meet the Captain of the sweeper. I ask him when the mobile crane is arriving, and he does not know. I phone the crane department in the dockyard. "Where's the crane for the yanks' boat?" I ask. The driver is on his lunch break, I'm told. "Sorry, I did not realize Portsmouth dockyard only had one crane driver; I must contact the Captain of the dockyard and rectify the problem." Within ten minutes a crane magically appeared. The old reel was lifted off the boat, and the new one fitted. Another job well done, now I had to trek back through the dockyard to Vernon and lunch.

The following week I am nominated as duty mess president; it's not an arduous duty, it just means keeping the Chiefs mess bar open, and locking up at closing time. At around eight o'clock a couple of Chiefs come in the mess covered in oil and grease. As they are not allowed in the mess unless properly dressed, I have to refuse them entry. However, I am able to get them a couple of pints, which they can legally drink in the hallway. I join them in the hall and start chatting to them; I ask them what they are working on. It seems the clutch has gone on their Mini; they have spent the last five hours trying to remove the old one, they have ruined a pair of pullers hired from the local tool shop, and got bruised and cut to bits in the process. Mr. Know It All with experience from Gibraltar offers to do it for the price of a couple of pints. They accept my offer; we head to the welfare garage, which is kindly provided by the navy for poor Matelots who can't afford to pay garages, e.g., do it yourself. Inside is the dead Mini, and I tell the guys I have no intention of getting dirty. I ask them to remove the starter motor, and they look at me with blank expressions. It's the clutch, not the starter motor, they tell me. "Trust me, I'm a doctor."

The starter is removed. "Now, you see the hole left by the motor?" "Yes." "Well, that toothed thing in there is the fly wheel, and that sits behind the clutch plate; now, if you get yourself a nice big hammer and give it a belt, then turn the engine over and repeat the process, you might be surprised with the result." Four bangs later, the clutch plate falls out. "Now, about those pints." Two gobsmacked Chiefs and me head for the mess.

One of the lads in the workshop appears to have a lump of hair stuck on the back of his head. I tug it, and a small pony tail drops down.

"What the hell is that?" I ask.

"It's for when I go ashore," he tells me.

"Well, unless you've put in a request form to grow it, and have it tarred, as per naval regulations, I'm afraid it's coming off."

He was a big bugger, and it took three of us to hold him down while I removed the offending locks with a pair of sharp scissors. No Christmas card from him this year then.

The main mine detection sonar in the mine sweeper is situated in the middle of a mess deck; the transducer is held in place with a ring of studs and bolts, and a block and tackle takes the weight off the transducer while the ring is unbolted. I left one of my lads to slacken off the bolts while I got the block and tackle. By the time I got back, the lad had removed all but two of the bolts; another two minutes and the sonar would have been on the bottom of Portsmouth Harbour. I spent the next ten minutes explaining the difference between slackening and undoing to my little friend. Fortunately, we managed to get the block and tackle attached before any harm was done to either the sonar or my career.

Chapter Sixteen

March 1982, the Argentines invade the Falkland Islands, and Maggie Thatcher organises an invasion force to recapture them. On the fifth of April, I am standing on the quayside along with the ship's company of Vernon waving off the biggest task force since the Second World War. Everyone seems excited and in anticipation about what is to come, but I personally felt despair, as I had mates on the Glasgow and Coventry. No one ever wins in a war, why these politicians could not have sorted it out before it came to this I do not know. Give them the left island (uninhabited), and keep the right one—there, how easy would that have been.

Over the next few months I was proved right to worry, as ship after ship was sunk. I often wondered if that Admiral at Portland thought about what I said about the old fashioned training in damage control, as ship after ship was hit with Exocet and bombs, and sunk.

Back at work, the sweepers are coming in for repairs at a pace; it's like trying to keep a Morris Oxford going that travels from lands end to John O'Groats every week.

Chain hoists arrive at the workshop; unfortunately, we ordered resistors, and trying to return them proved almost impossible; the Chief stores did not want to know. This is the same prat who refused us tools a few months ago because he did not want to empty his store. In general, the stores are taking ages to get, all due to the priority of the task force in the South Atlantic. We are getting to the stage of cannibalizing boats in refit to keep the sea going ones going, not an ideal situation.

Back at home, I draw plans up to build a conservatory; I send them off to the council for building approval. They come back a month later giving me the go ahead, so I order bricks, shingle, and cement. The foundations are dug and the concrete laid; I start the brick work, the damp course is in, and I complete up to the window level. I go and price up the door and window frames. I'm thinking maybe a couple of hundred quid would cover it. The truth is, they seem to cost as much as a small house, and that's without the glass. Time for a re-think, I head for a place called Inkster's at the back of Asda in Havant, where they sell seconds from leading manufacturers. I purchase five windows, a door, and frame for a hundred and sixty quid; unfortunately, they don't match up to the drawing sizes submitted to the council.

The conservatory is two thirds finished when the building inspector arrives; he queries the plans, I told him that I had phoned his department to explain the windows would be different to the plans, and was told this would be ok. He accepted this and told me to carry on with the project. Phew, that was a close call; I just hope he does not check it up when he gets back to his office. After five weeks, with only the glazing, the plastic roof and guttering to go, I'm finished with the building bit; a coat of white paint completes the job. Within a few weeks, it is converted into a place to stow anything from beach chairs to the kids' toys. If only my wife had said the word, I would have bought a shed and saved myself all the trouble. Our two cats also seem to think it's a good place to bring dead mice, crows, and seagulls. I wouldn't mind if we didn't feed the beasts, the murdering little buggers.

My mother-in-law's neighbour asks her if I can fix her dripping bathroom tap, so I pop round to have a look. The thing's been leaking so long I have to re-seat the tap with a cutting tool before fitting a new washer. I charge her a fiver; she accuses me of robbery, so I let her have it for two quid. I tell my mother-in-law that I won't be doing any more jobs for her. Two weeks later her neighbour's kitchen tap starts leaking, and I am asked once again to repair it, bloody cheek. I tell my mother-in-law to tell her to phone a plumber, and this she does. After two days he arrives, and five minutes later he is presenting her with a bill for £35. My mother-in-law informs me her neighbour nearly had a coronary. I said to tell her to get out more, and check the prices of things—fish and chips have gone up from the shilling she last paid for them, tight old bitch.

The Royal family are to pass through Vernon on their way to boarding the royal yacht from the quays. The usual grass is painted green, the establishment is spring cleaned, and sailors are ushered from their slumbers to press number one suits so they can look smart. They are now ready to line the road while the Royal Rolls passes through. The big day arrives, the still is piped, the ship's company stands to attention, the entourage sweep by, and I swear the Queen winked at me as she went by; anyway, I got a dirty look from the Duke as I winked back.

A call comes in to our office from the dockyard, a Royal navy MFV (motor fast vessel, yes, I know, you think they would call it an FMV) in Swansea harbour, has been blown out of the water after its anchor chain set off a Second World War mine. The hull remained intact, but the fixtures and fittings are smashed to bits. My job, should I choose to accept it, is to make her sea worthy enough to get her back to Pompey. This phone will self destruct in ten seconds time—well, not quite, but you get the gist of it.

A lorry is ordered, and loaded up with spares and tools; I leave my right hand man, Ray, in charge of the sweeper squadron. Dixie, the other chief on the section, has the only HGV licence, so we climb in the lorry and both head for Swansea. We arrive mid-afternoon at the jetty alongside the MFV, we board the boat and have a look round, and what we find is mission impossible. The motors, generators, engines, light fittings, navigation equipment, toilet pans, are all in bits. I choose not to accept the mission. I phone Portsmouth dockyard telling them to either write the thing off, give me £2,000,000 and a couple of years, or send a tug round and tow her back for a major re-build. I am informed a tug will be sent—bugger, we were looking forward to staying in Swansea, for a while. We drive back that evening, our spares and tools unused, the lorry is returned, and we go home to our families.

With the war now over, spares are now back to normal, e.g. we only have to wait three or four months instead of eight for our orders. The Public Works department is in Vernon rewiring our workshop, re-roofing blocks of accommodation flats, and renewing the galley equipment. They spend £1,000,000 on a new gate at the back of the establishment; this all seems a little odd as the place is due to close in the future? I ask one of the guys in charge what is going on, and he informs me their department has under spent this year, and the money has to go before the new financial year. Evidently, any money left will be deducted from the New Year's allowance. Typical government, save money and you are penalised, loads of incentive to be careful with tax payers' money there then.

Winter arrives with a vengeance, the temperature drops, and we get a call from HMS Bronnington—she is in Liverpool with a broken contactor.

This bit of kit connects the power from the generator to the sweep cable; the heavy duty copper contacts have probably burnt and require renewing, so we rummage in the spares box for a set. Dixie collects a lorry from the dockyard; we load up with the spares and tools, and I go to the pay office to get some money for our accommodation and food for the next two or three days in scouseville. The journey up the M6 to Liverpool is trouble free; the weather is cold, but bright and sunny. We dump the lorry off under the shadow of the Liver Building, which just happens to be alongside the dead ship Bronnington berthed alongside.

We inform the ship's quartermaster to keep an eye on it, and to inform the police if he sees more than one scouse with bricks anywhere near it. We go and see the skipper, and inform him that we are here, and that we will start work after we have got some accommodation sorted out. Dixie and I head into town to look for a bed and breakfast. The hotel we eventually decide on is at least minus one star; our budget after food and beer does not leave much for accommodation. We are greeted at the reception by a Panzer tank commander, a lovely twenty stone German lady with attitude. She points in the general direction of the stairs to the whereabouts of our rooms on the third floor. Our bedroom consists of a double room, cleverly partitioned into five individual slots, with a single bed and a chest of drawers in each. The bedding does not look over clean; I must remember to stay in my clothes when I come in and go to bed tonight. The bathroom is on the next floor, the sink and bath plugs have either been removed to save water, or stolen. This goes for the toilet paper, just as well I took the *Sun* in with me to read. We clean up as best we can and head into town; the pubs have all got bouncers on the doors, so we find an Indian restaurant and order a few beers, followed by chicken Vindaloos and poppadoms. I must admit it was rather funny being served by scouse talking Indians, "Yoos want chutney with that ar lar?"

On the way back to the concentration camp, we run into happy locals offering us a fight, just to finish off the evening. We hurry on and find Hilda has locked us out. I suppose with it being eleven o'clock we should be in bed before the guards change shifts. A six stone black guy lets us in, presumably the night porter; he informs us that we should have been given a key—that's nice to know. After a noisy night listening to drunks singing and shouting, we head downstairs for breakfast. I say breakfast, if that's what they call cold tea, burnt toast, crunchy bacon and rubber eggs. "Everything or'right, gents?" asks this greasy, spotty, smelly shit bag, who I presume is the manager. I tell him I have stayed in better and cleaner accommodation in a cave in the lake districts; he is not amused, and goes back to his slum of an office.

After breakfast, we head for the docks; it's bitterly cold, and a white frost covers the city. People are going to work, heads bent against the wind, steam clouds blowing out of every mouth, Christ, it's bloody cold. The lorry still has all its wheels, the doors and glass still intact; that's a result. The quartermaster in his heavy serge overcoat greets us on the gangway, "Morning, chief, fancy a cup of coffee?" This guy's a star. After warming up, me and Dixie unload the tools and spares from the lorry and head for the quarterdeck. Everything is covered in frost—boy, this is going to be fun—after an hour we have the lid off the contactor box. We isolate the power, the inside is a molten mass of copper, most of the electrical contacts have burnt out, and cables have been stripped of insulation by the heat. This is starting to look like a dockyard job; the skipper pops along and tells us it is imperative that he sails on Monday with the sweep cable in working order. Oh well, in that case, Jesus and I will perform the miracle you require.

All the molten crap is removed, and the cables are stripped clean to the copper; we use plastic shrink fit to temporarily insulate the bare cables. New contacts are fitted, and the box weatherproofed; its four o'clock, too late to flash up and try out our handiwork. We secure our tools in the lorry, and it's now time to eat, so we grab some fish and chips at the local chippy, and make for our rooms in the stalag. Helga the Hun is back on guard duty and gives us our keys. We have managed to procure some toilet rolls, cleaning paste, and a plug for the bathroom. After de-scumming the bath, I fill it up; surprisingly, the water is hot, and the management must have accidentally knocked the thermostat up from tepid.

Dixie is not so lucky; it seems I must have used all the water from the one hundred and twenty bedroomed hotel's only emersion tank. He is not happy—let's face it, for £7.50 a night you expect a bit more. We finally get ready, and make our way to reception; the stairway is lit by single 20 watt lamps. I guess that's so you can't see the peeling wallpaper and the threadbare carpet. We ask Helga for a key, and it's slammed on the counter. I say, "danker," and she actually smiles, "yor velcom," bloody hell, I almost clicked my heels but thought better of it.

Dixie and I wander around for half an hour before finding a pub without twenty stone heavyweights on the door. It turns out to be full of Irishmen; now, after recent bombings on the mainland I am feeling a little apprehensive about mixing with potential killers of servicemen. Dixie, on the other hand, had no qualms about striking up a conversation with a couple of micks from Belfast. Strangely enough, after we had been there for an hour, and had three pints of Guinness, things seemed to be like any other pub, e.g. normal. At closing time we fell out of the pub, and went to look for the Indian restaurant we had found the night before; they had obviously moved shop, or we had lost our way. We ended up with a Chinese take away, a sodium glutamate special—I must have drank six pints of water that night; I kept dreaming I was in the desert for some reason. Next morning with a head like Birkenhead, I headed for breakfast. Four cups of coffee and three fags later, I was getting back to normality. Down at the reception we paid our dues and clocked out. I thought about leaving a tip, but unfortunately, I couldn't find a farthing in my change so I thought better of it.

Outside it was starting to snow. Jesus, give us a break, not only are we going to freeze our balls off, we're going to have trouble getting back to Pompey. Back on the quarter deck of the minesweeper, we clear the snow from the contactor box. Dixie replaces the fuses, and we hit the on switch; the copper contacts crash together and immediately open again, oh joy, it's still fucked. We try again, same result, and by now the new contacts are starting to show the same signs of the previous set, e.g. burning, time for a re-think.

We disconnect the outgoing circuit from the contacts, and use a bridge megger on the sweep cable; it appears to have a short circuit. With it still disconnected we try the contactor again, and this time it stays connected without arcing, perfect. Time to tell the skipper the bad news, "Good morning, sir, the good news is we have found the problem; the bad news is you need a new sweep cable." He replies, "It's strange you should say that, the problem started when a fishing boat ran over our sweep." I'm thinking, well thanks a bunch, you stupid bastard, that little snippet of information could have saved us two days of pointless work. I phone HMS Vernon and tell them to prepare for a cable change. The lid on the contactor box is refitted and we pack up our tools, bits, and pieces and load the lorry; it's time to head for home.

The snow is getting heavy as we make our way to the M6 motorway; visibility is down to a few feet, and we pass several lorries, all tits up, having skidded off the road. Dixie is determined to keep going, even though we are having trouble going in a straight line, especially up hills, this is like the dodgems at the fair. How we never hit anything is beyond me. Fortunately, a snow plough passed us, and we followed him to the junction for Gloucester. The snow eased off through Swindon and Newbury, and by the time we reached Portsmouth we were in the clear. By now it was dark, and we were tired; the lorry was parked in Vernon, and we headed home.

October 1983, my draft comes through; I am to join flag officer sea training's staff at Portland. I now recall the Admiral's nod to his Aid on the Cardiff when I asked about the old fashioned method of damage control they were still teaching. This is his way of getting me to see the errors of my ways; the bastard wants to brainwash me. Either that or after the Falkland episode he realises I was right and he needs my expertise to re-train the Navy in damage control, nineteen eighties style. As luck would have it, a friend of mine who lives in Portland phoned me up and asked if I would like to swap drafts. He had been assigned to HMS Torquay, an engineering training ship day running from Portsmouth. Now then, would I like to get up at five every morning, catch a boat in rough seas to a waiting ship, return to shore at ten, and write out a report ready for the next morning, all this weather permitting? Or day run from my home port and be home every night? Let me see, tough one this. I nearly climbed down the phone and kissed him, boy, was that some let off or what.

The last few weeks at Vernon are spent handing over the job to my relief; he too arrives without any pre-joining courses, and hasn't a clue about sweepers. He is a nervous wreck till I tell him he is only a figure head and that Ray and Dixie are the brains of the outfit. My last day, I take all the lads to the local pub at twelve o'clock, and we have a few beers and reminisce about the last year or so. I am presented with a pewter mug by the lads, and I am touched.

It's 7.30, Monday the 14th of November. I arrive at the main gate of the dockyard, produce my joining papers to the dockyard police, and they issue me with a temporary car pass. I park the car on South Railway Jetty; alongside is HMS Torquay, F43. She cost £3.5 million in 1954; she now has a navigation room fitted in place of the forward triple mortar. One can't help but notice that the ship seems to be held together with paint and rust, the superstructure tends to be bubbly instead of flat; I just hope the hull has seen better days. I board the ship and make my way to the regulating office; I am met by a stroppy leading regulator, who seems to be up himself. I ignore it this time, but make a mental note for future reference. Having had a coffee in the Chiefs mess, I head for the tech office, my place of work. There I meet up with my boss, Dinga Bell, and a few heads of department, some I know already from past ships. I commandeer the office writer to do my joining routine and start my take over of the job; the guy I am relieving has today to hand over before going into barracks for discharge. You can imagine he is full of enthusiasm, not for the hand over but to get into civvies and home. By three o'clock he has gone and I am left to it.

The next day we sail so the navigator midshipmen can practice with their compasses and pencils on charts of the Solent. We also have some young trainee engineer officers on board, so breakdown drills are common place throughout the day. I did overhear one of the young lads talking to his mate after coming up for air from the engine room, "this engineering lark is a piece of piss, you only have three questions to worry about: one, what's the problem, Chief; two, how soon can you fix it, Chief; three, let me know when you have, Chief." He is a quick learner that lad.

Over the next few months we are in and out of harbour training these young future Admirals. I am, during this home time, able to get an extension done over my garage, and I now have a five bedroom, two bathroomed house—the bed and breakfast trade is about to pick up.

The ship has an invite by the mayor of Torquay, but unfortunately, when we arrive we have to anchor out as the new jetty has not been completed. The Chiefs mess has invites to a hotel owned by an ex-Matelot; his ulterior motive is to get repair jobs done for free by our expert craftsmen. The jobs range from fixing the hotel's central heating to fitting a new commercial gas cooker in the kitchen. We also had a go at fitting solar panels to heat his swimming pool—we reckon the temperature went up by maybe .0006 of a degree. Considering it cost him £4,000 in parts, we suggested he spent his money on wet suits to give his guests when they wanted to go swimming. I'll give him his due, at the end of the day he did give us a slap up feed and free drinks all night. The trip back to the ship was a bit hairy as the weather had got up a bit, and when you're a bit unsteady on your feet anyway, getting on and off a bouncing whaler is a bit precarious to say the least. After the weekend we sailed back to Pompey, and we hear news that a trip to the states by HMS Fearless and HMS Intrepid had been cancelled; they had been called to the Middle East for some reason or other. Damn shame, the good news was, we and a couple of other frigates were to take their place on this good will mission. The next few weeks were spent preparing the ship, loading stores, and getting machinery ready for the long voyage, bearing in mind this heap only did day running in sight of land for the last how many years.

We eventually get under way on a Monday morning; the weather is fair, and a few family and friends are there to wave us off along with the tourists. I hate leaving my family on these occasions. I feel we are missing out on family life, but I guess that goes with the job.

After a day or two we lose sight of the other ships in our convoy; the weather is up to force eight, and the old heap is groaning with every wave. My mess is right up forward, and there are twelve of us living in a space the size of a large living room. Twelve bunks in threes are down the ship's side; a three foot passage separates them from stainless steel personal lockers on the inner bulkhead. I have a middle bunk and a pretty brass window (commonly called a scuttle) with a view of the sea. Across the main passage is the other half of the Chiefs mess, which consists of more bunks and the bar, this being the main resting place of Charlie the chief Mechanician. If it wasn't for the cheap booze, his bar bill would run into hundreds, if not thousands every month.

He had a nasty habit of coming back to our mess and pissing in some unfortunate's locker; we would leap out of our pits and steer him so he could piss in his own locker, and we would then take his bedding to soak up any spillage. Next morning he would wake up on his bunk springs wondering what had happened; needless to say, his and anyone else's laundry bill would be added to his beer bill.

After many days of being pounded by massive waves in the Atlantic, we arrive at Charleston, South Carolina, and we tie up in the naval base, home to twenty-two thousand American sailors. The berthing ropes are tied up; telephone and shore supplies are connected, and all is well with the world when, "HANDS TO EMERGENCY STATIONS, damage control parties close up," is piped on the main broadcast.

Now what—evidently, the engine room has sprung several leaks; fountains are seen bursting from the ship's hull, pumping parties are organised to hold the flow; meanwhile, the engineering officer is on the phone trying to organise some fast setting ready mix concrete, and within an hour, five ready mix lorries are on the jetty pumping concrete into the engine room's bilges. I guess we were lucky it happened here, and not in one of our dockyards; they would still be doing the paperwork as the ship sank. Fortunately, concrete sets under water as it is a chemical reaction, not air, that causes it to set, and within four hours the hull was once again solid—we were almost seaworthy again, fingers crossed for the trip home, eh what.

Once the state of emergency is over and the clearing up has been done, leave is given to the non-duty parts. The locals as per usual were lined up in their cars waiting to take jolly Jack home for a beer and a barbie; I think the reason behind it all is for the invite back on board. They are fascinated with British war ships and their crews—we are indeed a rare breed. The ship's crew is advised not to go outside the dockyard gate on foot, as mugging and armed robbery are the norm between the dockyard and town. A couple of guys from the mess and I are invited to an old hillbilly's homestead on the outskirts of town, so we climb into his Dodge pick-up and head out. His family greets us with a beer and a glass of moonshine, all made on the premises. There appears to be a cow on the spit, seems like they are expecting a few more people than us three. Sure enough, half of Charleston's folk on welfare arrive over the next hour or so. Strangely, we did not see any coloured folk amongst these Southern redneck rebels. I can't say I was very comfortable with these people, as most of them were smashed out of their skulls within two hours. Understanding them when they were sober was bad enough, but now, yee har ya'll got me there. By twelve o'clock our hosts were unconscious; we borrow the old feller's phone and try to order a taxi, and we are told no can do, as the area is out of bounds due to the high crime rate, oh dear. We eventually get through to the navy base and explain the situation, and they ask us the road number and name, and there isn't one, as we're off the road. However, there is a brewery on the next plot. They recognize the name and tell us to stay put; they are sending a patrol wagon to pick us up. Half an hour later, a mini bus arrives, and two smart MPs call us over, "You guys should not be here, even the police don't come out here." Thanks a bunch. Still, they did not rob or kill us, so I guess we got a result, and I have to say they were very hospitable.

Back on board, the engineers and heavy electric departments are still working down the engine room clearing up and drying out electric pumps and motors. The next day divers are sent down to have a look, things don't look good, and the hull seems to be wafer thin. Still, forty tons of concrete should do it. Just hope the trip back to Blighty is nice and smooth. Over the next few days we are inundated with visitors; luckily, my friends from the back of beyond didn't turn up, so my mess bill was not too bad. Charlie the chief Mech was in his glory; permanently pissed for the whole stay, he seems to enjoy himself, but never remembers anything the next day. He also seems to have got over his incontinent problem; he was, I think, the original binge drinker. Stores and fuel are loaded up and we are ready to sail.

The ship sails for Fort Lauderdale on the Monday at eight in the morning—no ceremonies this time, it's all very low key. Special sea dutymen are piped to close up and we are ready to be under way. A few dockyard workers are there to remove the berthing wires. They don't exactly wave us goodbye. The local pilot is on board to take us down the river; at the estuary he disembarks; out at sea we head north.

Our arrival in Lauderdale is a muted affair, with no crowds to greet us. My last trip there was on the first Royal navy ship to visit the place in many years, hence the novelty. Since the Falklands, every bloody RN ship in the navy appears to have gone there. I expect the locals have had their belly full of drunken Matelots from the good old United Kingdom. A few tourists come and look at our rust bucket; the newest thing on the ship is the bright new ensign fluttering in the breeze—the rust and peeling paint is a bit of a give away to the age of the old girl. Another run ashore and the lads are having a good time; some are going to Disneyland, and Cape Kennedy, and most are hitting the bars in the resort and enjoying wet t-shirt competitions in seafront bars, and trying exotic cocktails in posh hotels. After a week, our goodwill visit is over and we prepare for home.

We sail into the teeth of a gale—the ship is battened down to condition Zulu, which means every door and hatch is shut down, just to be on the safe side. Many prayers are said over the trip home, I think the thought of the ship breaking in half might have something to do with it. We are treated to pot mess during the trip back; gets a bit boring after a few days, and the poor chefs try to vary it by adding chili or curry powder, they just keep adding more tins of meat and vegetables to top up the huge stew.

A few days away from home and a split in the superstructure and funnel appear; in the engine room there seems to be more movement in the hull than is usual. Things are getting worrying, to say the least. We finally find some calm weather going up the English Channel, and as we round the Isle of Wight people start to relax, realizing we are going to make it in one piece. A few family and friends are there to greet us on our return, but as we've only been away for a short trip, most people have stayed at home, happy to wait till we go on leave.

The following day we are tugged into dry dock. The structural experts arrive, and after their inspection with X-ray equipment they are amazed we made it back. It seems the ship had broken its back, and a fracture right round the ship was found. The only thing holding the front and back together was the pipe work, cables, and of course, the forty tons of concrete in the bilges. Over the next two weeks, welders are busy plating over the cracks, sort of gluing the two halves of the ship together. The dockyard experts tell our Captain that we are advised not to go out of sight of land when we sail, and of course in not more than a force five. We all wonder why? Surely, if the ship isn't safe we should not be allowed to leave the dockyard wall, let alone go to sea. Anyway, being our Captain, he has us set sail into a force eight gale—this should prove the new repairs, eh what.

Not only do we sail in rough weather, he heads for the open sea. I make a point of digging out my life jacket, just in case, you understand. After a few weeks of day running training our young navigators and engineers, we get ready for Navy days. The ship is tarted up; new gray paint is slapped over rust, and many tins of Brasso are used to buff up green verdigris-covered scuttles to a high polish. At last she is ready for the invasion of civilians who are about to inundate the ship tomorrow. I find I have been nominated as officer of the day, "cheers boss!" — I'm basically put in charge of the duty watch, and the ship, just as well it's not worth much.

The crowds start to come on board; routes have been roped off to stop spies looking in compartments at top secret equipment; you're right, I am joking. A few of the lads who live on board take willing young girls down to their mess, no doubt for a cup of tea, or to be shown the golden rivet. I stay on the gangway; to make sure we don't end up like a Filipino ferry; I have lads controlling the flow on and off the ship. I make sure everyone with a camera has a photo of me with them coming up the gangway. After a few hours, I get the duty seaman petty officer to take over from me on the gangway. I wander down to the mess and grab a cup of coffee and a fag. After half an hour, I take a wander round the ship, and I just happened to look over the ship's side, when I noticed the tide was going out—the ship appeared to be in the final stages of hanging off the jetty via the berthing wires. I quickly piped for the duty seamen; I said to the Petty officer "is it normal for the ship to be dangling off the jetty via the wires?" He replied, "Christ, I forgot to slacken them off!" I said, "might I suggest you do it now, before the ship ends up on its side, or the bollards on the ship or jetty give way."

Luckily, there was just enough slack to divert a catastrophe. An hour or so later my boss arrived; he had been to see his mate for a few drinks on another ship. I then find out he is in fact the officer of the day, not me, he just passed the responsibility over to me, bless. He nearly shit himself when I told him what had happened, and he promptly invited me into the wardroom for a drink, and I think he needed one more than me. I made a point of telling the seaman PO to forget the incident and not mention it again, and he gladly agreed. Health and safety eat your heart out.

A few days later, the stroppy leading regulator got his comeuppance; he was in his tiny office alongside the master at arms doing a spot of paperwork, when the door slid open a few inches. What appeared to be a hand grenade bounced on his desk, a voice then said, "this is for you, arsehole." The door was then jammed shut. What happened next was related to us later in the mess by a bruised MAA. First, the leading regulator screamed and made for the door which was jammed; he then literally climbed over the master at arms to get to the scuttle, which happened to be open. That fat bastard had no chance of getting through it, so he hid behind his boss, waiting for the grenade to go off, which of course it didn't, as it was a novelty cigarette lighter. You would have thought he'd have got the grenade and thrown it out the window, but hey, who am I to suggest what he should have done. No bravery medals for that fat twat then; in fact, when the story got round the mess decks he was very low in the sailors esteem. Oddly enough, after that episode he eased up on the lads with regards to picking them up for their dress and haircuts. Harmony and morale was restored on the lower deck. The master at arms made a few enquiries for the culprit, but did not push it.

Over the summer leave period, my wife and I fly to Vienna, Austria. My mother and sister live in Graz. They meet us at the airport and we drive back to their home. The reason I am there is to purchase a 3 litre, diesel,

240D Mercedes off my sister—in her letter she assured me it was a good car. My first view of it made me think otherwise; there were holes in the floor and it generally looked in a state as it had not been used for eight months. My sister assured me it was a good car, and got her boyfriend, Robert, to weld up the problem areas—trouble was, he didn't have a clue how to weld. He thought you could weld rust to steel. Anyway, after four days of botching the job, I took delivery. It seemed to run all right, so we did the paperwork at the local licensing office and got the thing transferred to me. The drive back to the UK was a bit traumatic; every border crossing consisted of the Spanish inquisition, *vi are you driving an Austrian car, vi is the tax out of date, vi are you looking scared, just because I have a gun and a typical officious Nazi German attitude*. Back in Blighty I am informed I must pay tax on this classic. They didn't mention this in the brochure; I must also get it registered with UK number plates, and taxed. This done, I am now clear to drive legally on our roads.

The ship is in a routine of day running from Portsmouth, fair weather or fowl, our captain didn't care. Now and again we pop over to France to show the flag and have a run ashore; this is also done so the young lads can't sue the navy under the Trades Description Act. As the advert goes, join the Navy and see the world. The mayor of Torquay invites the ship for its final visit; we are to be given the freedom of the city. This means the ship's company will have to march through the town, with a guard and fixed bayonets. No doubt, with this freedom we will be able to legally bring our sheep to market on a Wednesday through the town center and Maypole dance every other Friday.

Saturday morning the ship's company falls in on the jetty. I muster my lads and get them lined up in three columns, ready for the Chief gunnery instructor to take charge of the whole proceedings. Someone has hired the royal marine band for the parade, to add a bit of noise, and give us a rough idea how to keep step. The order is given, "ship's company Ho, move to the right in threes, right turn. By the right quick march," and off we go, Ambassadors of the Queen, proudly strutting our stuff in front of thousands of cheering holiday makers and locals. You would have thought we had just come back from the Great War, instead of a farewell visit. I just happened to be the last man at the back of this cortege marching through the town. The Trafalgar class submarine HMS Torbay will be taking over from us as the newly adopted vessel for Torquay; they obviously want to go up market, bloody snobs.

On Sunday, the chefs produce T-bone steaks for supper, with one alternative for the fussy buggers who don't like meat; this is accomplished by the caterer being honest, and capable of doing his job, a rare thing in the

Navy. Mind you, trying to feed people three meals a day on £1.25 a day can't be easy. Monday morning we sail to do replenishment at sea for fuel, a couple of lads have missed the ship; no doubt we will pick them up back in Pompey, that's going to cost them, big time.

Chapter Seventeen

February 1985, another draft comes through; I am to join HMS Andromeda in September, having completed five months of pre-joining training in Collingwood first. My last few months on Torquay are used preparing for my future in Civvy Street in a year's time—my wife and I decide we would like to buy a restaurant when I finish my twenty-two in the mob. We put the house up for sale. We spend the following weekends going round various business agencies; there appears to be a shortage of restaurants for sale in the Portsmouth area, bugger.

One agent did offer for us to go and look at a fish and chip shop called Churchills, and this we did out of curiosity more than anything. We arrived on a Saturday at lunch time, and the place appeared to be busy. The owner had only been there for eighteen months, but had personal problems and needed to sell; we had a look at his books, and agreed it was a good little business. We agreed to keep the staff on, if and when we took over. He was asking £75,000 for it freehold; our house was on the market for £72,000, so all we needed would be a £30,000 mortgage, and it seemed like a bargain.

We went back twice before shaking hands on the deal; this guy was a mason so you would have thought the deal was struck. Not so, this slime ball phoned us up to say we had been gazumped by two grand; we should have told him to stuff his shop, but being naïve we matched the so called offer. We asked him if he would spend our first week in the shop training us, offering to pay for him and his downtrodden wife's hotel accommodation. He agreed. The house sale went through smoothly, the furnisher lorry was loaded up, and we headed for the shop, but found it was locked up, and no one in sight. The agent arrived and informed us the cash had not come through yet so we could not have the keys. Two and a half hours later we get the keys—the previous owner had long gone, and he obviously had no intention of staying to train us suckers, the mason bastard.

Moving in was a bit hectic, as we had moved from a five bedroom house to a two bedroom flat. Theresa, my youngest, hated us for moving, having left all her friends on Hayling Island, Helen, my eldest, on the other hand was indifferent. I was on leave for the first week of the move which gave me a chance of getting used to frying and preparing. My wife Hermione also got stuck in, as did the kids. Carol, the lady we bought with the shop, was a peroxide blonde, overweight, with thin legs, and a mouth like a trooper; every word of her vocabulary was interlaced with the F-word, but, she was a good honest worker. The family and I soon got into this catering lark; the temperature for frying was upped from the 320 degrees the thieving mason told us to fry at, to 420 degrees. This, we found, sealed the fish, rather than it sitting there soaking up grease. It also stayed the same size rather than shrinking as before. The batter we thinned down, making it more palatable, and the chips we blanched, and crisped up and sold as required, rather than frying a whole bucket full and leaving them in the chip bin till sold. In general, common sense took over from the so called expert's advice given previously by the thieving mason.

At the end of April 1985, I leave the Torquay and join HMS Collingwood for courses. I am now trying to run a business and my naval career at the same time—day time I am plowing through electronic circuits and paperwork, evenings are spent frying. Quite a contrast in styles, to say the least. After a few weeks, Theresa is settling in at her new school and making new friends. Helen is working full time, and is going steady with her boyfriend, Steve, a proficient amateur golfer who later became a Ryder cup player. The shop is a busy one and I fear my wife will have her work cut out when I join the Andromeda, especially as I will be based in Plymouth doing a refit. No doubt there will be a Plymouth-based ship doing a refit in Portsmouth, and we will be passing their crews on the road each weekend as we head home. The Navy has a funny sense of humour like that; they think we like to travel in our own time.

I eventually finish learning circuits on equipment I can't repair, and administration that is of no relevance to me. Collingwood has done it again, filled my head with bullshit, and kept some civilian in a job. The middle of September arrives and I head for Plymouth. After a long drive on pathetic main roads, I book myself into HMS Drake, the local shore base. I am given a grotty cabin where I unload my kit, and after a coffee in the chiefs mess, I head for the ship in the dockyard. She is in dry dock in one of the new sheds, purpose built to keep us dry, bless.

I meet my new bosses and associates in the electrical department, quite a few I know from old commissions. Its not long before I am getting stuck into sorting out the admin side, and the junior rates watch and quarter bill, and training. Weekends are spent driving home, and frying; Sundays are a blessed relief after a hectic week. Most weekends I have a passenger, Billy

Wiz , a mate of mine, the idea is he keeps me company on the trip, however, by the time I've started the car and reached the gate of Drake, he is fast asleep, the lazy bastard. However, one particular weekend I was travelling along a straight bit of road at dusk, when I leaned over to the right (the Merc is left hand drive) to look round the car in front to see if it was clear to overtake. It seemed clear, so I pulled out, and just at that moment, Billy woke and shouted, "pull in!" Instinctively, I did, just as a black Jaguar shot past in the opposite direction. Fekin hell, that was a close one.

"What in God's name made you wake up?" I asked.

"Buggered if I know," he replied. Needless to say, the rest of the journey was taken at a more leisurely pace, and Bill made a point of staying awake for the rest of the trip.

That Christmas, my wife and I headed for Austria to see my mother and sister. The weather was below freezing, and our first stop in Germany was in a town called Bhul in the Black Forest. The hotel we found was superb, great food and beer, and a bed to die for after a long, hard drive through France. The next morning everything was covered in two inches of frost; the Merc was a pig to start, but we eventually got going and headed east. We arrived in Graz at around eight in the evening; a hot meal went down a treat.   My lovely sister, as usual, was rowing with my mother; this seemed to be the norm over the rest of our stay. My wife and I spent our time looking round Graz—the city is wonderful, trams and bendy buses weave through the streets, the trees are all lit up with fairy lights, and the absence of litter is a joy. The temperature is minus ten, but it is a dry cold, much more bearable than the English damp type. We frequent a café at the end of Hachergasse, my mother's street; the locals find us amusing, and are very friendly. The lagers go down very well with smoked sausage and fresh crusty bread. My wife had them in stitches one day; she was overheard to say her foot was hurting, but unfortunately, a foot in Austria is a swear word for a lady's private bits—I guess they must have thought I had given her a good bonking last night.

After three days I attempt to start the old Merc—no such luck, and the bitch would not fire up even with a can of ether sprayed in the air filter. By now every Austrian mechanic in Graz had come and given their expert opinion; it was like an Irish parliament. Unfortunately, none of them solved the problem, the thing was dead. The truth was, the compression in the cylinders was low, and the extreme cold added to the problem. We eventually decided my sister would lend me her car, a 450 SEL Merc, six and a bit litres of muscle. She wrote out a letter in German for the border guards, explaining I was not actually stealing it, but borrowing it to get home. She was to get mine repaired and drive it back to England and pick hers up at a later date.

After our week in Graz was over we set off home; the borders were no problem, as there weren't any. It was now January and all EEC borders were opened to freely drive through. The next problem was going to be the ferry, but obviously the loading guys don't know the difference between an English registered 240D, and an Austrian registered 450 SEL, which was lucky. The trip over was no problem, however, the customs in Portsmouth pulled us over—oh shit, here we go.

"Good afternoon, sir, is this your car?" After I explained the situation, he asked how long it would be in this country. I told him about six weeks. Surprisingly, he let me drive home, result.

The chip shop was going well, but things were getting a bit much for my wife, and it was time to get a fryer in to take the pressure off. As luck would have it, the shop next door was a job agency; I popped in there and got a young lad off their books. He was a good little worker, but unreliable—he would be crying on the stairs because his girlfriend had upset him, or he would arrive late for work, a real little pain in the arse. Still, we plodded on. The refit was going well in Plymouth; the big Merc was proving to be a bit juicy, averaging 17mpg on the run to and fro.

I was ashore at a mate's house removing a ceiling one night, when I got a message to contact the ship. I phoned through, and was told there was a huge fire at the shop, which was scary, as I had not got round to doing the shop insurance. I legged it back to the ship and got changed; I popped in to see my boss and told him the problem. He asked me if I had any leave left, and I said I don't know and quite frankly I didn't care, I was going home regardless. With that, I said goodbye and jumped in the Merc; I stopped for fuel and gunned it towards Pompey; 171 miles, and two and a half hours later, I pulled round the corner of the shop.

I breathed a huge sigh of relief as I saw my wife, the deputy electrical officer, who was on leave, and firemen in the shop. I parked the car and came in the shop with a huge grin on my face; my wife was not amused, till I explained I was told it was our shop and not next door that was on fire, and a lack of insurance might have been a problem. After the fire brigade had damped down next door, we spent the rest of the night cleaning the smoke damage. Next morning, I phoned the health and safety department up to see if we could open for business, and no problem, we were back to frying again. My boss gave me the rest of the week off, which gave me a chance to get next door's insurance to pay for cleaning in my flat, and to sort out some insurance of my own.

Back on board, my boss tells me my name has been put forward to do the flight deck officers course at Portland. This involves controlling the safe landing and taking off of the ship's helicopter. It seems like none of the officers on the ship want to do the job. I tell my boss it will be a waste of £12,000, which is the cost of the course, as I am due to finish my time in the navy in six months. He tells me it's too late; as I am down to go next week. Well, at least I will be able to drive home each night for a week.

I arrive at HMS Osprey, a royal naval air station on Portland bill, on a cold, wet, and windy Monday morning. I am joined by eight other chief petty officers. It seems like someone in authority at last deems chiefs are capable of doing officers jobs—people with no authority have known this for hundreds of years. We are ushered into a classroom, and shown films of helicopter accidents, and this makes my mind up—there is no way on this planet I am going up in one of those things. Over the next few days, we are trained to work out wind speeds and direction, using anemometers (wind speed and direction meters, and a gadget that works out the safe parameters) so the helo heli can take off and land safely into the wind. This often means ordering the ship to alter course, or in exceptional circumstances, landing the helo from the side of the ship.

Communications are next; this involves the use of a headset, and a key box which can be connected to speak to the pilot, the ground crew, the operations room, and the bridge. A pair of bats is used to signal the pilot; these indicate to him to hover, take off, and go left or right, and land; illuminated night sticks are used for night flying. Safety is paramount, and everything is taught from earthing the helo when transferring personnel or stores, to the ground crews training, and FOD,(that's the pre-takeoff litter collection) foreign object damage. The last two days are practical; we are shipped to the middle of Portland Harbour and dumped on a barge; it's freezing cold and blowing a Hooley, a Wessex helicopter is flown out to us and we take it in turns to land it; the instructor informs us we must do transfers to the helo, yeah right. I inform him I have a fear of flying, and that does the trick. Next day, a wasp and a lynx are sent to try us. The afternoon of the last day is spent on a written exam, which determines whether we become FDO's or not. An hour after the exam we are informed of our results; I, and five others, pass, two fail. I head home for the weekend.

Back in the chip shop things are busy. I now employ a staff of five, including my two daughters; the spuds are rumbled and every eye and black mark removed, it's a time consuming job, especially at this time of year, when the spuds are not at their best. We have a visit from the health inspector; he dons his white coat and goes round the business, torch in hand, he is a fussy little twat, and his thing is the fridge and freezer door seals. The patronizing sod suggests I use a toothbrush to clean them; oooh, what a brilliant idea, why couldn't I think of such a clever thing? After half an hour he departs, having given us a pass for another year.

A little old lady sits down and orders a plaice and chips, and with two mouthfuls left on her plate she calls me over, "Excuse me, young man, I think this fish is off." I excuse myself and go out the back to get a plaice straight out the freezer. I return to the old dear.

"You see this fish, this was yours half an hour ago, this is how we cook plaice, frozen, so if you have a complaint, I suggest you go to your local church and have a word with God, that will be three pounds please." She apologizes, saying she just thought it had a funny flavour, yeah, right. Carol, our Amazon swear machine, is brilliant, her only fault is her chip portions. Nobody is buying the large portions, mainly because she is giving enough to feed a family with one small portion. This is my profit; you can't tell the tax man you're a very generous man, because he won't believe you. I then went out and bought a stainless funnel with a handle, for a reasonable size portion; try overloading that, you generous minx. Over the next few months I have a garbage disposal fitted in the prep room; this gets rid of the batter scraps and food waste, and a washing machine is also plumbed in. In the shop's kitchen I fit a hob, a dishwasher, a rubbish compactor, and a decent sized sink—now we're cooking.

After driving the big Merc for five months with no English road tax or insurance, my sister phones and informs me my car has been fixed in Graz. New pistons and cylinder sleeves bring it up to spec, at a cost of £750. She will drive it to England with my mother, stay for a few days, and then take hers home. The following weekend she arrives at the ferry port in my 240D, we go to our shop and give them a feed of, you've guessed it, fish and chips, and they are well impressed. I take my sister round to her car; she is not over impressed with the ten gallons of water behind the front seats, as if five months of my driving it had caused the problem, der. She then informs me that I must never take the car back to Graz due to the fact she had been using it, and accumulated over forty parking tickets—cheers.

The ship's refit over, we set sail for trials, all the usual stuff, fire drills, action stations, emergency stations, and man over board drills, machinery, and power failures, you name it, nothing is missed out. My big day arrives, hands to flying stations is piped; I head for the hangar, and change into white overalls and a yellow bib. I don the FDO's headset and key box. I test communications between the relevant stations; I check the wind speed and direction meters, and then work out with my plastic gadget whether the ship's course is ok for a takeoff.

The helicopter is strapped onto the deck on four corners, just as well as the sea is a little on the rough side. My bats in hand, I check the ground crew is in position, one on each strop. The bridge gives the ok for takeoff; I signal the pilot to start his engines using a circular motion of my right bat, and he gives me the thumbs up, telling me he is ready. I signal the ground crew to unhook the helo and bring the strops to the front of the helo, in view of the pilot. I then point to each one, and the pilot acknowledges one to four strops. Both he and I are now sure the helo is free to fly. My arms now go horizontal, indicating he is ready for takeoff, when I judge the ship's flight deck is on an upward roll. I put my arms vertically, indicating to the pilot to lift and take off. I then point left or right of the ship to clear his takeoff.

After an hour of flying he returns, and he hovers on the port side of the flight deck. I signal him to come over and hover over the flight deck; my arms are once again horizontal. I am waiting for the ship's roll to be high, so I can land him as the ship's deck is on its way down, and this I do, but the bastard ignores me, and three seconds later he goes for the landing, just as the deck is on its way up—how the helo did not disintegrate, I'll never know—the suspensions on each wheel nearly collapsed, and everyone including me dived for cover waiting for the explosion. He had landed way off the central position; my only option was to send the ground crew out and try and lash it down with the nylon strops. I then signalled to cut the engine. The chief of the flight was way ahead of the ground crew; he had the pilot by the throat within ten seconds of coming to a halt. It was like you had lent someone your Rolls Royce and they had painted it pink and gone banger racing in it. It was his baby, and no one messes with his baby. I was sure I had made a balls up of it all, but was reassured by the flight crew I had done a good job for my first attempt. The pilot came to see me after he'd had a few whiskeys in the wardroom; he was still shaking from his near death experience, and he could not apologize enough; he assumed as it was my first go I was not experienced enough. I told him, experienced or not, I would not risk his and his navigator's life if I was not one hundred percent sure of doing the job properly.

Back in Portsmouth, we ammunition ship, having ordered everything from the Argos catalogue months before, my twenty odd million quid's worth of gear was waiting for us, and arrives by road and lighters. Shells, cordite, bullets, and missiles are all loaded into the magazines; it takes a day

209

and a half to complete the exercise. Over the next few months we visit Newcastle and Grimsby for good will visits, not the most exotic of runs ashore, but for the young lads it's a welcomed change.

I get my final draft through to HMS Nelson, royal naval barracks, its nearly time for my discharge; I have two weeks left in the Navy, after twenty-five years as man and boy. I join on a Monday, and I go round the usual places telling everyone I am about to become a civilian; jealous looks follow me. I see an old mate off the Andromeda and he invites me round for a drink and a farewell run ashore that evening. This I accept, and I tell my wife I will be a little late home tonight. That evening at six o'clock I arrive at Unicorn gate, and my mate is there to escort me on board. We arrive in the Chiefs mess; all my old mates are there. The whiskeys are flowing like water, twelve tots and three pints of courage sparkling bitter later, six of us decide to head ashore and hit the Savoy for grab a granny night. We pay our entrance fee and make our way through the Pompey beauties to the bar, and with a pint of bitter in one hand I stagger towards the dance floor. I approach a couple of eighteen stone lovelies with acne, tits round their waists, and a smell problem, sit at a side table, "fancy a dance?" I ask.

"Fuck off, jack." Charmed, I'm sure, I tell you, try and do them a big favour and that's what you get. How did they know I was a sailor? By now, the alcohol is kicking in big time, my legs don't belong to me any more and my vision is blurred. I decide to phone a taxi, and in the foyer I manage to locate a pay phone—only trouble is I can't get a fix on those damn moving numbers. I give up and head outside, it's bloody freezing, and I temporarily come to my senses, enough to work out the route back to the shop. The route I decide on is through Buckland council estate, notorious for muggings, burglaries, and the odd stabbing. As it turns out, the streets are empty, due to the cold. Half way home I decide to have a lay down on a bench, but just as I am about to get comfy I spot a police car coming down the road. It probably saved me from dying of hypothermia, as I made an effort and staggered the rest of the way home. I reach the shop and have trouble finding my key; eventually, it appears, but now I have trouble lining it up with the key hole. At last I enter the shop and make my way up to the bedroom.

My wife appears to be asleep. I now attempt to undress, but trying to get my trousers off over my shoes proves to be a bit of a problem. After five minutes of hopping round the bedroom, I eventually get undressed. By now my wife is awake; she calls out, "did you have a nice time?" I slurred my reply, "I'll tell you in the morning." The next day I woke with the mother of all headaches. I spend the next few days doing my leaving routine in Nelson.

I have an appointment to see the Commodore at ten o'clock. He greets me with a smile and a handshake, thanks me for my service to the navy, and presents me with a cute little card, a certificate which states that the Admiralty board wish to express their appreciation of my long and devoted service. This, I believe, is a new thing, after people who were leaving complained of being tossed out like some discarded litter, with no appreciation of their service to Queen and Country.

I have one more week to go. I enter the ship's office for a few more stamps, and see an old shipmate, the chief writer; he asks why I am there. I explain I am doing my leaving routine; he tells me to return my gas respirator, then come back to see him. I now have to get back to the shop as the respirator is at home. I park out front on double yellow lines, and leg it upstairs. Respirator in hand, I head back for the car, and there parked behind me is a police bike—the jackbooted Nazi officer is waiting for me.

He lectures me on the Highway Code, and why I should not be parked there. And being a naughty little boy with no knowledge of these things, I humbly apologize, saying I promise I will never ever park on double yellows again. The patronizing twat lets me off with a warning. Back in Nelson, I return my respirator, and get a stamp confirming it. In the ship's office, my mate the chief writer asks for my identity card, and I explain I will still need it for coming in next week.

"No, you won't, you're done," he tells me, "No need to hang about here." With that he shakes my hand and bids me good-bye. That's it; twenty five years done, my next career waits—from fish and ships, to fish and chips.

Glossary of Naval Slang Words

Blue liners	Navy brand cigarettes
Boot neck	Royal Marine
Boundary cooling	Cooling all sides of a ship's fire to contain spread
Bulkheads	Ship's steel walls
Bunk	Shelf for sleeping on
Civvies	Civilian clothing
Coxswain	Captain of sail or rowing boat
Defaulters	Sailors awaiting trial and punishment
Dhoby rash	Sores between legs caused by lack of rinsing clothes
Dhoby	Laundry
Divisions	Mass mustering of ships' company
Doubling	Naval running
Fags/dog ends	Cigarettes
Fish head	Sailor
Galley	Kitchen
Gash	Rubbish
Greeny	Electrical Engineer
Housewife	Sewing kit

Jack	Sailor
Kit muster	All kit laid out in regulation size
Knocking ten bells of shit out of	To hurt someone to the max
Make and mend	Originally given to take the afternoon off to make repairs to kit. Now just an afternoon off with or without leave.
Matelot (mat-lo)	Sailor
NAAFI	Navy, Army, Air force Institute. Armed forces shop
OD/AB	Sailor
Passing Out Parade	Final divisions on leaving a training establishment
Pinky	Radio Engineer
Pissing one's self	Something very funny
Pot belly stove	Wood burner
Pussers hard	Hard yellow soap
Pussers issue	Navy issue
RAS	Replenishment at sea
Request men	Sailors asking for permission
Re-scrub	Do an inspection again
Rifle drill	Using the rifle to slope, shoulder, or present arms
Seamanship Manual	Book on all you need to know to become a sailor

Set	Beard
Sickbay	Medical Clinic
Slop room	Clothing issue store
Station card	Red or green booklet indicating which watch you are in (Port or Starboard)
Stoker/grease monkey	Mechanical Engineer
Superstructure	Everything above ship's hull
Switchboards	Electrical distribution centre
The Andrew	The Royal Navy
The Dogs bollocks	looking good
Tickler	Navy brand rolling tobacco
Watches	Duties over and above day work, done in 2 or 4 hour shifts

Alf Pickup (center)

Alf Pickup